AF654401

Gender and Health

By the Same Author

1. Contemporary Indian Society: A Gendered Perspective with Sweta Prasad (Edited).
2. Gender: Themes and Issues (Revised and Enlarged Edition).

About the Editor

Dr. Jyoti Prasad Saikia is currently a Professor in the Department of Sociology, Dibrugarh University. He is working in the field of Gender Studies. He has written and edited a number of books. Among these, "Gender & Health: A Sociological Insight", "Gender: Themes & Issues", "Youth and Career Aspiration", "Problems of Education in Rural Women", "Gender Trouble: A Study in North East India", "Flash From North-East India," "Rendering Gender", "Sociology of North-East India", "General Sociology" are significant. Apart from these, he has also written a good number of text books of sociology both in vernacular and English language.

Gender and Health

A Sociological Insight

Edited by
Jyoti Prasad Saikia

CONCEPT PUBLISHING COMPANY PVT. LTD.
NEW DELHI-110059

© Editor

All rights reserved. No part of this work may be reproduced, stored, adapted, or transmitted in any form or by any means, electronic, mechanical, photocopying, micro-filming recording or otherwise, or translated in any language, without the prior written permission of the copyright owner and the publisher. The book is sold subject to the condition that it shall not, by way of trade or otherwise, be lent, resold, hired out, or otherwise circulated without the prior publisher's written consent in any form of binding or cover other than that in which it is published.

The views and opinions expressed in this book are author(s) own and the facts reported by him/her have been verified to the extent possible, and the publishers are not in any way liable for the same.

ISBN-13: 978-93-86682-83-3

First Published 2019

Published and Printed by:

Concept Publishing Company Pvt. Ltd.
A/15-16, Commercial Block, Mohan Garden,
New Delhi-110059 (INDIA)
T: +91 11 25351460, +91 11 25351794
E: publishing@conceptpub.com, *W*: www.conceptpub.com

Cataloging in Publication Data--Courtesy: D.K. Agencies (P) Ltd. <docinfo@dkagencies.com>

Gender and health : a sociological insight / edited by Jyoti Prasad Saikia.
pages cm
"... RC-10 (Gender and Society) of Indian Sociological Society decided in its business meeting held during the 39th All India Sociological Conference in Mysore to bring out a publication on gender and health ..."--Preface.
Includes bibliographical references and index.
ISBN 9789386682833

1. Women--Health and hygiene--India--Assam. 2. Women--Health and hygiene--India. 3. Reproductive health--India--Assam. 4. Reproductive health--India. 5. Women employees--Health and hygiene--India--Assam. 6. Women employees--Health and hygiene--India. I. Saikia, Jyoti Prasad, editor. II. Indian Sociological Society. RC-10 (Gender and Society)

LCC RA564.85.G46 2019 | DDC 362.10820954 23

In the fond memory of my teachers
Sharmila Rege
and
Anuradha Bhoite

Prelude

The emphasis and focus on various gender related issues have been witnessed in the recent times in many countries, including India. Critical analyses of these issues have brought home the fact that human development in its true and real sense is not possible in any country as long as the disparities and discriminations towards woman persist. In many countries and that includes our own country India, these issues have deep cultural roots resulting in complexities for any instant remedy. The sad reflection of this is there in the Human Development Reports prepared by the United Nations since 1990s. India ranks 132 in the Gender and Development Index (0.828 *vis-á-vis* 1.00 of Slovakia and 0.997 of Norway) in 2013 as published in the report for 2014. It is also pertinent to mention that world's first Family Planning Programme in 1951 was launched in India. Also, this is despite an array of such other national programmes under the various national policies like the National Population Policy, the National Rural Health Mission (NRHM), Reproductive and Child Health Programme and Janani Suraksha Yojana etc., launched since early 2000.

The stark reality pertaining to the gender issues, therefore, call for serious deliberations and in depth critical analyses of the multiple dimensions related to these issues. The nine odd presentations of the research work edited by one of my young colleagues Professor Jyoti Prasad Saikia of the Department of Sociology at Dibrugarh University, Assam, for the volume on "Gender and Health: A Sociological Insight", being published under the aegis of the RC-10 (Gender and Society) of Indian Sociological Society is indeed a relevant and timely intellectual exercise. I am pleased to write a few words as Prelude to the volume and believe that all the articles in this volume shall go a long way in the contemporary understanding of the issues being covered in the studies on Gender and Health in the Indian perspective.

I congratulate Professor Saikia for his notable efforts in undertaking such an academic exercise involving a significant issue. This volume, I do believe, will serve the interest of students, teachers and scholars of Gender Studies as well as Sociology.

(Alak K. Buragohain)
Former Vice Chancellor, Dibrugarh University,
Dibrugarh, Assam

Foreword

The Research Committee (RC) 10, "Gender Studies" of the Indian Sociological Society (ISS) remains committed to its goal of bringing gender concerns centre-stage to various topics covered in the All India Sociological (AIS) Conferences organised by the ISS in different parts of the country every year. Gender cuts across various dimensions whether social, economic, political, cultural or psychological and forms of social inequalities like caste, class, race, religion or region. To work towards a more inclusive and gender just society, it becomes imperative, therefore, to address, understand and analyse these issues.

The RC 10 adopts different methods and strategies to bring its members and other interested people on one platform to take the lead. Besides having technical sessions in All India Sociological Conferences, it organises mid-term conferences and seminars every year. It has its Newsletter that disseminates information about the activities of RC-10 as well as those of its members. In every AIS conference more than 100 papers are presented. There are around 250 active members in RC-10. In the 39th All India Sociological Conference held at Mysore in December 2013, a decision was taken by the RC 10 members in its "Business Meeting" to bring out some publications. One of the Volumes suggested was "Gender and Health". Professor Jyoti Prasad Saikia from the Department of Sociology, Dibrugarh University, Dibrugarh, Assam, most sportingly took the responsibility of bringing out this volume by next year to be released at the time of the 40th All India Sociological Conference. The same was announced and communicated to the ISS members during the Valedictory Function of the ISS Conference in Mysore. It gives me an immense pleasure to write the Foreword of the Volume

"Gender and Health: A Sociological Insight" edited by Professor Jyoti Prasad Saikia.

Gender equality is still a far-fetched dream in India despite several changes that have been brought about through legislative and political initiatives. Women continue to suffer from deprivation, discrimination, humiliation and denial of basic human rights in varying degrees, almost at every stage of life and in nearly all situations. They face violence which is the breach of the Fundamental Right to life, liberty, security, dignity, equality, non-discrimination and physical and mental integrity. Women and girl-child often become victims of domestic violence, dowry harassment, female-foeticide and sexual abuse leading to severe health repercussions.

Gender and Health are inextricably related. Gender equality is important to attain good health for all women and men of all ages irrespective of their socio-economic background and sexual identity. It is equally essential for the health of the nation and society in general. Thus, it is important to address the issue of gender discrimination in society and make gender sensitive policies and programmes which still are not impartial processes. In fact they help to sustain the unequal power-relations between men and women, from the fundamental level of the family to the highest levels of decision-making. Therefore, the demand for women's rights to equality has become central to the growing demand for women's empowerment and their consequent ability to meaningfully participate in, and benefit from, development process.

Gender disparity is most glaring as reflected in declining sex ratio particularly among children. It declined from 927 girls per 1,000 boys in 2001 to 919 in 2011 (Press Information Bureau, 2014). The existing sex ratio imbalances in our country are generally due to a traditional preference for a son along with a speedy decline in fertility and Information Technology (IT) allowing sex selective prejudices against females. The Global Gender Gap Report published by the World Economic Forum ranked India as 141 out of 144 nations in terms of gender equity in health (World Economic Forum, 2018). The Maternal Mortality Ratio (MMR) of 121 maternal deaths per 1,00,000 live births during the period of 2007-2009 is also quite high (Census: 2011); although it has come down to 178 per 1,00,000 live births in the period of 2010-2012 (Press Information Bureau, 2014).

Thus, the sex ratios at birth, infant and child mortality by sex, and low ages at marriage for women constitute the health and population indicators that depict gender-based inequalities Further, at the household level, disempowerment of women results in their lowers access to resources such as education, employment, and income, and limits their power over decision-making and freedom of movement. It also makes them vulnerable to violence and prone to health problems. In all such situations women's health—physical, mental, psychological and occupational is affected severely. This edited volume "Gender and Health: A Sociological Insight" examines these and related aspects to provide an understanding of health related issues of women in different parts of the country.

Though gender refers to women and men differences, the articles in the book focus on women owing to the glaring inequalities in matters of health. Not only women and men have dissimilar rates of different diseases, and seek medical care differently and in varying amounts, the way society treats them and the manner in which they suffer and face violence is markedly different. India has made considerable progress in the social and economic spheres during the last century. Life expectancy, infant mortality, and literacy rates have improved. However, progress in the area of sexual and reproductive health has been slow. HIV epidemic is steadily spreading from high risk to low risk population, maternal mortality rate continues to be high and sex ratio is declining in many states. Traditional ideologies of masculinity/femininity often push men and women to unsafe sexual behaviours. A "culture of silence" about women's health problems still prevails which often restricts women's access to health care.

The book consists of nine Chapters. Each one of them points to a unique and specific situation, yet certain inferences are derived from them focusing on the need to examine the matter more seriously and make necessary efforts in that direction. The Chapters deal with the health aspects of widows, health hazards and safety measures of women workers in garment industry and health issues concerning women working in the construction sector, urbanisation and its effects upon women's health, and life expectancy, medicalization and commodification of women's bodies through reproductive technologies, women's reproductive health and rural women's awareness of reproductive health issues.

This book will provide new insights into the fields of gender, health and medical sociology and would be immensely useful to the readers. I am sure it would be accepted and appreciated for its worth. On behalf of RC-10, ISS, I gratefully acknowledge the work of the Editor of the volume Professor Jyoti Prasad Saikia and marvel his efforts in carrying out the assigned task meticulously and painstakingly. The task of the reviewers and the contributors to this volume is praiseworthy and needs special thanks. I am equally thankful to all the office bearers and members of RC-10 for their consistent and concerted support to me in carrying out our plans in a conducive and academic atmosphere. The annual conferences of the Indian Sociological Society provide us a forum to come together and discuss our ideas and plan and execute our activities. To them, I owe a great deal. This book is an example of such fruition.

Prof. Abha Chauhan
Head, Department of Sociology,
University of Jammu, Jammu
Former Secretary,
Indian Sociological Society

Preface

Today, we do not need to invest much effort to understand the importance and seriousness of an issue as sensitive as health. Health and various aspects related to it determine not only the present, but also the future of a people and a nation. The issue becomes even more critical and complex when it comes to health of women. Being a student of Sociology and working in the field of gender provides one a certain perspective which helps us to observe this issue of women and health in a different light and recognise the importance of a gendered perspective to understand it. That is why, I was very happy when the RC-10 (Gender and Society) of Indian Sociological Society decided in its business meeting held during the 39th All India Sociological Conference in Mysore to bring out a publication on Gender and Health and I was humbled with the honour the Committee bestowed upon me in the form of the responsibility of editing and bringing out this volume. Hence, at the very beginning I would like to thank all the members of the executive body of RC-10 (Gender and Sociology) of Indian Sociological Society for their faith in me and for entrusting me with the difficult task of bringing out an edited volume on the issue of Gender and Health. I am not sure to what extent I have been able to live up to their expectations. However, I have tried my best to this end. I am also very grateful to them for their abundant trust in my abilities and for providing me a wonderful opportunity to work on an issue of great practical and academic importance. I must also take this opportunity to offer my sincere thanks to Professor Abha Chauhan for her boundless trust in me in terms of bringing out this volume and her constant support along with her words of encouragement. I am truly grateful for her guidance and generous support in writing the foreword for this volume. I am truly indebted to Professor Alak

Kumar Buragohain, Honourable forme: Vice Chancellor, Dibrugarh Univervisity, Assam and a renowned intellectual; for his trust and words of encouragement. I must offer my sincere gratitude to him for taking the pain of writing the prelude for this volume at my request despite of his tremendously busy schedule. I owe a great deal of gratitude towards Prof. Bishwajit Ghosh of University of Burdwan, West Bengal and Prof. B.N. Borthakur of Dibrugarh University, Assam for their kind help and valuable suggestions while preparing this volume. I must also offer my thanks here to my research scholar Hriday Ranjan Kalita for his invaluable help and efforts in bringing out this volume. My sincere thanks and gratitude also goes to all the contributors for their precious works and for their patience since I started working on this volume. I also offer my sincere thanks to Ranjit Saikia, Hemonta Kumar Hazarika, Mitali Gogoi, Mridul Phukan, Charuprasad Saikia, Ruhit Dutta and Parvez Hussain for their cooperation in attaining my goal. I will always remain grateful to them. Finally, I would also like to thank to Ashok Kumar Mittal, Concept Publishing Company Pvt. Ltd., New Delhi, for recognising the importance of the issue this volume have attempted to study and for taking the responsibility of publishing it. This volume has an aim to highlight various aspects of women's health and critically examine them at its heart. While doing it, certain unintentional mistakes may have occurred. I hope that the intellectual society will embrace this work and will be kind enough to point out the errors so that we can modify them in the next edition of the book.

Jyoti Prasad Saikia

Contents

List of Contributors

Ashwini Jain. Assistant Professor, Department of Studies and Research in Sociology, Tumkur University, Tumkur.
E-mail: *ashwinibjane@gmail.com*

Ayushi Agrawal. Doctoral Student, School of Interdisciplinary and Trans Disciplinary Studies, IGNO.
E-mail: *ayushi.agrawal03@gmail.com*

Gargee Gayan, Assistant Professor, KKH State Open University, Guwahati, Assam.

Hriday Ranjan Kalita. Assistant Professor, Department of Sociology, Kaziranga University, Jorhat, Assam.
E-mail: *hriday.ranjan@gmail.com*

Jyoti Prasad Saikia. Professor, Department of Sociology, Dibrugarh University, Dibrugarh, Assam.
E-mail: *jpsaikia.2012@gmail.com*

Kuki Boruah. Assistant Professor, Department of Sociology, Women University, Jorhat, Assam.
E-mail: *kukiboruah.87@gmail.com*

Labani Dey, Research Scholar, Department of Sociology, Vidyasagar University, West Bengal.

Pooja Bhalla. Research Scholar, Department of Sociology, Delhi University, Delhi.
E-mail: *pooja.bhalla03@gmail.com*

Purabi Bhagawati, Research Scholar, Tezpur University, Assam.

Rabin Deka, Associate Professor, Department of Sociology, Tezpur University, Assam.

Rekha K. Jadhav. Research Guide, Department of Studies in Sociology, University of Mysore, Manasagangotri, Mysore.
E-mail: *salmasyed33@yahoo.com*

Rekhamoni Gogoi. Assistant Professor, Borpothar College, Golaghat, Assam.

Salma Bano. Research Scholar, Department of Studies in Sociology, University of Mysore, Manasagangotri, Mysore.
E-mail: *salmasyed33@yahoo.com*

Sudeshna Mukherjee. Assistant Professor, Centre for Women's Studies, Bangalore University, Bangalore, Karnataka.
E-mail: *sudeshna_socio@rediffmail.com*

Upasana Borthakur, Research Scholar, Indira Gandhi National Open University, New Delhi.

Vikas Saharan, Research Scholar, Jawaharlal Nehru University, New Delhi.
E-mail: *vikas.sw18@gmail.com*

Introduction

Women, Gender and Health: The Indian Scenario

Jyoti Prasad Saikia

Sociological study of health and women's health in particular aims at reaching beyond the obvious and seemingly normal phenomena of women's health problems and explore the unseen realities of such problems and their origin. Health is one of the most important aspects of sociological enquiry, especially when it comes to health of women. Health is defined by the World Health Organisation (WHO) as a state of complete physical, mental and social well-being, and not merely the absence of disease or injury. This definition emphasizes the fact that health is not merely the absence of negative traits such as illness or injury, but requires the presence of positive traits such as feelings of well-being, traits which are social and psychological as well as physical (Cockerham and Ritchey, 1997). On the other hand, illness is a state or condition of suffering as a result of a disease or sickness (Cockerham and Ritchey, 1997). In sociology, an illness is a subjective state, pertaining to an individual's psychological awareness of having a disease, symptoms or pain and typically modifying his or her social behaviour as a result. This definition contrasts with that of a disease, which is physiological dysfunction within an individual. Health behaviour is an important aspect of health for both males and females which is defined as the behaviour undertaken by a person who believes himself or herself to be healthy for the purpose of preventing health problems (Kasl and Cobb, 1966). Health behaviour involves all kinds of activities, habits and lifestyles that healthy people pursue to stay well. Health Belief Model which is a social psychological model of health behaviour designed to explain the motivation and activity of healthy people to avoid the threat of illness based on the work of Irwin Rosenstock (1966) and his colleague Marshall Becker (1974) and derived to a great extent from the theories of psychologist Kuurt Lewin suggests that people live in a life space consisting of regions with both positive and negative values. An illness would be a negative value and will push the person away from its region, unless it would cause the person to enter the region of even greater negative value. The person's behaviour is, therefore, oriented towards finding regions with the positive values. According to the Health Belief Model, the preventive action taken by a person to avoid any disease is due to that particular individual's perception that he or she is personally susceptible and that the occurrence of the disease would have at least some severe personal implications (Cockerham and Ritchey, 1977).

Health Care is defined as the medicinal and preventive measures taken by the self or others to maintain functional health status. Again it is also defined as the society's cultural and organisational arrangements directed at maintenance of the health status of its population. Health Care is distinguished from Medical Care, which is a more narrowly defined concept. Health Care refers to any behaviour or institutional functions aimed at maintaining or enhancing health status, including preventive measures such as brushing teeth, exercising, dietary practices and injury prevention. The term 'Medical Care' refers to only those practices and institutional functions controlled by medical practitioners. Health status of an individual or a group of people as a whole gives us a complete picture of the health of that group or individual. And individual's health status can be judged by their self-assessment of his or her health condition. Studies of the validity of self-reported health status typically find it to be an accurate assessment of an individual's state of health (Cockerhamand Ritchey, 1977). Health ideology plays a very crucial role in shaping the health status of a people in any given society. Within a society or social group, the ideas, values and doctrines about health care that legitimise or justify health norms and behaviours can be called health ideology of that particular society. Ideologies are often shaped by the particular group interests of those in power yet must appeal to the basic values of the society (Bray Brooke, 1967; Edelman, 1988). Health ideology is a broad term referring to how a society comes to socially construct is so widely held believes about health and sickness behaviour. Health Care accessibility is another very crucial aspect of health. It is defined as sufficient availability of personal and health system resources such that individuals are able to obtain Health Care in accordance with their needs (Aday and Andersen, 1975). Accessibility is analysed which distinctions among the need, demand and utilisation of services, between process and outcome indicators, between characteristics of the health system and those of the population at risk, and between behavioural (utilisation) and subjective (satisfaction) outcomes of care seeking (Aday and Andersen, 1975). Thus, as an ideal type, a truly accessible Health Care System is one in which appropriate services are available and easily obtainable in an area and in which individuals in the area have the knowledge and Financial Resources to utilise services in accordance with their true needs.

There are various theoretical perspectives that have developed and have been used to understand health and women's health related issues in the sociological discourse. One such perspective was forwarded by Talcott Parsons under the banner of Functionalist Perspective. Parsons regarded medicine as an instrument contributing to the maintenance of social order. He said that illness is dysfunctional and a mechanism was necessary to separate this dysfunctionality as a temporary social state. Parsons gave the idea of Sick Role as a solution in which a ill individual is exempted from his other roles in the society as he assumes the sick role when ill. Here, the person must wish to get better and must acquire help in order to get better. However, this concept of sick role has been questioned by many. Issues have been raised such as, not everyone might wish to assume the sick role or might be unable to do so. An individual might not be completely free from his/her other obligations, even if he/she assumes the sick role. Moreover, an important question has been raised that such a concept gives tremendous power to the doctor who will have the ability to declare a person sick and thus controlling that individual completely.

During the 1960 and 1970, many critical perspectives on medical power came up. These perspectives saw medicine as something that was having power over society that replaces other authorities such as religion. Illich (1977) presented a well-known critique of medicalisation by saying that medicalisation poses a major threat to health as it has the ability to generate new diseases which would have not emerged without medical intervention. Although, in this critique it has not been answered how we are going to legitimize denial of medical attention to someone; however it is surely explicit that we must not and be very careful in overstating the benefits of medical practices. Marxist and Political Economy perspectives also emphasize the negative impact of medical practices. However instead of blaming the medical power in the hands of medical professionals, it concentrates upon a deeper set of power relations that fuel the power of medicalisation (Nagla, 2013). This perspective suggests that the structure of society that is built around the needs of capitalism as an economic system should be the starting point of analysis on Health and Health Care. Interactionist perspective on the other hand concentrates upon the role of social interaction in terms of identity construction, stigma and its impact upon experiences of illness and health. This perspective, inspired by the works of George Herbert Mead and symbolic interactionism talks about how interaction between individuals and shared meaning created by it influences individual perception regarding illness and health and in what ways stigma concerning a particular health issue not only affects the way people see an illness but also the way that sick person sees himself or herself. Social Constructionist perspective also examines the impact of social processes on the meaning of health and illness. This perspective suggests that health and illness can not be understood as fixed entities. Instead the meanings changes with time and space. Thus, the meanings of health and illness may differ according to society, culture, race, sex, religion and over time.

Gender perspective threw new light on the issue of power of medicalisation and social control in specific terms of woman. This perspective shifted the attention from power of medical professionals upon women's bodies to control over women's bodies by men through unequal gender relations between men and women present in the society. Gender perspective emphasized the control of women's reproductive abilities. But, instead of concentrating upon just how medicalisation and its power control women's reproduction, it also explored the question of why it is controlled. The quest to answer this question led gender perspective to discover the fact that along with the power exerted by medicalisation over women's reproductive abilities, patriarchal control over women's reproduction and sexuality, their productive labour and their mobility must also be taken into consideration and that these factors also affects women's health and their experiences of health and illness.

Gender inequality is one of the most important variables when it comes to women and their health. In order to understand what gender inequality is, it is important to take into account the various theories and perspectives that have emerged in Sociology and other academic discourse. The status of women is a very complex issue. It depends upon a complex web of variables cutting across each other. There are various theories that have emerged to explain why women stand in an unequal position in comparison to men. Theory of cultural dualism argues that women are a culturally constructed gender category. This idea rejects biological determinism in terms of defining the differences that exist between men and woman. Ortner (1974) in order to avoid biological determinism and at the same time retain the universality of women's subordination asked what it was that would lead every culture in this world to place a lower value on women than on them. She concluded that every society made a distinction between nature and culture. Simone de Beauvoir is one of the chief proponents of cultural dualism finds the origin of women's subordination in her relation to nature and nature's relation to culture. She shows that men controls nature through culture and hence men is superior to both nature and culture (Nagla, 2013).

Social evolutionary theory tries to answer the question if women's position in society is getting better or worse with changes in society as a whole through time. This theory suggests that with changes in society, every society seeks for greater productivity and hence seeks to acquire greater level of specialisation. This theory suggests that in this context women have always stick to work with less productivity and because of that they suffer inequality. The social inequality also affects the participation of women in public life as woman stick to more domestic work than in the public sphere.

The idea of developmentalism came with the recognition of differential impact of modernisation upon man and woman. This recognition led to the belief that necessary steps must be taken in order to integrate women into the development process for ensuring socio-economic equality between men and women. In a similar context, dependency theory focused upon the impact of international forces upon the development in the so called Third World countries. Dependency theory talks about the hegemony of developed nations in terms of development and technology and the dependency of the nation's which were earlier colonised upon developed nations in terms of development strategy. Following this model, Marxist feminist thinkers suggested that patriarchy is one such system which upholds the hegemony of developed nations in terms of development and thus has emerged as a mechanism through which women are placed in an unequal position in terms of development and the impact of development in comparison to men (Nagla, 2013).

Biological perspective traces the roots of inequality between men and women in the biological differences between them. The most influential and controversial theory in this context comes from Sigmund Freud who considers the source of gender differences and gender inequality between men and women lies in the possession and absence of male sexual organs and the experience of this possession or absence in infants and young children. Sigmund Freud argues that this experience leads to socialisation of men and women on the basis of their gender and formation of gender based roles in society and in this way the biological differences leads to the emergence of social inequality between men and women.

Marxist theory explains gender relations as a result of specific relations between production and reproduction in a specific context. According to Marxist theory reproduction is not just biological reproduction and also the entire maintenance prices that keep workers functional and this process is maintained primarily at home by women. The most vivid manifestation of this Marxist idea can be seen in Frederick Engels work, the origin of the family, private property and the state. Frederick Engels suggested that the hierarchical nature of the relation between men and women originated in the sexual division of labour between the two in which men had to engage in work outside the home while women and their work was confined to home with the coming of agriculture. This initial segregation in terms of work led to the emergence of patriarchal social structure in future.

Sylvia Walby said that it is important to understand patriarchy as "a system of social structures and practices in which men dominate, oppress and exploit women." Garda Lerner proposes that the appropriation and commodification of woman's sexual and reproductive capacity by men lay the foundation of private property and class society. Control over one's own reproduction and freedom of information is a concern for all women throughout the world. Thus, reproductive health is one of the most important aspects of women's health. "Patriarchy" literally means the rule of the father. The concept of patriarchy was earlier used to demonstrate a particular kind of family. Now, however, it is used by feminist scholars as a theoretical construct to explain the structure beneath the subordination of woman. Madhu Nagla writes, "...the roles women play in the society and the images that have developed of them, are not simply from exigencies of biology and social situations, but are rather deeply rooted in the myths, legends, religion and culture" (Nagla, 2013).

Health is an aspect of human life today which is given paramount importance. It is considered to be a primary indicator in terms of the overall development of a nation. It is probably safe to say that health has always been given considerable priority throughout the history. However, it will also not be wrong to say that never before the issue of health has been given attention and concern to such extent and with such intensity from both the Government and policy-makers and the academics alike. Such attention and concern directed towards health, we must say, are well justified. However, it is seen that the status of the health of men and women remains still on unequal grounds, especially in the so called 'developing' countries; such as India. Much research effort has been already dedicated to exploring the various aspects of the health of women and the specificities of their health problems, particularly in the last couple of decades. This interest in the issues relating to the health of women was initiated the development in the feminist thinking which made scholars throughout the world to take into consideration the unequal gender relation between men and women and the contextual realities of women in terms of various issues and problems concerning them; including their health.

Gender inequality is embedded in Indian social structure. Indian social structure is hierarchically organised on the basis of unequal power relations between unequal genders. This inequality is produced, sustained and reproduced by the patriarchal social structure and while doing it the patriarchal social structure which defines Indian social structure ensures its own survival. The presence and extent of the gendered inequality in Indian society has severe consequences in terms of the health of women in the country. This gendered inequality manifests itself in various women specific health issues in India such as poor health and nutritional status, inadequate reproductive health awareness and behaviour, low life expectancy and survival rates etc. It also manifests certain basic issues which leads to health related problems among women such as inadequate access to health facilities, self-denial and ignorance towards own health, prejudicial treatment of girls in terms of food and health care and many more.

In India today, the health sector has exhibited marked improvements in terms of health of both men and women. However, as encouraging as it may be, the sad fact remains that women in Indian Society are still unequal in terms of health status, availability and accessibility of Medical Care etc. The reason behind this trend is the overall low status of women in our society. According to UNICEF, 12,000,000 girls are born in India each year out of which 25 per cent do not survive beyond the age of 15. The reason behind this trend is a higher mortality of girl children in the age group of 0-5 years. Life expectancy among women is still low in comparison to men. In terms of sex ratio, the trend in India has always been negative towards woman. The adverse sex ratio in our country is mainly because of high risk of female death from infancy to the end of the productive period (Ghosh, 1985). Another reason for adverse sex ratio in India is a strong presence of male child preference and sex selective abortion and female infanticide. Lack of widespread availability of safe abortion services also has adverse impact on women's health. According to some estimates, roughly five million abortions are performed annually in India, the large majority about 4.5 million illegally. As a result, abortion related mortality contributes 10 per cent of the total maternal mortality figures (Nagla, 2013). The gender inequality also persists among the elderly woman. India currently might be a young nation. However, it is going towards having a huge population which will consist of elderly men and women in our future and the problem of ageing is becoming more and more distinct. Ageing is often perceived as deterioration in health and this phenomenon is much more harmful for women in comparison to men because of the existing inequality and disadvantages that women in Indian Society have to face. Even though growing old brings certain improvements and for women, these benefits disappear as they become older or when they are widowed (Rao and Townsend, 1999). As women in Indian Society derives her power by being associated with the male head of the family, went widowed she loses this power and that makes her vulnerable (Nagla, 2013). Nutritional status is another very important issue concerning health especially of women. Madhu, Nagla (2013) writes, "in Indian Society poor nutrition is caused not only by lack of food or poverty but there are also many socio-cultural factors which are responsible for this. Today, India is in the bottom of world's maiden nutrition barometer, announced by 'Save the Children' recently. The report says that children in poor households were more than twice as likely to be stunted as those in affluent ones." In India, nutrition programmes are directed towards the needs of pregnant women. But despite these efforts, they are not yet free from under-nutrition. This has devastating impact upon the health of pregnant women and their children. And if the child is female, she is again forced into the vicious circle of malnutrition since her birth to her infancy, adolescence and adulthood. Indian social values give highest priority to adult men and male children in the family and their food and nutritional needs are fulfilled first. Still today, in many parts of the country women are expected to eat only after their husbands and other male members of the family have eaten. Such social values and cultural traits place woman in a very disadvantageous position in terms of nutrition and health. When it comes to access to Healthcare women are again placed at the receiving end in Indian Society where they are unequal and disadvantaged. Because of lower socio-economic status in comparison to men, women are dependent upon men for accessing Health Care Services. Most often woman requires permission to access Health Care, because of their secondary position in the family and society, there required to be accompanied while seeking Health Services because of restrictions upon their mobility and they are also dependent in terms of financial resources to access Health Care Services. The inadequate availability of Health Care Services and lack of knowledge regarding the facilities available for them also puts woman in a position where they remain disadvantaged and vulnerable. The unequal gender relations present in our society results in the lack of decision-making abilities among women in the family. This lack of decision-making capability results in the lack of their control over their reproductive capabilities which in turn adversity affects their health. Woman in India still have hardly any say in terms of having children and other decisions in terms of family planning, use of contraceptives etc. Such realities expose the very vulnerable condition of Indian woman when it comes to their health. Thus, it is seen and proved time and again that health status of women in India is influenced and implicated to a great extent by the various socio-cultural and economic factors along with gendered inequalities present in our society.

This reality in terms of women's health in India necessitates the application of a Gender Perspective in order to unravel the contextualities and complex realities of women and health in India. Keeping this fact in mind this edited volume has attempted to bring together various studies covering various issues related to women's health in different parts of India. Despite the heterogeneity of issues covered in these studies based on different areas in different context, the perspective these studies have used to explore these various problems remain the same. As the title of the volume "Gender and Health: A Sociological Insight" suggests, the studies included in this volume have looked upon various issues they have covered from a vantage point of Gender.

The chapter by *Pooja Bhalla* titled, "New Reproductive Technologies: A Sociological Study on the Control of Women's Body in the Social Perspective" presents a very critical analysis on the role of Science and Technology leading to the coming of New Reproductive Technologies. She has also very beautifully analysed how such reproductive technologies have helped men to gain control over the sexuality and reproduction of women, which was until recently was a sole domain of women. This study, along with presenting a very clear understanding of the various Reproductive Technologies, has very carefully discussed the various ways such technologies are affecting the women's experiences of sexuality and reproduction. In this way the work by Pooja Bhalla has forwarded a very strong argument against the belief that the New Reproductive Technologies are providing control over their sexuality and reproduction of women.

The Chapter, "Widowhood, Gender and Health in Nalbari District of Assam: A Qualitative Analysis in Sociological Discourse" by *Hriday Ranjan Kalita* is a qualitative analysis of the status of widows in terms of their health in the Nalbari District of Assam. The study tries to find out the issues related to the health of the widows and to ascertain the sources of such issues. Using a gendered theoretical perspective the study has found that gender and gendered inequalities plays a crucial role in generating such health issues among widows and that the origin of such health issues are not only physiological but also socio-cultural. The study argues that widowhood has many indirect affects upon the health of the widows and stresses the importance of gender as one of the primary factors which determines the nature of widowhood and the quality of the life of the widows and consequently their health. This study concludes that widowhood and gender are two of the most important factors that influences the ways in which widowhood gathers the potential to adversely affect the health of the widows.

Rekha K. Jadhav and *Salma Banc* in their chapter, "Working Hazards as Indicators of Occupational Health and Safety of Women Workers of Garment Industry" has attempted to make a meaningful inquiry into the health status of women working in the garment industry and has provided an account of the trends in employment and integration of women in the labour market and explore how they impact on their occupational safety and health. This study with a careful observation of the healthcare system of women workforce, occupational health and safety aspects and stress and psychological distress in Garment Industry has argued that the health condition in these industries are very poor. Along with that lack of education, unawareness of hazards of their occupations, general backwardness in situation and poor nutrition aggravates the health hazards from work environment. Further, this study argues that lack of effective legislation and punitive measures to confront the factories that violate occupational health and safety regulations must be checked. The study suggests that medical surveillance for assuring healthy workplace environment along with proper counselling and health education can improve the condition of these women workers.

The Chapter "Urbanization, Gender and Health" by *Vikas Saharan* has focused upon urbanisation and its effects upon the health of women living in urban areas. The chapter argues that the urban poor, especially women face health risks often high and sometimes worse than those of rural residents, despite the availability of modern health services and they are vulnerable to the negative health effects of rapid urbanization. The study stresses the urgent need to understand the impacts of urbanization on the health of poor women and to design appropriate planning of public health interventions considering the dynamic relationship between urbanisation and their impact on vulnerable urban women.

The Chapter "Medicalisation and Commodification of Women's Body through Assisted Reproductive Technology: A Feminist Review of Indian Infertility Trade" by *Sudeshna Mukherjee* has made a qualitative study to trace how post-liberal, market friendly Indian state is promoting foreign revenue earning ART and surrogacy at the cost of commodification, objectification and medicalisation of impoverished Indian women. The study argues that surrogacy and donor egg IVF are transforming the moral and ethical dimension of the society and women are pitched against women as commodities and consumers. Mukherjee stresses the obvious danger that economic problems may force some women to enter surrogate agreements when they might otherwise never have entertained the idea. The study also argues that all women should have access to the knowledge and resources to judge its uses of reproductive technology and to use it wisely, in keeping with their own particular needs.

The Chapter "Reproductive Health Awareness among Rural Women in India: A Sociological Study" by *Jyoti Prasad Saikia* and *Rekhamoni Gogoi* primarily focus upon the women's reproductive health awareness. The study argues that in rural areas, a good number of women have no adequate knowledge of the causes and consequences of their diseases, and reproductive health issues in particular. Based in Kekuri Borchapori Village of Golaghat District of Assam, the findings of this study suggest that though the women have some knowledge about reproductive health, they are not sufficiently aware of it. Awareness and the knowledge of Reproductive Health and its related diseases are highly absent due to lack of education and poor socio-economic condition of the respondents. The study also argues that Reproductive Health Awareness Among Rural Women is highly essential for the development of civilised human society.

Ashwini Jain's Chapter, "Women and Health: A Study in Gulbarga District" focuses on rapid changes in the health care system and its flaws in terms of women's health. The study shows that with rapid changes in health care system, basic issues such as patient care, establishing intimate doctor-patient relationships, time for trials and testing and sometimes even the development of confidence in the whole system are ignored. As a result health care has become a very big industry, putting profit before health of women. The study stresses the urgent need to devise and implement comprehensive health awareness and educative programmes the increase general level of understanding about health related issues.

The chapter, "Decent Work is a Distant Dream: Study of Women in the Construction Sector, New Delhi" by *Ayushi Agrawal* has shown implicit gender-based discrimination in the world of informal sector, where women got stuck in the lower end of the job hierarchy and men are doing the skilled and technical jobs. The chapter focuses on the women experiences in construction work and migration to other city which is full of difficulties and adjustments and argues that under such a condition the issue of women health is mostly overlooked. The study also shows that while there is no one interested in their health problems, the women themselves ignore their health and show greater concern for their family members and their health.

Kuki Boruah in her chapter, "Health Status and Life Expectancy among the Women of the Tai Khamyang Community in Assam—A Sociological Study" has presented an interesting account of the relation between health status and life expectancy of women of Tai Khamyang community of Assam. This study stands apart in comparison to the other studies in this book as this is the only one focusing solely upon the health status of women of a single tribal community in Assam— the Tai Khamyang. The empirical investigation conducted for this chapter has highlighted the nuances of the health status and health behaviours among the women of this community. With a careful observation of various aspects of the lives of these women and their health, this chapter finds that life expectancy among the Tai Khamyang is more favourable in case of women than men.

Rabin Deka in his article 'Political Economy of Population Control and Women's Reproductive Health" has strived to critically assess the family planning policies of the Government of India from the gender perspective. The views of Thomas Mathus that human population growth invariably leads to famine and poverty gave rise to genesis of various misconceptions regarding population growth among intellectuals and political leaders in the 20th and 21st centuries. This paradigm started influencing the economist planners and social activists in India right from the pre-independent days and consequently the sterilization of women has been the main method used in India population control policies. In the recent times, many Indian women have become the victim of the Governmental initiative for family planning to control increased population.

The article of Rabin Deka is completely based on secondary sources and he discussed how women have become victims of coercive family planning policies supported by male dominated medical system throughout the world. He mentioned that the government is accountable to every death of women due to family planning surgery during recent years. It needs a serious study to find out the reality in India. However the author rightly observed and suggested that the population control measures should not be imposed coercively without any holistic national policies.

Labani Dey has given an interesting view on gender discrimination in terms of healthcare expenditure on female child in the household level and for this she has done a field study in Purba Medinipur district of West Bengal. Significantly, she provides some major issues in regard to gender disparity prevails at the household level.

India is a country with enormous resources. But one of the resources which still remains untapped is none other than the human resource. In order to natural human capabilities to transfer into human resource, improving the quality of life is essential. This aspect is very critical for the progress of any nation. This approach stresses ensuring availability of choice for all since choice is not biologically given. It is socially determined in a much disguised manner. Gargee Gayan in her article "Reflection on

Social Structure: Women's Health in Assam" focuses on the state of Assam and strives to examine how social structure influences the choice of people in term of health practices they opt. In this context she tried to engage in informal conversation with people to get an insight about their everyday health practices. She also made an effort to understand those mundane choices and health practices by taking into consideration so of the dominant narrative and normative literature celebrated in Assam. In this Gargee Gayan has employed content analysis as a technique to elicit data.

Purabi Bhagawati has expressed her deep concern to health-seeking behaviour of the rural women in her article. It is also an empirical study and she has done the field work in three villages of Nalbari District. Nalbari District is situated in Assam. She selected marginalized women as sample respondents from these three villages and considered marginalized women who belong to poor socio-economic condition, living geographically excluded and environmentally in the danger area. To understand health seeking behaviours of rural women, she appropriately took help of Pierre Bourdieu's concept of habitus and symbolic interaction perspectives on health. According to findings of his empirical study, culture has played an important role in term of women's health. The villages's cultural construction of health has made significant impact on women's health seeking behaviour. Concluding remarks of her article provides a new insight regarding various factors which have been continuously determining the women's health seeking behaviour.

Upasana Borthakur in her article "Women and Health: A study of Women Labourers in a Tea Estate of Assam" has tried to examine health of women workers among the tea garden communities. She interviewed 122 women workers in a tea estate of Dibrugarh district and found that majority of workers are prone to malnutrition, anemia, tuberculosis, high blood pressure gastroenteritis, maternal mortality, hypertension she mentioned that there is a close connection between socio-economic condition and ill health among the plantation labours, especially women workers. Their nature of work, living conditions, type of food intake, poverty, lack of nutritious diet, lack of hygiene and sanitation, illiteracy etc. contribute to ill health among the women workers. As per her findings, lack of qualified doctors and nurses and health care centres in the tea estates to contribute to ill health among the women workers. Thus, women's health is affected not just by their biology, but also by their social conditions, such as poverty, illiteracy, families' responsibility and ignorance of proper sanitation etc. Moreover, the women workers have been enjoying low status in the patriarchal plantation society.

This volume was proposed in the RC-10 (Gender and Society) of Indian Sociological Society with recognition of a very vivid problem of women and health. The studies in this volume have followed systematic methodological guidelines which are essential for any sociological research. The volume manifests pressing concerns in terms of women's health and has attempted to highlight the various aspects of this issue in the specific context of Indian society. I am absolutely sure that the articles in this volume have succeeded in doing that and this volume will be able to provide a meaningful insight into the issue of Gender and Health in India.

REFERENCES

Aday, L.A. and R. Anderson (1975). *Access to Medical Care.* Ann Arbor. MI: Health Administration Press.

Braybrooke, D. (1967). "Ideology". *The Encyclopedia of Philosophy.* (Ed.) P. Edwards. Vol. 4. pp. 124-127. New York: MacMillan.

Cockerham, W.C. and F.J. Ritchey (1997). *Dictionary of Medical Sociology.* London: Greenwood Press.

Edelman, M. (1988). *Constructing the Political Spectacle.* Chicago: University of Chicago Press.

Ghosh, S. (1985). "Discrimination Begins at Birth". Paper Presented for UNICEF Journalist's Workshop on the Female Child. New Delhi: UNICEF.

Illich, I. (1977). *The Limits to Medicine.* Harmondsworth: Penguin Publications.

Kasl, S. and S. Cobb (1966). "Health behaviour, illness behaviour and sick role behaviour", *Archives of Environmental Health.* Vol. 12. pp. 246-266.

Nagla, M. (2013). *Gender and Health.* Jaipur: Rawat Publications.

Ortner, S.B. (1974). "Is female to male in nature is to culture", In: Rosalde, M.Z. and L. Lamp here (Eds.). *Women, Culture and Society,* Stanford, C.A.: Stanford University Press.

Rao, S.R. and J.W. Townsend (1999). "Health Needs of Elderly Indian Women: An Emerging Issue", In: M. Krishnaraj, R.M. Sudarshan and A. Shariff (Eds.). *Gender, Population and Development.* New Delhi: Oxford University Press.

Saikia, J.P. (2017). *Gender: Themes and Issues,* New Delhi: Concept Publishing Company (P.) Ltd.

1

New Reproductive Technologies

A Sociological Study on the Control of Women's Body in the Social Perspective

Pooja Bhalla

Introduction

Technological development is a growing process. In addition to the advancement of existing technologies, the present scenario witnesses the growth and development of new technologies. The same is witnessed in the medical field also. The expansions of New Reproductive Technologies[1] (NRTs) have added new dimensions to the humanity. The present scenario witnesses the technological ways of controlling conception procedures, gestation periods, and even child delivery procedures. These technologies are now getting infused into the medical profession into an accelerated pace (Snow, 1994). Gupta (2000) states that while in earlier times the term covered the "technologies such as contraceptive pills, intra-uterine devices, as well as sterilization and abortion (through dilation and curettage, or through suction" in the present scenario the term defines itself to be a medical procedure related to in-vitro fertilization (IVF), contraceptive vaccines, diagnostic technologies for pregnant women as well as birth technologies (*ibid.*, 15). The ability of women to bring forth children has been seen both as a capacity and as a source of women's power and status in society—basically as something positive poising themselves to empower women with the necessary choices available to them either in the form or reproduction or contraception. But does the scenario only reflects a picture of empowering women for a better health or is it something more to this?

The concept of NRTs being a subject of women only, differentiates men from women. The technologies, therefore, designed to interfere in the process of human reproductions[2] are classified in particularly three areas:

(i) **For Directing Birth**—These include contraceptives and pregnancy termination methods.

(ii) **For Assisting Reproduction**—These are technologies designed to aid or stimulate conception. Technologies ranging from artificial insemination, which are low tech involving least or no medical intervention to variations of In-Vitro Fertilization, using high tech medicine involving very complex medical, surgical and laboratory procedures.

(iii) **For Genetic and Prenatal diagnosis (including sex detection, and pre-selection)**—The aim being improving the health and genetic characteristics of foetus and the new born with the search for a healthy child.

In all ages and in all places there have been attempts to control women's reproduction both by others as well as women themselves. As pregnancies take place inside the women's bodies, control of fertility and reproduction is closely looked to control over women's sexuality; this argues for the changes in the meanings of reproduction which these technologies have produced. Gupta (2000) states that while these have made possible to have "sex without reproduction, artificial insemination and *vice versa* through in-vitro fertilization", it also became possible to have "reproduction without sex" (*ibid.*, 595). A child can now be created without recourse to sexual intercourse. Though this has been presented as liberation for women making her free from the "tyranny of reproduction" yet what is witnessed is the development and application of these reproductive technologies creating contradictory possibilities for women (Firestone, 1971: 88). Being associated with undesirable health and social consequences for women, for their fetuses, and for society at large, these offer 'choice' to some women; at the same time are potential sources to take away rights and other choices from other women. This work by briefly describing some of the prominent technologies available in the field reflects the ideas about the roles of women and men from which these technologies emanate and the 'politics' of reproduction within which these technologies are used (Spallone, 1986: 543).

Different Types of NRTs

The NRTs comprise technologies associated with Artificial Insemination, IVF fertilization, Super Ovulation, Embryo Evaluation, Surrogate Mothers, Ectogenesis, Sex Pre-Determination Tests and Egg Donation.

Artificial Insemination (AJ) is a process related to assisted reproduction used to alleviate infertility in women. It involves partners or donors sperm. This is placed into a gun and the gun is inserted into a rod. The rod is inserted into the wombs for insemination. A more broader use of the process constitute it use for treatments like including ovulatory dysfunction, cervical factor infertility and infertility caused by endometriosis, male, and immunologic factors. In-Vitro Fertilization (IVF) is a process of providing "new means of preconception genetic diagnosis and preservation of fertility" (Huang, J. & Rosenwaks, Z., 2012: 778). This involves fertilization outside the women's body. The egg and sperm (which could be of the donors or couples) are placed in the medium where fertilization occurs. When the technique is used for in infertility treatment, the resulting embryo is transferred to a women's womb. It is the most efficient treatment option for couples with multi-infertility problems. The Technique of Super Ovulation[3] involves the release of more than one egg during one menstrual cycle. Super ovulation of very young and very old females can extend the period of their egg production. Embryo Evaluation is the inspection of embryos under dissection, microscopy, eliminating those considered unfit for transfer and ranking the acceptable ones according to quality. Surrogate Mothers carry her pregnancy for other women. Through the process of 'flushing' she may provide the egg and be artificially inseminated or may receive an IVF embryo, if another women's egg is used (Rowland, 1987: 522). Ectogenesis is the scientific term for the possibility of the growth of the foetus outside the human body in an artificial womb or foetal incubator without the need of the artificial womb. Oxygen and nutrients are pumped into it that keep it alive. Sex Pre-determination Tests[4] can be used during pregnancy. Amniocentesis can be used to assess the sex of the foetus. It involves a procedure in which a needle is inserted into the cavity of the womb and the amniotic fluid around the foetus is withdrawn. It was developed to help women detect genetic abnormalities and terminate the pregnancy, if deemed necessary. It was developed to help women detect genetic abnormalities and terminate the pregnancy, if deemed necessary. It also provides information on the sex of the foetus. Egg donation is the procedure through which the woman capable of carrying eggs are implanted with eggs for IVF in case they themselves fail to develop so within their own bodies.

While these NRTs are a source to achieve self-determination and control over their bodies yet they easily become the instruments of those in power to exercise control when used either within the patriarchal ideologies or in the ideologies of population controls. This study examines the 'role' of groups as related to involvement in the issue: experiments by medical researchers, profit-making by manufacturers/providers of NRTs, agendas of population controllers and the feminists worried by the increase in medical control over reproduction. It discusses the underlying interest that each group has in its own particular construction of the issue; revealing the "politics of reproduction" within which these technologies are used thereby revealing the manner the women's body being sociologically controlled.

Population Control Perspective

Recent demographic factors reveal the population control to be a must for the country and for the wider world. As Srinivasan (1995) mentions, in spite of India being the first among the countries which adopted an official family programme as early as 1950s, "to lower fertility levels and population growth rates, this seems to be a contrary situation where fertility declines have been tardy in population" (*ibid:* 4). The situation has not prevented India touching figure of one billion. The figure reflects a failure of all efforts to achieve the goal. However, to control population, the present scenario relates the concept of population control to the new aspects of reproductive health focusing around females (United Nations, 1994). The concept encompasses the different health requirements of women before, during and after the menstrual cycle. Stressing this, it is evident that the population control measures and reproductive health are one and the same things. The success of family planning measures are intricately linked to the reproductive health of a woman. In the words of Dixon-Muller (1993), for women it encompasses that every women should have the "right to control her body, that is her right not to be alienated from her sexual and reproductive capacity, and the right to the integrity of her physical person" (*ibid.,* 5). This also includes the right to regulate her fertility effectively and safely by being free of infections, diseases and disabilities. The reproductive health framework provides her with the necessary opportunities to broaden the scope of "family planning and planned parenthood" to "the realm of individual rights to sexual and reproductive health" (Gupta, 2000: 148). It is believed that birth control can liberate women from being overburdened with unwanted children, provided contraceptive measures are brought within the reach of women, they are safe and effective and controlled by women themselves.

But in practice, as evidenced in the Third World countries, the contraceptives are provided within the population programmes which are reduced to birth reduction programmes rather than creating conditions of facilities which make considered choices possible. Control over women's reproduction is often exerted by secular state in terms of pro- or anti-natalist population policies either for the general population or differently for different groups in society. Within the context of population issues these technologies are advocated to achieve the goals of national and international control policies. Keysers (1982) argues:

> The merging of birth control with its emphasis on family planning at the small scale level and eugenics, with its emphasis on large scale population policies fitted very well in the development of capitalism in the twenties and thirties. The birth control ...were directly and indirectly supported by capitalism, driven not so much be humanitarian ideals as by the need to safeguard their commercial interest and stability [to safeguard their dominant and profitable position] (*ibid.,* 90).

These policies treat women as instruments for managing population growth and reduce her status to fertility factors alone. Investment in schemes focused on women is propagated to achieve population targets and reduced fertility rates in the context of national development goals where women find themselves caught between contradictory pressures—on one hand from the state which propagates couple for fewer children and on the other hand from the patriarchal family structures which demand from them a certain number of children and preferably sons.

Controlling the productive capacity of women is considered as necessary to achieve the solution to the problems of hunger, poverty and economic backwardness; the population growth being treated as a key factor influencing and influenced by these. In such macro-level perspectives, individual desires (reasons for having children) find little place. The state policies being contrary to the idea of women's autonomy where the emphasis rather than on being health and safety of users is laid on the efficacy of contraceptives; leading women to get abused in the clinical trials of hormonal contraceptives thus neglecting or dismissing their adverse effects as experienced by them.

Science and Technology

Science and Technology is playing a major role in controlling the lives of women. As cited by Gupta (2000) "the technological control over reproduction occurs through—the fragmentation of the process of procreation: sex without reproduction and reproduction without sex, delinking biological parenthood (motherhood and fatherhood) and reconstituting it and the manipulation of the female body by those who control access to female technology" (*ibid.*, 593). Reproduction is medicalised at different stages, both to avoid pregnancy (through contraceptive technologies) and to induce pregnancy when it is desired (through assisted reproduction and genetic and prenatal screening technologies. Now, the ultimate project of science seems to be ectogenesis[5] (reproduction outside women's bodies), i.e. in laboratories for instance through cloning.[6] Further, for women child birth is a continuous experience; they participate in intercourse, the embryos grows inside their bodies for nine months, give birth, nurse and raise the child. But, for men, reproduction is a discontinuous experience. After intercourse, their role disappears till the time the women give birth to a child. This raises the questions about paternity being considered only an idea before the birth of a child, men being not related to the process of birth, therefore, not physically attached to the child as the women are; while maternity being an experience felt by women throughout the beginning of conception till the birth.

But now, because of NRTs today women's claim to maternity has also been weakened. As Shore (1992) argues by challenging "our most established ideas about motherhood, paternity, biological inheritance, the integrity of the family, and the naturalness of birth itself", it has divided the whole motherhood experience into bits and pieces, leading to the loss of the integrity of the experience when because of these new technologies one woman donates eggs and becomes the genetic mother, another women carries the child becomes the physiological mother and the third one who raises the child becoming the social mother. Maternity now is in question too, as paternity used to be (*ibid.*, 295). The interventions in women's bodies are undertaken as a solution to male infertility. Through prenatal diagnosis technologies, pregnancy is supervised and if it is continued, the delivery is induced and conducted under a supervision of gynaecologist. The pregnancy and child birth have become string of medical events with pregnancy being viewed as a disease and pregnant women as needing control and supervision, which starts even before conception. The development and application of these technologies is practiced by mostly men to bodies of women where these are applied reducing "the bodies of women to become the sites on which the power relations are played out and transforming their role from women as subjects to women as objects" (*ibid.*, 594). Further, not only the techniques like cloning and ectogenesis are posing great social and psychological problems by undermining the role of women in natural reproduction but also the milder technologies like X-rays and ultra sounds are reducing the status of women into reproductive machines. The impact of ultra sounds extends beyond the medical risks or benefits for individual women for it is significant in presenting a powerful; visual image that of fetus as self-sufficient, free floating and making it a public presence, thus tending to discredit the women's felt experience of pregnancy in favour of the objective data. The scenario argues that the claim to increase choices for women towards the use of NRTs approach in clandestine manner for intensification of exploitation women's body as objects of control.

The Commercialisation of NRTs

A major concern as revolving round the issue is the use of these new technologies for the commercial interest. As Rowland (1988) argues, "the booming of reproductive supermarkets in United States is one example of the misuse of technology for pure financial gain" (*ibid.*, 105). They have turned the precious gift of a baby into something which money can buy. It is a whole "baby business" which has emerged in the present scenario (Sengupta, 2010: xxxi). "The child is now viewed as a product. And the product must be perfect and, as far as possible, consumer designed" thus allowing babies to be created as per the parents want and economic power (Rowland, 1988: 105). There is a whole gamut of Multinational Pharmaceutical industry involved in the development and distribution of NRTs. Gaining profit from the proliferation of NRTs, the multinationals emerge to be expanding at a speedy rate as compared to the past scenario. Hormonal contraceptives have emerged to be a source of huge profit for pharmaceutical companies. The commercial firms are active, through their subsidiaries in the field of fertility drugs as well as in biotechnology. As Gupta (2000) defines, Organon and Serono are the major two pharmaceutical companies that manufacture hormones for hyper ovulation and control of ovulation (*ibid.*, 597). Considering the case of India, at International level India has become a site of government supported reproductive tourism. Sengupta (2010) depicts the scenario of this government led reproductive tourism, which allows the surrogates to be recruited from poor villages, housed in four walls, supervised and monitored clinically till they give birth to a child that is handed over to couples monitoring pregnancy. Sexton (2010) also argues on the Indian Governments support to the process of using Indian bodies as commodities of export. The government has entered into agreements with Indian IVF clinics, laboratories for exporting the parts of the bodies like stem cells for research and development. The untreated patients in India are advertised for further research and clinical procedures at the cost sponsored by US and Western Europe.

Use of NRTs: The Feminist Assessment

While for the infertile women the use of NRTs is not less than a miracle to treat infertility, the feminists stand on the issue move between the cure of infertility being acknowledged as a matter of "self-determination" (Rothman, 1989: 140) and the so called new technologies which threatens her role while being an instruments of procreation (Corea, 1985). Thus, the issues reflect a two way application of feminist standpoint with some coming out in support of these NRTs in contrast to others raising questions on the issues of sexuality and reproduction. The literature on reproductive technologies' is sprinkled with arguments advocating the use of these technologies. Major advances are seen in the facets of women's life getting changed under the umbrella of these technologies. The technologies have proved significant in freeing the women from the painful procedures of child delivery. As related to pregnant women, the healthy pregnancies and healthy babies are all boon of the new advanced technological processes. it is now possible to detect and remove unhealthy foetus from the body. When seen in relation to the infertile women, the technologies have made possible to conceive in a natural manner. The changes in technology are a precursor of changes in society. It is assumed that with the change in the application of the new methods of reproduction, the position of women will also get changed. They will get the necessary rights related to reproductive procedures. The use of the contraception and abortion method will allow women gaining a full control on their bodies.

Thus, some feminists regard these as scientific and technological progress, generally positive and benign and claim the justification of developing these technologies by stressing the need for liberation of women from child bearing. In this respect Firestone (1971) emphasizes the need for the development of these technologies so as to free women from the "tyranny of reproduction by every means possible" (*ibid.*, 88). She argues that women's subordination and oppression lies in the fact that women bears children, "pregnancy is barbaric...the temporary deformation of the body of the individual for the sake of species" advances for the "real test tube babies" as the solution to this, thereby urging women to seize the means of reproduction (*ibid.*, 193). Relating patriarchy to control of women's body/sexuality by men, she favours the process of ectogenesis because it would make "a fundamental contribution towards human sexual equality" (Singer and Wells, 1984: 137) and favour for further research at an accelerated speed. The technologies have made possible to induce pregnancy in or outside the women's body. The prominent availability of contraception and abortion procedures has allowed women the supremacy of their bodies. Expanding the traditional rights of women in relation to her body, these are "about fulfilling rather than rejecting the traditional feminine roles" (Sen & Snow, 1994: 156). In contrast to these, the women health advocates point towards the abuse of these technologies, the violation of women's rights and the risks to women's health. They view these NRTs as sexist, racist and eugenic which are aimed at reducing women's control over their bodies, thus undermining their autonomy. Relating the impact to the social scenario rather than simply to the medical interventions, they argue the ways, the physicians force women for caesarian section delivery procedures, the un-wilful sterilization of the poor, uneducated women thereby highlighting the male control over the reproductive choices rather than a means of increasing women's autonomy. Ruth Hubbard (1981) by supporting the view point argues that these technologies like, IVF on the grounds that it ties women's reproduction to marriage alone. Its complicated and closed training programmes exclude women from administering and controlling it, locking women into a male-controlled high technology model of birth, offering minimum health care to her. Further, the development and application of these technologies is practiced by mostly men to the bodies of women, where these are applied and therefore Rowland (1987) considers the issue of male control of reproductive technology as the issue of control over women by men. The issue has changed from one of 'choice' to one of 'control' (*ibid.*, 518).

The process of surrogacy establishes the identity of "women as working laboratories" is leading to the methods of divorcing her parts from the whole. As Rowland (1988) argues "the language of surrogacy itself is the part of women splitting" (*ibid.*, 102). The doctors talk about the "uterine environment" or the womb as their own right. In fact, the surrogate mother is no surrogate at all but is in fact the biological mother. "By calling her as surrogate, commercial agencies can more easily divorce her from her child" leading into the market of commercialisation where child is viewed as the object of 'deal' (*ibid.*, 102). To the extremes, the NRTs are also mixed with the surrogate process, to yield a better result. An example can be of USA where super ovulations of the surrogates are done so that the women may produce twins. Sangeeta Udgaonkar (2010) highlights that without taking the least health care of women; the process establishes no limits to the number of times that a woman may sell her ova. She may be subjected to repeated hormone injections and ova extraction procedures a number of times. The process has no limits to the numbers. Even the three pregnancy rule does not include her pregnancies before becoming a mother. The surrogacy contract ends in transferring all the rights to the child she delivers (*ibid.: xxxii*).

Surrogacy is the final and grossest exploitation of women and their bodies. Although, it is a fact that the NRTs are purportedly directed towards helping the infertile yet it is not to be denied that it the social and political implications which stand the technology in a controversial aspect. Not only do they reflect a social and political struggle over sexuality, reproduction and gender structures, but they challenge our conventional notions as related to maternity, biological inheritance and the process of natural birth. With the development and use of these NRTs the debate on these issues takes on a new and more complex turn. A significant issue which emerge gets is about the ideology and experience of motherhood been affected by the use of these NRTs.

Motherhood as an Ideology and New Reproductive Technologies

Motherhood[7] and the reproduction process is very much related with each other. The idea of motherhood is mostly influenced by the reproduction process. Motherhood ideology is mostly spoken about the social world of mothers and their mothering activity. The traditional ideology of motherhood considered it to be a patriarchal construction. The institutions of patriarchy looked motherhood as celebration, as a value and principle which every mother obeyed and followed. Meillassoux (1981) argues that the conventional motherhood ideology demanded every woman to stay in house and her main work to be the raring and caring of child and other family members. The notion was criticized by various feminist scholars (Ortner, 1974; Brown, 1970). It was argued that motherhood is an act, as social relationship and it is not biological but social and historically created during the passage of time. They argued the patriarchal ideology of motherhood is the major source of women powerlessness and it suppress and exploited the women potential and devalued women. The present view looks motherhood as an inspiration for women empowerment, it as a source of women status and demand for equality and liberty in every field and also the freedom and choice in reproduction.

However, the modern reproductive technologies have not made vast change in the convention motherhood ideology. By commodifying reproduction and treating pregnancy as disease they give power to male to dominance over women and reproductive decision. The NRTs are posing challenges to definitions and the dominant ideology of mothering and motherhood. By manipulating embryos from some women, implanting those in other women, the technology is gaining an exemplary control over the process of motherhood. Motherhood as a process is getting spit into pieces with the process witnessing the ovarian mothers who donate eggs, the surrogate mothers who carry pregnancy and the social mothers who raise a child. The technology thus is challenging the conventional ideologies of motherhood and the relationship of women in larger way. Stanworth (1987) argues that motherhood is seen more than in the past as a full time occupation. Today women spend less time in pregnancy and breast feeding than in recent past, the care of children has come to be defined in a more rigorous way. The technologies for managing pregnancy and childbirth are often embedded in a medical frame that defines pregnant women as patients, pregnancy as an illness and successful childbearing in terms that de-emphasis the social and emotional dimension and emphasizes the domination of reproductive technology so much with the medical profession and the state to exert control over women's lives (*ibid.*, 15). The definitions of mother and mothering are co-opted by scientific and medical experts and determined by legal contracts, thereby making the process of birth giving and motherhood to get 'commodified'. The desire of the product in the form of a perfect child underestimates the maternal experiences of women and reduces her status similar to that of a machine producing finished products. Rather than affording reproductive freedoms, technologies are countermanding the women's choices and behaviours thereby further reinforcing male dominance and reinforcing women's oppression.

Conclusion

However, through the emergence of reproductive technology and the social and cultural ideology of motherhood has been changed and reformed. Adaptation of new form of technology and the mobility of women care create new forms of motherhood that challenged reformed and disrupted existing expectation and norms. It is a fact that the NRTs may make a positive effect on mothering with women getting more interested 'in being' a mother of a child even they are barren or infertile or lesbian, yet it is argued that these treat pregnancy as disease and have commodified the reproductive activity. It is impossible to withdraw from these technologies once they are in market. People find it difficult to deny access to the use of a technology once it has been established and a need is created. They are leading us essentially to change the face of humanity. We are now involved in a process which creates children out of a sexual relationship. Though for many it may seem to be a liberating force, but an analysis of the power dimensions involved, particularly in relation to women indicates that they lead more to a loss rather than to liberation. These have increased the male dominance both over reproduction and women.

These technologies are legitimized by those who try to sell them through humanitarian arguments of helping infertile couples to have a baby of their own, to help women avoid bearing handicap children and to minimize the hazards of pregnancy and child bearing. The technological advancement is not a precursor to women's independence as these do not better the sexual/gender relations. The emphasis should be shifted to variety of choices to social conditions in which these choices should be carried out. The argument that the NRTs will increase the choice for women rests on the assumption that women should have control on them. But today women still do not control contraception and abortion. They use what is available, but do not control it. The numbers of women who have access to these NRTs by choice are few in comparison to those who access these by coercion. The search for solutions to infertility should not be reduced to technological fixes "but should include non-evasive methods (e.g. massage) as well. Women, in particular, need to take a close and critical look at these technologies because it is the women's health which will only be at stake through the use of these technologies. Although, these might be presented as "new and varied choices" for women, yet their consequences in limiting opportunities for women as a social group should also be taken into perspective.

NOTES

1. "As Khanna (2010) defines New Reproductive Technologies (NRTs) refer to "medical technologies specifically used for prenatal imaging, in utero diagnosis of birth defects, and assisted reproduction." Although, they are still referred to as 'new', they were first developed in 1960s as medical diagnostic tools for prenatal examination and treatment of infertility. Having made staggering advances in the past forty five years, new reproductive technologies provide live and vivid images of the intra-uterine world, and a broad range of reproductive choices" (*ibid.*, 85).
2. As per the words of *Encyclopaedia Britannica,* Reproduction is the process of making a copy, likeliness and thereby providing a continued existence of species. It is the production of off springs in animals and plants. In both the species the concept encompasses the features of child care and child rearing. O'Brein (1981) argues that "reproduction in the biological sense, however, is necessary social from any perspective, practical or abstract" (*ibid.,* 40). The term has been referred in the same sense in this study.
3. In the words of Genoveffa Corea (1985), Normally animals release (ovulate) only a single egg in a month. Reproductive engineers want a number of eggs for research and birthing procedures. The process of super ovulation increases the efficiency because "hormones produced by the pituitary gland affect the ovaries. It occurred to men that they could inject such hormones into a female and force the growth and ovulation of eggs from an abnormally large number of follicles—the small sacs which enclose the eggs. This is super ovulation... The super ovulation of very young and very old females can extend their period of their

egg-production and hence, of their usefulness to brothel-management" (*ibid.*, 300).

4. As Rowland (1987) defines, "Sex Predetermination before conception is being developed as a method to separate out the male-determining from the female-determining sperm. In fact a sperm-washing technique is being used in North America in at least seven clinics by a company called Gametrics Ltd. It is 75 per cent successful for selecting boys. The company has patented this method.

   Most societies have indicated that most societies male preferring. With the introduction of these techniques the sex-ratio balance may be severely disrupted. In India, where amniocentesis followed by the abortion of female foetus is on the increase, this is already happening (*ibid.*, 523).
5. In the words of Rowland (1987), "From the birth end of the continuum of pregnancy, younger and younger premature babies are now kept alive in increasingly sophisticated artificial environments, possible now from twenty four weeks into the pregnancy....when this succeeds, an egg could be fertilize and brought to term within an artificial or glass womb. Development of the artificial womb has been promoted as having the following advantages: foetal medicine would be improved; the child could be immunized while still inside the womb; the environment would be safer than a woman's womb; geneticists could programme in some superior trait on which society would agree; sex pre-selection; woman would be spared the discomfort of child birth; woman could be permanently sterilized; and finally, a man would be able to prove beyond doubt that he is the father of the child. Children may then be created who are neither born by, nor born of, woman" (*ibid.*, 524).
6. As Grossman (1971) defines, the process of cloning describes "that an individual 'previously' unique and mortal, may be rid of its uniqueness and have immortality conferred on it" (*ibid.*, 542). Further, the "process places a doubt on the reality of experience of parenthood and would be an alternating experience for both male and female partners" (Grossman, 1971 as cited in Rowland, 1987).
7. Ideology of motherhood is not a one-dimensional concept. It forms a complex whole, composed of assumption and ideas regarding the reality of the mother-child relation which develop over times. Ideology of motherhood has been used in feminist writings to explain the power inequalities between man and women in different societies. The ideology of motherhood as the belief that the quality of maternal sensitivity and attachment, and only that maternal quality, is directly and integrally related to the ideal growth and development of children, and which conceptualizes women primarily as producers of children.

Motherhood shapes not only the relationship of women with her children, but also the relationship between her and the father of her children. The process of reproduction is very much necessary for the stability and continuity of human existence.

Gupta (2000) argues that the concept of motherhood help us to understand more about the power relations between women and men than perhaps any other concept (*ibid.,* 80). The concept of motherhood is mostly associated with the reproductive activities of women. She states that to be mother is associated to the traditional role of mothering. As consequences of the control exercised over women's reproductive activities and their reproductive roles is that their mobility is reduced, which makes the household their primary sphere of concentration as compared to men who are free to participate in social production (*ibid.,* 80).

REFERENCES

Brown, Judith K. (1970). "Economic organization and the position of women among Iroquois", *Ethnohistory,* 17 : 131-67.

Correa, Genoveffa (1985). "How the reproductive technologies could be used to apply. The Brothel Model of Social Control over Women," *Women's Studies Int. Forum* 8(4) : 29-305.

Firestone, Shulamith (1972). *The Dialectics of Sex.* London: Paladin.

Grossman, Edward (1971). "The obsolescent mother: A scenario", *The Atlantic,* 227 : 39-50.

Gupta, Jyotsna Agnihotri (2000). *New Reproductive Technologies, Women's Health and Autonomy: Freedom or Dependency,* New Delhi: Sage Publications.

Huang, Jack Yu Jen and Rosenwaks, Zev. (2012). "In-vitro Fertilisation Treatment and Factors affecting Success", *Best Practice & Research Clinical Obstetrics and Gynaecology,* 26 (2012) : 777–788.

Hubbard, Ruth (1981). "The case against in-vitro fertilization and implantation," In: Helen Holmes, Betty Hoskins and Michael Gross my *Women Centered Perspectives,* Clifton: N.J. Humana Press.

K. Srinivasan (ed.) (1995). *Population Policy and Reproductive Health*: Proceedings of the seminar on Policy Direction and Strategies of Action in Population and Reproductive Health in India.

Keyser, L. (1982). "Does family planning liberate women?" M.A. Thesis, *Women and Development,* Institute of Social Studies, The Hague.

Khanna, Sunil (2010). *Foetal/Fatal Knowledge: New Reproductive Technologies and Family-Building Strategies in India,* Wadsworth, USA: Cenage Learning.

Meillassoux, Claude (1981). *Maidens, Meals and Money,* Cambridge: Cambridge University Press.

Mueller, Ruth Dixon (1993). *Population Policy and Women's Rights: Transforming Reproductive Choice,* Westport : Praeger Publishers.

O'Brien, Mary (1981). *The Politics of Reproduction,* New York : Routledge Kegan Paul.

Ortner, Sherry B., (1974). "Is female to male as nature is to culture?" In: M.Z. Rosaldo and L. Lamphere (ed.) *Woman, Culture and Society,* Stanford, CA. : Stanford University Press.

Rachel C. Snow (1994). "Power and decision: The social control of reproduction", In: Gita Sen and Rachel, C. Snow (eds.) *Power and Decision: The Social Control of Reproduction,* The Harvard Centre of Population and Development Studies.

Rothman, Barbara Katz (1989). *Recreating Motherhood,* New York: Rutgers University Press.

Rowland, Robyn (1987). "Technology and motherhood: Reproductive choice reconsidered", *Signs: Journal of Women in Culture and Society,* 12(3): 512-524.

Sengupta, Amit (2010). "Emerging genetic technologies and research: The interlinkages with assisted reproductive technologies", In: Sandhya Srinivasan (eds.) *Making Babies: Birth Markets and Assisted Reproductive Technologies in India,* New Delhi: Zubaan Publications.

Sexton, Sarah (2010). "The regulation of oocyte donation and surrogate motherhood in India", In: Sandhya Srinivasan (eds.) *Making Babies: Birth Markets and Assisted Reproductive Technologies in India,* New Delhi: Zubaan Publications.

Shore, Cris (1992). "Virgin births and sterile debates: Anthropology and the new reproductive technologies", *Current Anthropology,* 33(3): 295-313.

Singer, Peter and Wells, Deane (1984). *The Reproduction Revolution: New Ways of Making Babies,* Melbourne : Oxford University Press.

Spallone, Patricia (1986). "The warnock report: The politics of reproductive technology", *Women's Studies International Forum,* 9(5) : 543-550.

Stanworth, Michelle (1987). *Reproductive Technologies: Gender, Motherhood and Medicine,* UK: Polity Press.

Udgaonkar, Sangeeta (2010). "The brave new world of neo-eugenics", In: Sandhya Srinivasan (eds.) *Making Babies: Birth Markets and Assisted Reproductive Technologies in India,* New Delhi: Zubaan Publications.

United Nations Report of the International Conference on Population and Development (1994). Cairo, Egypt (New York: United Nations).

2

Widowhood, Gender and Health in Nalbari District of Assam

A Qualitative Analysis in Sociological Discourse

Hriday Ranjan Kalita

Introduction

The widow or *'Vidhava'* can be defined as a woman whose husband is dead and who has not married again (Godavari, D., 2000). Silverman said, "The very word 'widow' has very negative connotations. Many widows feel as if it implies that they are damaged, a second class citizen" (Godavari, D., 2000). The origin of the word *'vidhava'* can be traced in the Sanskrit word *'dhava'* meaning husband. In the Vedic period, reference can also be found to a double negative term, *'avidhava'* meaning *sadhava* which implies a woman whose husband is still alive. Accordingly to L. Thara Bhai, "widowhood is the change in the status of the woman brought about by the death of the spouse in the marital relationship and which necessitates the establishment of new relationships within the family, within the kin-group and within the community" (Bhai, 2004).

In India, "Widowhood is one of the sad facts of existence" (Godavari, D., 2000), so has rightly been observed by H.H. Heyman and this is probably more true in India than any other part of the world. It is made as such by customs, taboos and social stigma that are attached to widowhood in India which puts woman in the periphery of society. Christianity has accepted widowhood and widow remarriage as natural. In Islam too, widowhood like divorce is a non-issue as Islam believes that its acceptability in society should be free from inhibitions and taboos.

Even in Jainism, though widow remarriage is not allowed, it is not a serious problem as they still enjoy freedom in religious, political and social field. But, as Uma Chakravarti says, "widowhood in India among the upper castes is a state of social death" (Chakravarti, 1998). Chakravarti has borrowed the concept of social death from Orlando Patterson's classic work on slavery. Even though Hindu woman are not equitable with slaves, her use of the concept that Patterson used for slavery rightly expresses the gravity of the matter.

However, the condition of widows in India was not always so denigrated. G.D. Patil, tracing the history of widowhood in India in her book, *Hindu Widows: A Study in Deprivation* suggests that, "...In some respects, the Vedic woman and widow enjoyed certain privileges which they were deprived of in a later stage" (Godavari, D., 2000). The status of woman was high. The number of widows was small because early marriages were not in practice. *Sati*[1] system was absent. Widow Remarriage was allowed. Restrictions on widows regarding cloths and food were absent. Hence, as L. Thara Bhai writes, "the Vedic period was golden for single woman" (Bhai, 2004). However, apparently, women in India were striped off the privileges of this 'golden age' by a patriarchal society and status of widows has been declining ever since. During the British period reformers like Raja Rammohun Roy, Keshav Chandra Sen and Ishwar Chandra Vidyasagar raised their voices against *Sati,* child marriage and for widow re-marriage. However, such attempts barely scratched the surface of the problem and definitely failed to free Indian society from the apathy it possesses towards widowhood.

After Independence, Constitution of India took the task of ensuring legal protection for the rights of women through Hindu Code Bill, Hindu Marriage Act, 1955, Hindu Adoption and Maintenance Act, 1956 etc. Before Independence, Hindu Widows Re-marriage Act, 1856 gave widows right to remarry and after Independence, Hindu Succession Act, 1956 ensured for the widows the right to husband's property. Such laws are meant to secure a widow's socio-economic rights. However, in reality, very few widows are equipped with the knowledge, resources and access to these laws. Lack of education and lack of knowledge of these laws make them unable to use these legal provisions in their own favour. Moreover, the social structure, which is patriarchal, also makes it hard for widows to secure their rights. For example, Constitution of India provides property rights to daughters and to widows. But the customary practice is to inherit family property by sons. Thus, widows in India still have a long way to go in terms of receiving their rights both from state and society.

Condition of women in Assam is supposedly better to some degree in comparison to the rest of the country. This belief is rather a popular notion than a statement based on scientific observation the base of which lies in the belief that the Assamese society is a 'liberal' society when it comes to women. From a layman perspective certain examples might indicate towards the validity of such a statement. But presently, critical scientific studies are being conducted to evaluate the true condition of women in Assam the results of which are presenting grave challenges to such statements. However, we cannot deny that certain practices such as dowry[2] (at least explicitly) and *Sati* systems are absent here and have been so throughout history. Skilful and hardworking Assamese women have always been active in society contributing to the economic sector through their weaving and labour in agriculture. However, being a Hindu Patriarchal Society, women in Assam too are living in a state of inequality. Gender inequality is deeply inherent in Assamese society which reflects itself in the lack of access to property, productive resources, say in the decision-making process in the family etc. on the part of the women. However, due to the assimilation of many socio-economic and religious norms and values, in general the social behaviour and attitude of the society towards women was liberal to some extent in comparison to other states of India. But, this "liberal behaviour and attitude" was not enough to provide better acceptance towards the widows in the Assamese society. In Assamese society like the rest of the country, widows are looked down upon and marginalised by society. Observing the isolation and taboo on widow remarriage which prevents widows from coming to the societal mainstream, Jeuti Barooah writes in her book, *Single Woman in Assamese Hindu Society,* "Sporadic cases of widow re-marriage continued, but society did not accept is as a usual phenomenon" (Barooah, 1993). Lack of property rights still haunts Assamese widows and they are burdened with economic obligations after widowhood.

As Martha Alter Chen points out, "The total number of widows in India is extremely large—more than 33 million at the time of 1991 Census (Government of India, 1993)" (Chen, 1998). According to Census 2001, there were 44,019,000 widowed persons in India out of which 9,729,000 were male (widowers) and 34,290,000 were female (widows). The contrast is striking; while widowers comprised only 22.10 per cent, the widows comprised 77.89 per cent of the total widowed population in India (Census, 2001). The Indian widows "comprise approximately 9 per cent of the population of women" (Khanna, 2002). Besides the large number, the complexity of the social and economic set up on which Indian widowhood lies makes it a pressing concern. But in spite of this, very little is known about the real conditions and state of widowhood in India. As Martha Alter Chen puts it, "Widows are rarely mentioned in the literature on poverty, in public debates on social policy, or even by the women's movement" (Chen, 1998). Such neglect has turned widows in India into a very marginalised and vulnerable segment of the population. In such a situation, looking into the ways in which widowhood might affect the health of the widows gain relevance. While doing that we must keep in mind the specificities of the nature of widowhood in India including the changes it brings about in the social relations for the widows. We must also keep in mind the complexity of social relationship in Indian society and its hierarchical nature based on gender. As Madhu Nagla writes, "The health of a woman is conditioned by her social, cultural and economic status in the society" (Nagla, 2013). Thus, an analysis of widowhood and health in India must be done incorporating both the direct and indirect ways in which widowhood might affect the health of widows and a gendered perspective might be a vital tool for such an analysis.

Widowhood and Health: A Review of Literature

The integral relationship between widowhood and health has been observed and studied by many scholars. Studies have revealed that widowhood is a very stressful life event which affects psychological well-being and increases the risk of mortality. Gender as a factor probably came into consideration in this context of increased chances of mortality in widowhood when striking contrasts were observed in terms of mortality rates between widowers and widows. However, the effect of gender differences upon widowhood and health goes far beyond this as we will see in this study. Nonetheless, it can be said that the link between widowhood and health has been extensively dealt with by various scholars. Widowhood has been considered as "one of the most stressful and disruptive transitions" faced by older individuals which results in grief and trauma and the loss of emotional support which was provided earlier by the deceased spouse (Holmes and Rahe, 1967). In addition, the surviving spouse must learn to bear the burden of daily decisions and responsibilities which were previously handled by the deceased partner (Wortman *et al.*, 1992). Furthermore, such burden of added responsibilities compounds the grief and increases the psychological stress for the surviving partner which may have adverse impact on his/her well-being (Martikainen and Valkonen, 1996). Many studies have proved that the widowed typically have higher death rates than married people (Berardo, 1968). It has also been observed that widowhood have greater impact on mortality among women than men. Even though both widowers and widows have higher morbidity rates than their married counterparts, widows are more prone to chronic, disabling illnesses than are widowers (Verbrugge, 1979). Mental illness also affects the widowed more than married persons. Depression is much more often experienced by widows than widowers (Clayton, 1974). It is also important to notice that such psychological impact of widowhood cuts across age, race and sex (Pearlin and Johnson, 1977). From the above discussion it becomes explicit that the relation between widowhood and health has been extensively explored. This relation has also been put under the gender lens to some extent. However, while the effect of widowhood upon psychological well-being and its effect upon morbidity have been stressed, an area which has been largely ignored is the impact of widowhood upon physical well-being. A few studies have covered this aspect though. M. Stroebe, H. Schut and W. Stroebe (2007) in their study, *Health Outcomes of Bereavement* have suggested that widowhood adversely affects physical health. However, the few studies that have attempted to explore the impact of widowhood on physical health differ in terms of their results. While some finds explicit evidences that widowhood affects physical health; some only suggests mild effects when it comes to widowed men. Such differences are indicative of the need of a careful inspection of how the consequences of widowhood upon physical health differ by gender.

Widowhood, Gender and Health in India

The effects of widowhood upon the health of widows are not always direct. There are various intermediate factors which shape the ways in which widowhood affect the health of widows and the manner in which it affects it as well. Alka Ranjan (2001) writes, "The state of widowhood is both a personal condition and a social situation. Widowhood brings about severe social, economic and cultural deprivation." Such deprivation forms the background on which widowhood acquires the potential to adversely affect the health of the widows. These deprivations have been very clearly depicted in Marty Chen and Jean Dreze's study, *Widows and Health in Rural North India*. While examining indicators (both direct and indirect) of the health status of widows in rural north India Chen and Dreze have discussed economic condition and the effects of economic deprivation on mortality rates among widows. They have discussed patrilocality, according to which the women accompanies her husband to his parental home after marriage, and patrilineal inheritance, which give only the sons the right to inherit family property. Chen and Dreze have suggested that such systems have the effect of isolating and dispossessing women and act as one of the fundamental sources of gender inequality in rural north India. They have further discussed restrictions over remarriage and employment (caused by strict rituals to be followed by widows and restrictions over their mobility) which have their origin in the patriarchal family structure and gender inequalities created and sustained by it. Another very important aspect that Chen and Dreze have covered is the social isolation of widows which has its roots in the gender inequalities in society and the stigma associated with widowhood in rural India (Chen and Dreze, 1992). Alka Ranjan, while studying the determinants of well-being among widows in Varanasi, has pointed towards similar issues (Ranjan, 2001). Chen and Dreze's study puts forward the widow in rural north India as a highly marginalised being who is vulnerable to multiple factors. They have concluded that "the consequences of this social and economic marginalisation are manifested, as far as one can tell from the limited evidence available, in poor health and high mortality levels" (Chen and Dreze, 1992).

Social relationship is another very important factor that determines how and to what extent widowhood affects health. Debra Umberson and Jennifer Karas Montez write, "Social relationships—both quantity and quality—affect mental health, health behaviour, physical health and mortality risks" (Umberson and Montez, 2010). Quality of social relationships depends upon positive aspects of relationships such as emotional support provided by significant others, and strained aspects of relationships such as conflict and stress. Social relationships suggest the lack of social isolation. Social relationships have both positive and negative impact upon health. Social relations ensure positive health behaviours. A relative may oversee the health behaviours of the widow which contributes towards maintenance of her good health. This is the behavioural explanation of how social relations might affect the health of a widow. This impact can also be explained psycho-socially. Social support, personal control, symbolic meanings and norms etc. falls under this category which shows how these psycho-social elements contribute towards better health behaviours. The relation between social relationships and health can also be explained psychologically. Social relationships between spouses or parents and children generate values and greater sense of responsibility which compels people to promote healthier lifestyles. Thus, social relationships contribute towards better health behaviour. However, it can also exert negative impact on health behaviour which makes social relationships a very important factor in terms of the health of widows (Umberson and Montez, 2010). Moreover, in our society gender plays a crucial role in determining the social relationships, which makes the analysis of social relationships and their impact on the health of the widows even more crucial. Hence, gender has been used as a vantage point in this study. It has been used as a theoretical perspective for the qualitative analysis of the effect of widowhood upon health of widows. It is explicit that society in India is hierarchically organised on gender lines. So, when we try to analyse the effect of widowhood upon the health of widows, the various factors that shape the nature of widowhood in India must be taken into account as they will determine how widowhood affects the health of widows. Gender acts as an important determinant of women's status in India, both before and after widowhood. Hence, it becomes imperative that we observe the impact of widowhood on health from a gendered perspective.

Objectives, Field and Methodology of the Study

The primary objective of this study is to explore the effects of widowhood upon the health of women. However, the question that this study has attempted to answer is 'how' rather than 'what'. Thus, the objective of this study is not to explore 'what' impact widowhood has upon the health of women. Instead, through a qualitative analysis of the state of widowhood and the health issues concerning the widows, this study has attempted to explore 'how' or in what ways widowhood causes the emergence of health related issues for widows. While doing this, this study has explored the complex socio-cultural relationships between the widows and their family members and relatives that determine the state of widowhood and the affects it has upon their health to a great extent. In short, it can be said that the objective of this study is to explore the indirect ways in which widowhood leads to health issues for the widows. To achieve this objective, this study has undertaken a qualitative study with the help of a gendered theoretical perspective.

The field of this study is the Nalbari district of the state of Assam that is situated in the North-Eastern part of India. Nalbari initially was a part of undivided Kamrup District and became a sub-division in 1967. In 1985 Nalbari was separated from Kamrup District and made a district with its headquarters at Nalbari Town. Nalbari district was further divided in 2003 for creation of Baska district in B.T.A.D. area. The north and west side of the district is bounded by Baska and Barpeta district respectively. The south and east side of the district is bounded by Kamrup district. Nalbari has 1 subdivision, 7 revenue circles, 7 development blocks, 5 police stations and 65 Gaon Panchayats. Road links to Nalbari is through National Highway 31 and broad-gauge Railway Line. Nalbari town is 2 km away from the National Highway 31. Nearest

Railway Junction is Rangia. Nalbari Town is situated 60 km away from Guwahati (Nalbari District Profile, Government of Assam). According to Census 2011, Nalbari has a total population of 7,71,693 out of which 3,96,006 are males and 3,75,633 are female. The district has a total area of 1,052 square km and a sex-ratio of 949. Average literacy of Nalbari district is 78.63 per cent (Census, 2011).

The respondents in this study have been selected using Simple Random Sampling method. 120 widows have been selected using this method as the respondents of this study. After that, these respondents have been divided into three categories on the basis of their age: Young Widows (20-40 years), Middle Aged Widows (41-60 years) and Aged Widows (61 years and above). The purpose of this categorisation is to highlight the impact of gendered inequalities upon the health of widows. As gender relations and the socio-cultural attributions vary from one age group to another, this categorisation was imperative to fulfil the objective of this study. After this categorisation the respondents of this study has been placed in these categories as 20-40 years: 30 Respondents, 41-60 years: 60 Respondents and 61 years and above: 30 Respondents. Thus, a total of 120 widows have been taken as the respondents for this study. The study is based primarily on Qualitative Data collected through Interview Schedule and Personal Interviews conducted with the help of Interview Guide. This marks the Primary source of this study. Along with that, secondary sources such as books, journals etc. relevant to the issue at hand have been used as the secondary source for this study.

This study is directed towards exploring the effects of widowhood upon the health of the widows and the complex social relationships which leads to various indirect ways in which widowhood affect the health of the widows. This study is primarily based upon qualitative analysis and the number of respondents is very small. In this respect, this study is limited in its scope in terms of its ability to make generalisations based on empirical evidence. However, the study surely attempts to deal with a very important and generally neglected aspect of widowhood and the health of widows and has tried to explore the ways in which health issues arise under widowhood using a gendered perspective. Thus, the subject of this study can surely be said to be significant.

Socio-economic Background of the Respondents

Social Background is of utmost importance as it is a factor that shapes the life and life experiences of any individual. As shown in Fig. 2.1, among the 120 respondents, 84 (70%) are Hindus and 36 (30%) are Muslims.

Community-wise, the respondents in this study are diverse. It was found that the respondents of these study comprises people from the Assamese, Bengali, Bodo and Muslim communities.

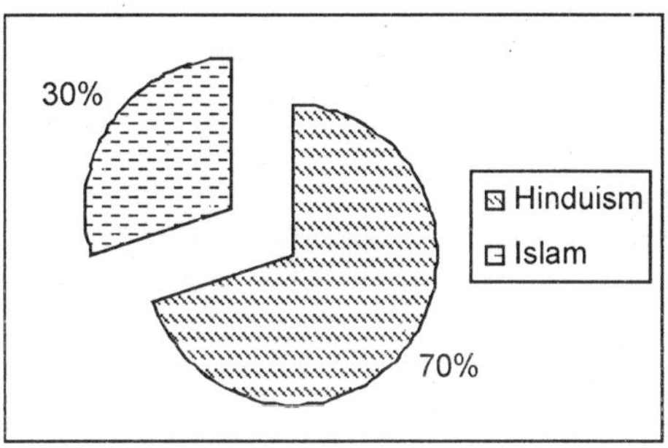

Fig. 2.1: Religious Composition of the Respondents

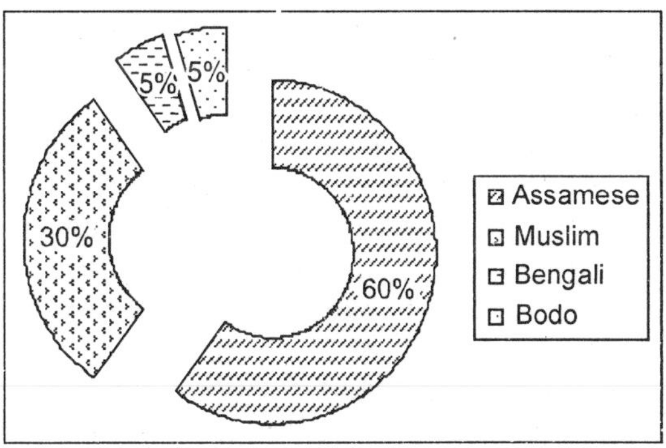

Fig. 2.2: Community-wise Composition of the Respondents

As Fig. 2.2 shows, 72 (60%) of the respondents belong to the Assamese community, 36 (30%) to the Muslim community[3], 6 (5%) to the Bengali community and 6 (5%) to the Bodo community.

While 90 (75%) respondents speak Assamese language, the respondents belonging to Bengali and Bodo community speaks Assamese along with Bengali and Bodo languages respectively. As far as the family pattern is concerned, among the 120 respondents, 78 (65%) respondents live in nuclear families and 42 (35%) respondents live in joint families. 105 (87.5%) out of 120 respondents have children, while 15 (12.5%) of the respondents do not have any children. It is noticeable that most of such respondents who do not have any children belong to the groups of Young Widows (20-40 years) and Middle Aged Widows (41-60 years). Among the 105 respondents who have children, 6 have single child, 81 respondents have 2-4 children, 12 respondents have 5-7 children and 6 respondents have 8-10 children. As far as the size of the family is concerned, 75 respondents have small family (2-4 members), 27 respondents have medium family (5-7 members) and 18 respondents have large families (more than 7 members). Among the 120 respondents, 87 (72.5%) respondents considered themselves as the head of their family, 9 respondents considered their sons, 9 respondents considered their mother-in-law, 3 respondents considered their father-in-law and 9 respondents considered their brother-in-law to be the head of the family. The remaining 3 respondents out of the total 120 respondents live with their parents and consider their parents as the head of the family. The large number of respondents considering themselves as the head of their families has its source in the wide prevalence of nuclear families, 65 per cent as have been found in this study. After the death of the husband who is usually the head of the family in a largely Patriarchal Assamese Society, the widow assumes her husband's position as the head of the family. The real power that they are able to exercise in the family, however, is another matter for careful observation.

Economic Background of the respondents also has been explored in detail in this study. Among the respondents, 36 respondents are illiterate, 15 respondents have studied up to primary level, 48 up to matriculation, 9 up to higher secondary level and 12 respondents have studied up to Graduate level.

Fig. 2.3 shows the educational status of the respondents explicitly. It has been noticed in this study that most of the

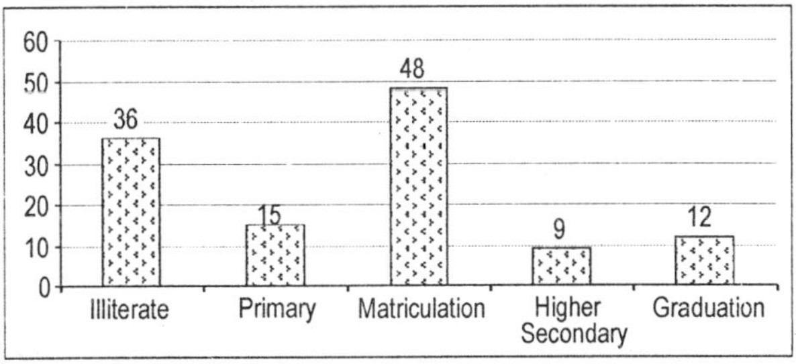

Source: Field Study.

Fig. 2.3: Educational Status of the Respondents

respondents, who are illiterate (24 out of 36 illiterate respondents) belong to the group of Aged Widows (61 years and above). Family source of income is a very important aspect in terms of the economic condition of the respondents.

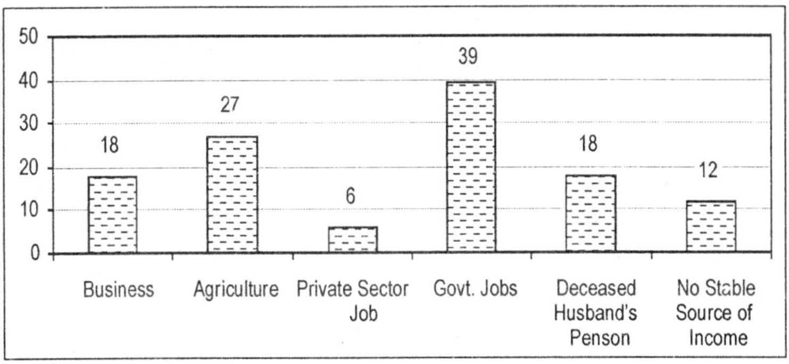

Source: Field Study.

Fig. 2.4: Family Source of Income of the Respondents

Figure 2.4 shows that among the families of the respondents, 18 had business as their source of income, 27 had agriculture, 6 had jobs in private companies and 39 had Government jobs as their source of income. Eighteen respondents' families are living on the pension of their husbands. The remaining 12 respondents had no conventional or stable source of income in their family. They are living by giving their cultivable land on lease (*Adhi* system)[4] for agriculture, giving their pond on lease for fishery, some worked as daily wage labour and some even worked as domestic help and did odd jobs in nearby families. The sources of income of the families in certain cases are multiple as those having jobs also have earnings from agricultural activities.

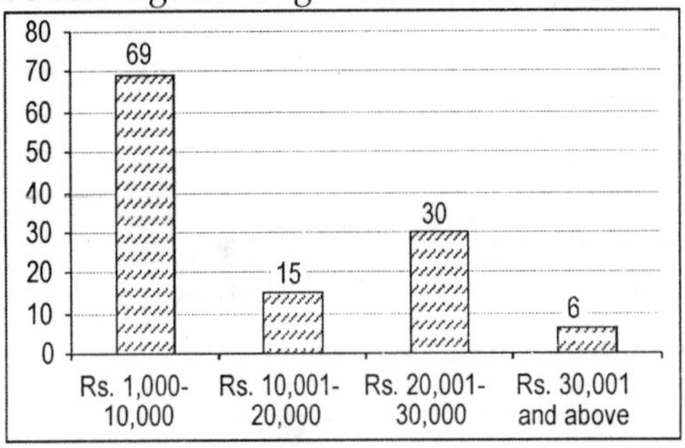

Source: Field Study.

Fig. 2.5: Family Monthly Income of the Respondents

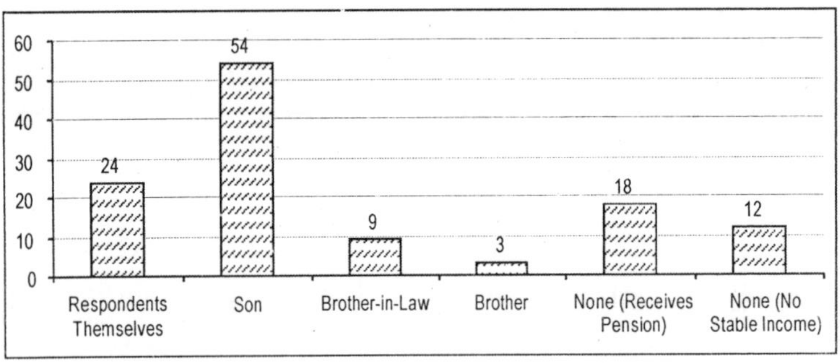

Source: Field Study.

Fig. 2.6: Engagement in Income Generating Activity

But, taking all these factors into consideration, as Fig. 2.5 shows, 69 respondents' families had a monthly income of Rs. 1,000—10,000. These 69 respondents also include the 12 respondents, having no stable source of income as mentioned earlier having a monthly income ranging from Rs. 1,000 5,000 only. Fifteen respondents' families had Rs. 10,001—20,000, 30 respondents' families had Rs. 20,000—30,000 and 6 respondents' families had a monthly income of Rs. 30,000 and above. In terms of family income, another important factor is the question; who is engaged in that income generating activity in the family?

As Fig. 2.6 shows, among the 120 respondents, in case of 24 (20%) respondents, the respondents themselves are engaged in income generating activity. In case of 54 (45%) respondents, their sons, and in case of 9 (7.5%) respondents, their brother-in-laws were engaged in the income generating activity. Three (2.5%) respondents who are living with their parents depend upon the income of their brothers, in case of 18 (15%) respondents, their families depend upon the husband's pension and in the families of 12 (10%) respondents there are no members involved in any proper or stable income generating activity. As far as the pattern of the houses of the respondents are concerned, 45 respondents live in *Kachcha* Houses[5], 54 respondents live in *Pakka* (Assam Type)[6] houses and the remaining 21 respondents live in *Pakka* (RCC Type) houses.

The social and economic background provides a very vivid picture of the socio-economic status of the respondents. It has been mentioned earlier that out of 120 respondents, only 24 are engaged in income generating activity. Of them, only 21 have proper jobs providing them with a steady source of income. The remaining 3 respondents are engaged in managing agricultural activities or other form of small business which they manage from home. A staggering 96 (80%) of the respondents have been found to be unemployed. These respondents without a source of income of their own were asked if they receive some money on a monthly basis for their personal needs. Surprisingly, all the 96 respondents commented that they do not receive any money from their family for their personal needs. Although, 69 (57.5%) respondents said that their family members take care of their needs to a certain extent, 21 (17.5%) respondents said that they are able to take care of their own needs to a certain level as they have some source of earning, 3 (2.5%) respondents said that they ask for money when necessary and the remaining 3 (2.5%) respondents expressed that their personal needs are not fulfilled as they have no source of income and their family members do not cater to their personal needs. In terms of property, 93 respondents had some form of property, primarily land in their name. It is interesting that 90 of these respondents inherited this property from their husbands. Only 3 respondents bought land themselves. None of the respondents inherited any property from their parents. 27 out of 120 respondents did not have any property. In their cases, either, the property has not been transferred to the respondent officially and the property will pass on to her son as custom dictates or in other cases, the husband's family refused her the share of her husband's property after his death. In terms of decision-making abilities, mixed responses were given by the respondents. Figure 2.7 will make the traits in terms of decision making abilities clear.

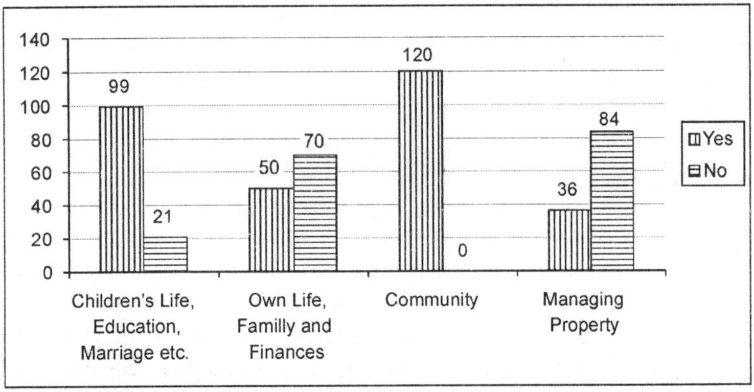

Source: Field Study.

Fig. 2.7: Decision-making ability among the Respondents

As can be seen in Fig. 2.7, 99 respondents said that they are capable of making decisions regarding their children's education, marriage etc. However, in terms of making decisions regarding their own life and various other matters concerning the family, especially finances; only 50 respondents responded positively. However, in terms of making decisions in the community level, all the respondents responded positively. Again, in terms of making decisions regarding managing property, only 36 respondents said that they have a say in this regard. It is important to remember that 93 respondents had property in their name. Moreover, it is also important to note that out of the 36 respondents having decision-making abilities in terms of property; most of them (27) belong to the Group of Middle Aged Widows (41-60 years). Again, out of 57 respondents without decision-making abilities in terms of management of property, most (27) belong to the group of Aged Widows (61 years and above). 111 out of 120 respondents said that the death of their husbands has caused financial hardship for their families and that it has resulted in a decline in the social standing of their family. Only 9 respondents responded negatively in this regard.

Interactions between Gender and Widowhood and Impact upon the Health of the Widows

The previous section has dealt extensively with the socio-economic background and the socio-economic status of the respondents. Such an in-depth analysis is essential for this study as the objective of this study is to explore the complex ways in which widowhood causes health related issues for the widows. As Madhu Nagla writes, "Sociological study often involves itself in investigating what appears at first sight to be natural, universal or common sense, only to discover that such behaviours or practices are fundamentally affected by specific social factors and influences. At the outset, any social phenomenon which appears to be natural or general or simply common, however, when these phenomena or behaviours or incidents are put for sociological inquiry, they are affected by certain social factors or certain other causative actors" (Nagla, 2013). As gender inequalities and the complex web of relationships formed around it contribute to the nature of widowhood to a large extent, it is imperative that the socio-economic status of the respondents in this study is taken into consideration.

The previous section throws light on many important aspects. It is seen that majority of the respondents were Hindu which means that they had to follow strict rules and regulations as widows. In fact, 81 out of 120 respondents commented that they had to go through various ceremonies and follow many strict rules and regulations which include not wearing *'sindoor'*,[7] wearing only white attires, not wearing any jewellery, having only boiled-vegetarian food, fasting, staying away from religious places and family ceremonies etc. Such norms associated with widowhood also severely restrict the mobility of the widows. Such harsh practices have a twofold effect. First, they isolate the widow from the family and society. Such isolation combined with the grief of loss of spouse and stress of changing role and status through widowhood affect the psychological health of the widows. Among 120 respondents, 80 respondents complained that they felt extreme loneliness while following such practices.

Restrictions on mobility also contribute to the felling of loneliness. Secondly, such strict rules and regulations for widows affect their physical health too. Many of the respondents admitted that they found maintaining rules and restrictions concerning food as they had to completely alter their previous habits. Some respondents also admitted that at the early period of their widowhood they found practices like fasting very difficult and they even fainted at times. However, such details were mentioned by the respondents after a lot of probing. At the beginning when the respondents were asked if the strict rules and regulations they follow as widows affect their health; most of the respondents responded negatively. The reason for such answers lies in the fact that the social custom associated with widowhood in the society has made the adverse effects of the practices of widowhood invisible for the respondents themselves. Their socialisation on the basis of gender has instilled a firm belief in them that following such harsh norms and facing the adversities caused by them is natural for a widow. Gender plays a crucial role in this regard. Strict rules and regulations for widows are intended to control their sexuality which without a spouse remains vulnerable and potentially harmful for the family. That is why, it was observed that while among Young Widows (20-40 years) and Middle Aged Widows (41-60 years) such practices were insisted on following religiously, in case of Aged Widows (61 years and above) these rules were loosely imposed and followed. The reason for this lies in the 'diminishing' threat of exposed and vulnerable sexuality of aged widows as they are seen as 'de-sexed' beings in our society.

Another fact that was observed in this study is that most of the respondents (78 out of 120 respondents, 65%) live in nuclear families. Further, the number of respondents who consider themselves as the head of the family (87 out of 120 respondents, 72%) echoes this trend. Being in nuclear families, the respondents had to assume the responsibilities of their husband as the head of their families. Many of the respondents commented that they were 'at a loss' at the beginning faced with such tremendous change in role. In a Patriarchal Assamese Society, the roles of women are still confined to their homes. It is clear from the data regarding education and employment among the respondents. With widowhood, the widows not only goes through a stressful mental period but also have to bear tremendous pressure of shouldering the financial and other responsibilities of the family, which were previously performed by their spouses. This change in roles puts excessive pressure upon both psychological and physical health of the widows. Most of the respondents commented that their lack of knowledge regarding banking and other official work created difficulties for them and they had to depend upon others for such work. Out of the 21 respondents who had jobs, 8 respondents started to work after their husbands passed away under the pressure of maintaining their family. Adjusting to such new role, as the respondents commented, was 'very stressful' for them and they had to face extreme role conflict trying to maintain their responsibilities at office and home. Such pressure has caused poor health behaviour among the respondents as they tend to ignore their health in order to fulfil their responsibilities.

It is surprising, although not unexpected, that none of the respondents remarried after their husbands passed away. All the respondents except 6 respondents belonging to the group of Young Widows (20-40 years) commented that they did not wish to remarry. The 6 respondents who wished to remarry but did not, said that they did not remarry because of their fear of what their families or people might say. In some cases the husband's family and in some occasions their own parents did not allow them to remarry. As Marty Chen and Jean Dreze writes, "The marginalisation of widows in north India is consistent with the traditional perception of Hindu widows as inauspicious and guilty women who, ideally, should lead a life of austerity devoted to the memory of their husband" (Chen and Dreze, 1992). Such perceptions make widows live a life of loneliness devoid of healthy social relationships. Again, it causes physical hardships for the respondents who are bound to take care of themselves for the rest of their lives, a task for which they are very ill equipped with because of their lack of education, employment and the lack of confidence caused by them. Another issue that surfaced during the interviews is the fear of the respondents regarding the hardships of old age without the support of their spouse. This fear is more potent among Young Widows (20-40 years) and worse among the widows without any children. Such fear has caused depression among the respondents. Out of 120 respondents 75 respondents said that they suffer from depression due to their present condition and in anticipation of what to come.

It has been already mentioned that widows are marginalised in multiple ways in Indian Society. The ideology, perception and stigma related to widowhood push the widows to the periphery of the society. However, another important factor that disadvantages them is their poor socio-economic status and this factor is very closely associated with the gender inequalities present in Indian society. As Marty Chen and Jean Dreze write, "This ideological influence, however, may be less crucial than the simple fact that widows are often seen as an economic burden. The most effective way of ensuring the social protection of Indian widows is perhaps to help them to be recognised as persons who have something important to contribute to the household economy" (Chen and Dreze, 1992). This problem has clearly been observed in this study. The socio-economic status of the respondents, as has been discussed before, is poor. They lack education, employment and in case of most of the respondents, they are valued for their traditional family roles. However, when widowed, they lose those roles and with that their social status and position in the family. As most of the respondents are unable to contribute to the family financially they are considered as burden on many occasions. Such conditions of these widows have its roots in the inherent gender inequalities present in the society which causes a tremendous emphasis on the gendered roles of women ignoring the need to equip women with other qualities such as education and ability to support them financially. Because of it, it was observed that the respondents lack confidence and self-respect. They are devalued not only by the society and family but also by themselves. Many respondents even commented that they are living 'being a burden' upon their family. It was also observed that many of the respondents who were unemployed engaged themselves in productive work such as helping in agricultural activities, cattle and poultry rearing etc. which generated periodic incomes for the family. However, when asked if they were engaged in any income generating activity almost all the respondents responded negatively. The unemployed respondents were completely dependent upon their family members as they do not receive any regular income for their personal needs. They lacked decision-making abilities, especially in terms of financial matters and property related decisions made in the family. The widows belonging to the group of Aged Widows (61 years and above) are the most disadvantaged in this regard. Thus, widowhood resulted for the respondents in a situation in which they are vulnerable and prone to neglect and the factors mentioned here makes them unable to assert their rights and demand their needs.

Living in such a condition has severe impact upon the health of the widows. Symbolic Interactionism propounded by George Herbert Mead suggests that human beings are distinctive as they are capable of reflecting on their own thoughts and actions. It emphasizes the ways in which people gain a shared understanding of the meanings. Using this perspective, sociologists have tried to study the changes in identity. Goffman's work on stigma shows that a person's sense of identity is formed in interaction with others and it is strongly influenced by other people's perceptions (Goffman, 1963). The same phenomenon occurs in terms of widowhood which makes a widow lose their sense of identity and worth which in turn affects their health negatively. In this study, it was observed that the respondents, devalued and lacking in self-respect and confidence in their own mind, fails to demand for their essential needs. They lack the ability to decide what kind of health facilities they will avail. More importantly they could not decide on their own when to avail medical help. It is truer in case of the Aged Widows (61 years and above) as they commented that on many occasions their family members ignored her complaints regarding her health and her request to visit a doctor. The problem in case of Young Widows (20-40 years) and Middle Aged Widows (41-60 years) surfaces somewhat differently. Unlike the Later Age Widows (61 years and above), they are not directly neglected in terms of their health. However, the sense of loss of status that these respondents previously possessed compels them to invest extra effort physically and psychologically for the family in order to regain that lost status at least to some extent, if not completely. Some of the respondents remarked that, "I am a burden on my family, so I try my best to be of some use for my family." Such a comment shows that with such efforts they gain a sense of self-worth, however, with dire effects on their physical and psychological well-being. On the contrary, the respondents who were employed exhibited far better levels of confidence and self-respect. They were able to make decisions regarding what health facilities they avail and when. They also exhibited very positive attitude towards maintaining good health behaviour.

The Health Problems that the respondents complained about included common problems such as Cold and Cough, Headache, Stomach Ache, Fever, Gastric etc. However, some of the respondents also complained of pressure, heart related problems, kidney related problem, nerve disease, diabetes, thyroid problems, menstrual abnormalities, orthopaedic problems, appendicitis, back pain and eye related problems etc. Due to the poor economic condition of most of the respondents, Government Hospitals are preferred for availing health facilities. However, in case of major health problems and surgery, health facilities in private hospitals have been availed, though not without much financial strain.

The respondents said that they use to ignore certain 'minor' diseases such as cold and cough, headache, stomach ache, light fever, gastric etc. and in most cases do not seek medical help. Figure 2.8 will help make this clear.

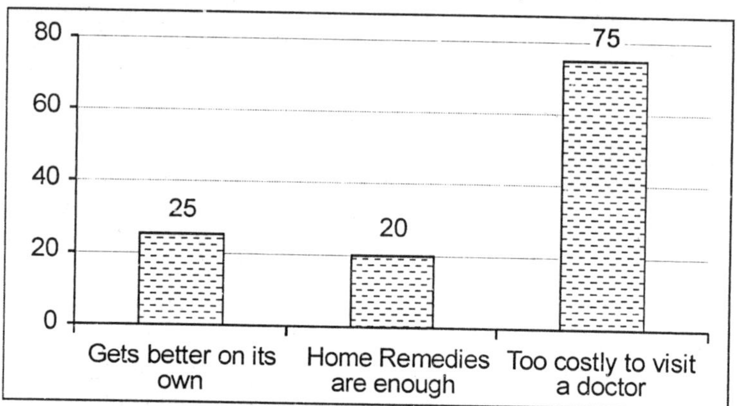

Source: Field Study.

Fig. 2.8: Reasons of Ignoring 'Minor' Diseases among the Respondents

As it is shown in Fig. 2.8 shows, when asked why they ignore such diseases, 25 respondents said that such diseases get better on their own, 20 respondents said that home remedies and indigenous medicines are enough to cure them. But 75 respondents responded that they do not visit a doctor and ignore such diseases as it is too costly to visit a doctor for such 'minor' problems.

Such approach towards health has given rise to practice of self-treatment (having medicine without consulting a doctor). All of the 120 respondents admitted that they resort to self-treatment for saving money of visiting a doctor, at least occasionally. Such approach also gives way for use of indigenous medicine and indigenous methods of healing.

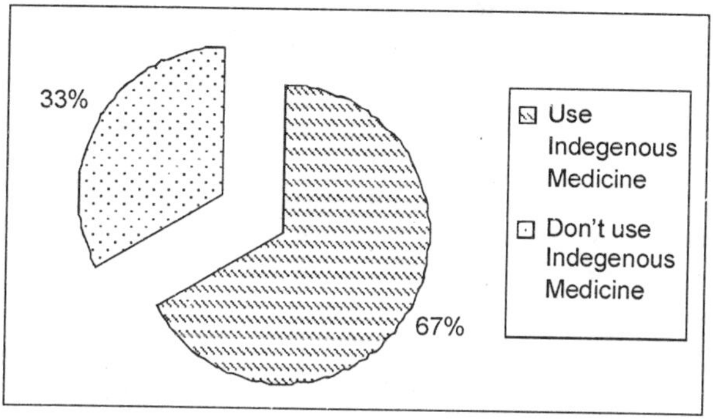

Source: Field Study.

Fig. 2.9: Use of Indegenous Medicine among the Respondents

As can be seen in Fig. 2.9, while 40 respondents said that they never avail indigenous medicine or indigenous healing methods, 80 respondents admitted that they do. However, there are many other reasons for ignoring health issues and they differ according to the age groups among the respondents. Ignorance of health issues is not always voluntary, but also involuntary at times as in many cases the family members of the respondents ignore their health problems even though the respondent herself do not wish to. The idea of 'need' of medical facilities is affected highly by socio-cultural norms and the status and perceptions of self-worth which it generates among the widows. In terms of health, "women are not only neglected by others, but they also neglect themselves." "Fewer women declare themselves ill as compared to men" (Nagla, 2013). It is evident in this study that the devalued status of the widows in family and society plays a crucial role in such behaviour. The evidence of such behaviour has been found in the case of Aged Widows (61 years and above). While, any specific association of any disease with widows of any particular age group cannot be made, it was observed that certain diseases like Diabetes, Orthopaedic Problems, Back pain and Eye problems are more common with the widows belonging to the group of Aged Widows (61 years and above). The prevalence of such diseases with this particular age group among the widows has significant consequences. It is explicit that such diseases increase the dependence of elder widows upon their family members and the absence of required care might result in psychological distress and worsening physical health as well. Among the 30 Aged Widows interviewed in this study 20 respondents commented that their family members "do not give proper attention towards the needs of their old age". They further commented that such neglect creates difficulties in terms of their day-to-day activities and they feel 'sad' as their family members do not care for them as they should. Thus, the dependence of these respondents upon their family members has explicit impact upon their health. This finding substantiates what Madhu Nagla writes, "Often women need permission and be escorted to seek health care. When there is dependence, either physical or financial, on care givers, access is determined by the willingness and ability of the care givers to provide treatment" (Nagla, 2013).

In case of Young Widows (20-40 years), the reasons for ignoring health issues were found to be much more subjective. Among the 30 such respondents, 23 are unemployed and live under varied financial constraints. Among these respondents those with children commented that they ignore their health issues at times in order to be able to provide for the health needs of their children. Moreover, those respondents with young children admitted that they cut on their share of nutritional food such as milk in order to provide the children properly. Besides financial constraints this problem has a vivid gender undertone. It is gendered socialisation that makes any form of sacrifice on the part of the mother for her children a very 'natural' phenomenon. Similarly, in case of Middle Aged Widows (41-60 years), most of them who are unemployed admitted that they ignore certain 'minor' health issues in order to carry on with their household duties. Such an attitude can only be explained with the help of the concept of gender socialisation in our society which makes such ignorance acceptable for themselves and for the people around them.

Social support is another factor that affects the health of women in widowhood. Silverstein *et al.*, writes that intergenerational social support plays a moderating role on widowhood and its health consequences and instrumental and expressive support can moderate the declines in psychological well-being in widowhood (Silverstein *et al.*, 1994). In this study it has been observed that the Young Widows (20-40 years) living with their husband's family after the death of the spouse have some kind of social support despite the fact that her life becomes much more difficult as she has to live in very strict social control and restriction. However, the numbers of such respondents were very small and a good number of respondents belonging to this age group are living separately on their own in financial terms. Under such circumstances social support becomes scarce. In most cases it has been observed that the contact with the husband's family becomes minimal and if any social support she receives, she receives it from her parents and siblings. However, such incidences are rather scarce.

Among the respondents who are living separately on their own mostly belong to the age group of Middle Aged Widows (41-60 years). Reasons for living on their own are various such as the respondent lived separately with husband since marriage, it was her choice to live separately, husband's family behaved badly and refused to support after husband's death, parents refused to help after being isolated by husband's family after husband's death etc. Whatever the reason is the respondents living separately on their own face tremendous stress of managing the family on their own, which affect their physical health. This has been discussed earlier. Further, living separately, in many cases results in a state of social isolation where social support and social networking becomes scarce. This lack of social support directly affects the psychological health of the widows.

However, living with husband's family does not automatically ensure the quality of the social support that the respondent is receiving. The quantity of contact has little connection with whether material or emotional support is exchanged (Umberson, 1992; Ward *et al.*, 1984). Quality of the relationship and social support is what that matters most. Many respondents in this study who lives with their husband's family commented that the members of the husband's family "tolerate" her as she has "nowhere else to go". It is truer in the case of the respondents living with the husband's family who are also unemployed. The respondents who are employed were observed to be maintaining much healthier relation with the members of their husband's family. This again proves what Marty Chen and Jean Dreze said about the importance of the ability of a widow to contribute to the household economy to ensure their social protection in India (Chen and Dreze, 1992).

In case of the Aged Widows (61 years and above) among the 120 respondents, it has been observed that they become dependent primarily upon their sons. The most important determinant of the health consequences of social support is the level of closeness of the older adult to the provider of social support. Aid from only the closest family members (e.g. adult children) reduced the influence of distressing life events on depressive symptomology (Strain & Chappel, 1982). The responses of these respondents in terms of the quality of relation with their children and other family members present a mixed picture. While some respondents said that they are satisfied with their relation with their children, others responded negatively. It was observed that the respondents judged the quality of the relation between themselves and their son and other family members on the basis of the care that they provide them. A respondent commented that, "My relation with my son is very good. He takes care of me to the best of his abilities." However, 11 respondents belonging to the age group of Aged Widows (61 years and above) remarked that their family members 'do not take care' of them 'properly' and that they are not satisfied with their relation with their son and other family members. It was interesting that the respondents based their judgement of the quality of relation upon the care that family members provided in terms of their health.

Respondents without children, whether living separately or with their husband's family, suffers from inadequate quality of social relation and social support. Even when they had family members to take care of them, these respondents expressed the neglect they feel for not having children and impending hardships in old age when without children they will have no one to take care of them. It was observed that in the case of these respondents, the quality of relation with the members of husband's family is usually poor. Such respondents also suffer more from depression. Further, childlessness and widowhood leave them in such a state where they have nothing to look forward to. In such a scenario, the health behaviour of these respondents is also affected adversely. Thus, respondents without children not only provide evidence of inadequate social relation and social support, but also reemphasises its vitality and importance.

Another very vulnerable section among the widows is the widows who are living with their parents after the death of their husband. The primary reason in such cases is usually the hostility and unwillingness of the husband's family to support the widow. In this study, only 3 such respondents were interviewed and all 3 of them were living with their parents because of the above mentioned reasons. Gender plays a crucial role in increasing the vulnerability of these respondents. The custom dictates that the widow remains with her husband's family after the death of her husband and live a life of control and self-restraint for the rest of her life. While widowhood takes away her status as a married woman, leaving her husband's family and living with her parents, snatches away the social status she had as a widow too. Thus, the widow living with her parents becomes an entity without an identity. Under such condition she not only loses her social relations and social support, she even becomes unable to live with her parents considering it her right to be there. All the 3 respondents in this study expressed a sense of 'guilt' for having to 'become a burden' on their parents and this guilt is intensified in case the widow becomes dependent upon her brother as after her parents he assumes the role of the head of the household. The respondents said that they feel 'depressed' and 'anxious' thinking about their own future. They also said that they hesitate in asking for money for fulfilling their requirements as they feel as they are putting 'more burdens' upon her father/brother. They even commented that due to this hesitation they sometimes ignore certain health issues too. Such vulnerability also affects their health behaviour. Thus, the respondents living with their parents are affected by their inadequate social relationships and social support both in terms of their psychological and physical health.

Analytical Observations

This study has been an attempt to make a qualitative enquiry in the question of how widowhood affects the health of the widows. While answering this question, the study has got inextricably attached to the understanding of the effects of gender upon the existing social relations and the nature and experience of widowhood itself. These two quests together have led to the conception in this study regarding the ways in which widowhood affects the health of the widows. The study has encountered various complex ways in which widowhood affects the health of the widows. It was found that while widowhood has certain direct effects on the health of the widows such as depression and other psychological problems; it has many indirect affects upon the health of the widows as well. It has been observed in this study that in this context of the indirect effects of widowhood upon the health of the widows; gender and its effects upon social relationships and the nature and experience of widowhood comes into play.

Gender determines the nature and scope of social relations in the Indian society. In the Nalbari District of Assam too, where this study is based, it is true. Because of this fact, it is undeniable that gender is one of the primary factor which determines how the nature of widowhood will be and hence it also determines what its effects will be; whether it be experience of widowhood, quality of social relations and social support for the widows, the rights and responsibilities of the widows, their access to resources, mobility, the extent of their duties and also the boundaries of her freedom to choose, to reject, to expect and their freedom of will in general. As has been meticulously probed, explored, examined and explained throughout this research work, what this study has observed is that these factors which determine the quality of the life of the widows have a strong gendered connotation in our society. At the same time, these and various other factors like these affect the health of the widows. Thus, widowhood and gender are two of the most important factors that impacts, shapes, influences, manipulates and finally, forms the varied ways in which widowhood gathers the potential to and ultimately does affect the health of the widows in adverse ways.

Concluding Remarks

A gender perspective has been said to have the potential to hand a researcher the ability to make visible issues and concerns which were previously invisible. Using gendered perspective, this study has tried to present an in-depth account of the interplay between widowhood and gender in terms of the impact of widowhood upon health of the widows. The findings of this study reveals that there are various ways in which widowhood affects the health of the widows and this study have been successful in enumerating some of them. However, it will be wrong to presume that this study presents a holistic and exhaustive account of the issue at hand. First, it must be admitted that this study has limitations in terms of its scope for making generalisations as the number of respondents is very small. Secondly, although, it can be said that this study has attempted and has been successful to some extent in highlighting the relation between widowhood and gender in terms of the impact of widowhood upon the health of widows, the issue of contextual realities can never be overlooked. India presents a tremendously heterogeneous social structure and with that the factor of gender also acquires its heterogeneity. The issue of widowhood and health is one of pressing concerns and gender as a factor presents a viable tool to understand this very complex problem. Hence, it will be adequate to conclude by saying that further studies conducted, keeping the contextual realities of the interaction between widowhood and gender in mind, might provide valuable insights concerning the issue of widowhood and Health.

NOTES

1. *Sati* is the Hindu custom of self-immolation of a widow by burning herself to death at her dead husband's funeral pier. *Sati* is legally banned in India. However, occasional incidents still occur.
2. Dowry refers to the custom of offering gifts to the bridegroom's family by the bride's family along with the bride at the time of marriage. Dowry could be in both cash and kind. Although, custom states dowry as a voluntary offering of gifts by the bride's family; in reality it is most often obligatory.
3. It is very difficult to demarcate distinctively between the people belonging to the Assamese and the Muslim communities in Assam. That is because Muslims in Assam are also seen and accepted as an integral part of a greater Assamese community. Not just Muslims, but the various communities living in Assam including the Bodos, Bengalis and many other are considered as a part of a larger Assamese community as a whole. However, the religious beliefs of Muslims and the Hindus who are the majority

surely remain distinct and so does the nature of widowhood among them. Hence, in this study, Assamese and Muslim have been kept as two distinct communities despite the fact that they share various traits in terms of community.

4. *Adhi* system is a system prevalent in rural Assam. According to this system those who own agricultural land use to give their land on lease to farmers without agricultural land. The farmer cultivates the land and in return gives the half of the produce of cultivation to the owner of the land, instead of money. The word *'adhi'* literally means half. This system represents the earlier nature of rural Assamese society which was primarily agricultural and self-sufficient.
5. The term *'kachcha'* in the context of a house means non-concrete. It is a type of hut widely prevalent in rural Assam. Bamboo and canes are used for the walls and they are coated with clay. The roof is also made using bamboos and a tall grass available locally.
6. *'Pakka'* house refers to houses made of bricks and concrete. Assam Type houses, however, carry certain unique features. It is a house made of concrete. However, instead of a concrete roof, a roof made of tin sheets, place pointing upwards and tilted towards the ground, is used. This type of house is ideal for the climate in Assam as it rains a lot in the state and the tilted tin roof lets the water flow away easily. Moreover, the cost is much lesser in comparison to a proper RCC Building.
7. *'Sindoor'* is a form of red coloured cosmetic powder worn by married women on their forehead in India. It represents the married status of women and after the death of the husband, the *'sindoor'* is ceremonially removed in public, marking the end of the married life of the widow and she stops wearing it since then. Although, this practice is not so prevalent now, it is still in practice.

REFERENCES

Barooah, J. (1993). *Single Women in Assamese Hindu Society,* New Delhi: Gyan Publishing House.

Berardo, F.M. (1968). "Widowhood status in the United States: Perspective on a neglected aspect of the family life-cycle," *The Family Coordinator,* 17 : 191-203.

Bhai, L.T. (2004). *Widows in India,* New Delhi: B.R. Publishing Corporation.

Census of India (2001). Government of India. URL: http://censusindia.gov.in/Census_And_You/age_structure_and_marital_status.aspx.Accessed: 02:00 PM 23-09-2014.

Census of India (2011). Government of India. URL: http://www.census2011.co.in/census/district/163-nalbari.html. Accessed: 02:01 PM 07-10-2014

Chakravarti, U. (1998). "Gender, caste and labour: The ideological and material structure of widowhood", In: Chen, M.A. (Ed.). *Widows in India: Social Neglect and Public Action,* New Delhi: Sage Publications.

Chen, M. and J. Dreze (1992). "Widows and health in rural North India", *Economic and Political Weekly,* Vol. 27. No. 43/44. (October. 24-31). pp. WS81-WS92. Published by: *Economic and Political Weekly*. Stable URL: http://www.jstor.org/stable/4399061. Accessed: 25/09/2014 12:01 PM.

Chen, M.A. (1998). *Widows in India: Social Neglect and Public Action,* New Delhi: Sage Publications.

Clayton, P.J. (1974). "Mortality and morbidity in the first year of widowhood", *Archives of General Psychiatry,* 30 : 747-750.

Goffman, I. (1963). *Stigma,* London: Penguin Publication.

Holmes, J.H. and R.H. Rahe (1967). "The Social Readjustment Scale", *Journal of Psychosomatic Research,* 11 : 213-228.

Khanna, M. (2002). "Trauma of taboos and tributations of widowhood in India", In: Giri, V.M. (Ed.) *Living Death: Trauma of Widowhood in India,* New Delhi: Gyan Publishing House.

Martikainen, P. and T. Valkonen (1996). "Mortality after the death of a spouse: Rates and causes of death in a large finnish cohort," *American Journal of Public Health,* 86 : 1087-1093.

Nagla, M. (2013). *Gender and Health,* Jaipur: Rawat Publications.

Nalbari District Profile, Government of Assam, URL: http://nalbari.nic.in/menu.asp. Accessed: 02:04 PM 07-10-2014.

Patil, G.D. (2000). *Hindu Widows: A Study in Deprivation,* New Delhi: Gyan Publishing House.

Pearlin, L.I. and J.S. Johnson (1977). "Marital status, life-strains and depression", *American Sociological Review,* 42 : 704-715.

Ranjan, A., (2001). "Determinants of Well-being among widows: An exploratory study in Varanasi", *Economic and Political Weekly,* Vol. 36. No. 43 (October 27 — November 2) : 4088-4094. Published by: *Economic and Political Weekly,* Stable URL: http://www.jstor.org/ stable/4411295. Accessed: 25/09/2014 12:04 PM.

Saikia, J.P. (2017). *Gender: Themes and Issues,* (Revised and Enlarged edition, Concept Publishing Company Pvt. Ltd., New Delhi.

Silverstein, M. and V.L. Bengtson (1994). "Does intergenerational social support influence the psychological well-being of older parents? The contingencies of declining health and widowhood", *Social Science and Medicine,* 7 : 943-957.

Strain, L.A. and N.L. Chapel (1982). *Confidants: Do They Make a Difference in Quality of Life?*

Stroebe, M., H. Schut and W. Stroebe (2007). "Health Outcomes of Bereavement", *The Lancet,* 370 : 1960-1973.

Umberson, D. and K. Montez (2010). "Social relationships and health: A flashpoint for health policy", *Journal of Health and Social Behaviour,*

Vol. 51. Extra Issue: What Do We Know? Key Findings from 50 years of Medical Sociology (2010). pp. S54-S66. Published by: American Sociological Association. Stable URL: http://www.jstor.org/stable/20798316. Accessed: 25/09/2014 11:55 AM.

Umberson, D. (1992). "Relationships between adult children and their parents: Psychological consequences for both generations", *Journal of Marriage Family*, 64 : 664-674.

Verbrugge, L.M. (1979). "Marital status and health", *Journal of Marriage and the Family*, 41 : 267-285.

Ward, R.A., S.R. Sherman and M. La Gory (1984). "Subjective network assessments and subjective well-being", *Journal of Gerontology*, 39 : 93-101.

Wortman, C.B., R.C. Kessler and D. Umberson (1992). "Widowhood and depression: Explaining long-term gender differences in vulnerability," *Journal of Health and Social Behaviour*, 33 : 10-24.

3

Working Hazards as Indicators of Occupational Health and Safety of Women Workers of Garment Industry

Rekha K. Jadhav and *Salma Bano*

Introduction

Garment industry is one of the many labour intensive sectors that provide a gateway for developing countries to the global market. It offers important opportunities to countries to start industrializing their economies and in due course of time diversify way from commodity dependence. Forty years ago, the industrialized countries dominated global exports in this area. Today, developing countries produce half of the world's garment exports. Though, the readymade garment industry caters to one of the basic needs of human beings, it came into existence as a industry, only at the turn of the century with industries of sewing machine on a commercial scale. In developing country like India, readymade garment sector plays an important role in the overall economic development. The garment industry has been expanding rapidly since late 1970s. As new industries expand, the labour force grew with the economy of the country, at the same time there are various occupational health hazards highly prevailed among these women workforce. Garment industries can be defined as sweat shops in which businesses that regularly violate multiple labour laws, including often, health and safety standards. Garment industries are known for their deplorable working conditions and rife with physical dangers to workers. The economic status of women is now accepted as an indicator of a society's stage of development. Women workers unlike the majority in the garment industry have been exposed to rigorous work discipline forced working hours, specific production norms and so on. The garment industry is an unorganised sector providing ample scope of employment to people from low socio-economic status involving largest number of women workers. Although such industries are identified with women employment—are subject to numerous workplace hazards and health hazards of women workers are special mention and have always been traditionally been underestimated. Women participation in labour force shows the importance and contribution of women to economic productivity hence, the need for occupational health and safety policies covering women workers. This is even more pressing with the feminisation of labour force in this sector. The occupational health problems affecting workers of our country, in fact workers of any developing country are liable to be much more complicated and dangerous as compare to that of developed countries because of poor health status due to poverty, overcrowding, illiteracy, malnutrition, higher prevalence of infections, parasite and other diseases, lack of adequate medical and health care facilities and a host of other factor. Industrial illness form a major part of the health problem of garment workers. Sickness absenteeism is the major contributory factor to absenteeism. Lack of laboratory facilities to monitor, analyse and assessing harmful contaminants in the work environment and their effect on heath of women workers is causing health hazards.

Conceptual Framework

The right to occupational health is an integral component of the right of everyone to the highest attainable standard of physical and mental health. It is the obligation of States to formulate, implement, monitor and evaluate national occupational health laws and policies. The lens of the right to health extends beyond the mere absence of injuries in the workplace and includes prevention of disease in workplace, environmental and industrial hygiene, and harmful substances affecting workers, emerging technologies, psychological hazards and occupational health services. In order to achieve the full realisation of the right to occupational health as a fundamental component of the right to health, a broad understanding of the relationship between work and health must be adopted. Accordingly, an examination of occupational health must include consideration of harmful exposures during work, specific varieties of working conditions, working environment, working relationships, and the social environment and political context in which work is situated. Since the establishment of ILO, the landscape of work and the relationship between workers and employers has changed dramatically as a result of, amongst other things, globalisation and the growth of transnational corporations. The phenomena have had a significant impact on the occupational health of workers. At the same time, the contemporary understanding of work has been enriched by the recognition and examination of the informal economy as a persistent and substantial portion of the modern, globalised economy, and the source of work for millions of individuals. This has been cause for the re-evaluation of traditional approaches to the promotion and protection of occupational health.

The right to occupational health is an integral component of the right to health. The International Covenant on Economic, Social and Cultural Rights addresses occupational health in Article 12.2(6) and (c) and establishes that—

> States must take steps towards the full realisation of the right to health, improvement including all aspects of industrial hygiene and the prevention, treatment and control of occupational and other diseases.

General Comment on No. 14 of the Committee on Economic, Social Cultural Rights interprets Article 12.2 (6) of the Covenant to include safe and hygienic working conditions, preventive measures in respect of occupational accidents and diseases and minimisation, so far as in reasonably practicable, of course, of health hazards inherent in the working environment. General Comment No. 14 states that Article 12.2(c) of the Covenant requires States to make available relevant technologies, using and improving epidemiological surveillance and data collection on a disaggregated basis. A number of international human rights instruments address the right to occupational health in variety of contexts. The Universal Declaration of Human Rights provides for the right of everyone to "just and favourable conditions of work"

(Article 23). The Convention on the Elimination of All Forms of Discrimination against Women establishes—

> Women's right to protection of health and to safety in working conditions, including the safeguarding of the function of reproduction" [Article 11.1(f)] and requires States to "Provide special protection to women during pregnancy in type of work proved to be harmful to them" [Article 12(d)].

The International Convention on the Protection of the Rights of All Migrant Workers and Members of Their Families obliges States to "take measures not less favourable than those applied to nationals to ensure that working and living conditions of migrant workers and members of their families in a regular situation are keeping with the standards of fitness, safety, health and principles of human dignity" (Article : 70). The ILO recognises both rights to safe and healthy working environment and the protection of the worker against sickness, disease and injury arising out of this employment to be fundamental human right (ILO, 2009). The ILO defines its Descent Work Agenda to require safe and healthy work that does not expose workers to health hazards. The ILO has adopted numerous instruments ratified by varying number of member States that directly address occupational health. These include the Convention Occupational Safety and Health, the Occupational Health Services Convention, the Working Environment (Air Pollution, Noise and Vibration) Convention as well as the Protection of Women's Health Recommendations. The ILO defines "health broadly in the context of work to indicate not merely the absence of diseases or infirmity but also the physical and mental elements affecting health, which are directly related to safety and hygiene at work."

> Industrial hygiene (or occupational hygiene) encompasses all efforts to protect worker's health through control of work environment, including the recognition and evaluation of those factors that may cause illness, lack of well-being or discomfort among workers or the community (Benjamin O. Alli, 2001).

Under the right to health, everyone is entitled to the enjoyment of the highest attainable standard of health conducive to living a life in dignity. The ILO Decent Work Agenda establishes the primary goal of the ILO to promote opportunities for women and men to obtain decent and productive work in conditions of freedom, equity, security and human dignity. The joint ILO-WHO social protection floor approach, a strategic objective of the Decent Work Agenda is committed to promoting human dignity and increasing the productive capacity of vulnerable groups. The ILO Convention No. 155 on occupational safety and health states that it applies to "all branches of economic activity" in which workers are employed, including the informal economy. The right to occupational health, as an integral component of the right to health thus includes the promotion of the dignity of workers realised in part through safe and healthy working conditions with a particular focus on vulnerable and marginalised groups. States may need to take a number of steps to ensure that women workers are brought within the protective reach of adequate health and safety protections. Based on the treatise and the guidance provided by the treaty monitoring committees, it is now clear that States may be required to adopt a range of measures to fulfil their obligations.

Healthcare System of Women Workforce in Garment Industry

The occupational environment of the worker is inseparable from his domestic environment. Both are complementary to each other. But for many people the boundary between their home and work environment is blurred, mainly in developing countries as they often undertake small scale industry activities within their home. Generally, there should be a scope for giving ample opportunity for welfare of workers engaged in garment industry. Musculoskeletal problem has been the most common health problem. Musculoskeletal disorders affect back, neck shoulders, hands and wrist among these garment women workers. These musculoskeletal symptoms at work, the common symptoms were pain over shoulder, lower back and ankle and upper back pain. A significant relationship was found to exist between occupational related events and musculoskeletal problem I this study. Intensive shoulder work is a risk factor for impingement syndrome of shoulder. There is a positive association between musculoskeletal disorders and work factors like awkward postures and high physical exertion. The risk of developing musculoskeletal disorders from an activity depends on frequency, duration and physical demands of the activity. It can be revealed that lack of time to take rest, to attend to personal health problems, social programmes, less time for relaxation, low wages, poor attitude of employers and these are simply observed in this study. Comment made by one of the respondent—

> Most of the time my whole body is painful. I suffer from backache, to constant bending and running the machine with my legs.....

Female workforce engaged in garment industry is generally suffered from malnutrition, anaemia, gastric dysentery, diarrhoea, respiratory problem, gynaecological problems, tuberculosis and urine infection. Moreover, gender equity status and existing disparity, indeed practically deprive female workers from public health care system. Garment workers working in urban centres and live around the slums of urban and semi-urban area. It is natural that when workers are sick, they go to the public hospitals. They cannot afford to receive health care from private clinics. On the other hand they are even not able to get proper health care from public hospitals. Thus, health care in public sector is quite costly for these low paid female workers. As a result more women workers suffer from different types of ailments and diseases. Married female workers suffer from various problems. These pregnant female workers suffer from malnutrition, anaemia along with other complication. But they do not have access to proper health care for kind of ailment. At the same time, they face serious problem to feed her and support the family. Female workers who have this kind of health problem are compelled to go to the village home, as because they are not in a position to live in the city, since they do not earn at the period, it becomes difficult for them to bear expenses. In the rural areas, they do not get any specialist or even a trained nurse to consult and avail health service. As a result, they are bound to go to half trained midwife or village quake. Due to lack of antenatal and post-natal check-ups, they usually do not take care of malnutrition and vitamin. Most of these women suffer from malnutrition, ill health, reproductive health problem and various community diseases, which they cannot address with low income. Another health problem facing by these women workers is bladder complication. It has been found that a number of garment women workers mentioned that according to their doctors they have developed bladder problems as a result of not drinking enough water also not urinating when required. They need to drink water at regular intervals. But the strict factory rules do not allow workers this opportunity to drink water and hydrate themselves and hence it has impact on the health of the workers. Injuries are common; especially puncture wounds from needles on the finger tips and nails as the cloth is passed through heavy vibrating mechanised machines. A worker can ill afford to report this as she may be declared unfit and removed from this job. In case of severe puncture wounds through the tip of the finger, women have to take to hospital and have had to stay away from work for at least a month.

Occupational Health and Safety Aspects

Occupational health and safety is one of the industrial workplace legislation. It served as the foundation for the establishment of the International Labour Organisation (ILO), which sought to establish occupational health and safety as not only as basic labour right but also as a fundamental human right. Occupational health and safety remain one of the ILO Constitution's main objectives, and as early as 1950, the International Labour Organisation and World Health Organisation (WHO) had already developed the above definition of occupational health and safety as a building block for labour legislation.

> "Occupational health should aim to promote and maintain the highest degree of physical, mental and social well-being of workers in all occupations, to prevent amongst the workers the departure from health caused by their working conditions, to prevent workers in their employment from risks resulting from factors averse to health, to place and maintain workers in an occupational environment adapted to their psychological and physiological capabilities, in summary, to adapt work to the workers and each worker to his or her job." Joint ILO/WHO Definition of Occupational Health

As women move beyond their traditional occupation, they meet new health hazards which either replace or add to their existing occupational exposure. Women labour force participation rates have increased steadily; a dramatic economic success is a reflection of increasing feminisation of labour. Female workforce participation rate has increased far more rapidly since 1960s, although their jobs are largely less-skilled and poorly paid. Women workforce form the largest pool of workers in these export oriented garment industry which underpinned economic expansion. Occupational health and safety as a set of coherent measures designed to protect workers from sickness, disease and injury arising from their employment. But the steady improvement of workplace practices and declining rates of occupational disease and injury in the global North has meant that the most dangerous and unregulated working conditions shifted towards cheap labour markets of the current garment producing countries.

Occupational health and safety is one of the corner stone of industrial workplace legislation. It served as the foundation for establishment of the International Labour Organisation, which sought to establishment of occupational health and safety as not only as a basic labour right but also as a fundamental human right. Occupational health and safety remain as one of the ILO's Constitution's main objective and as early as 1950, the ILO and the World Health Organization had already developed the above definition of occupational health and safety as a building block for labour legislation. Occupational health and safety as a set of coherent measures designed to protect workers from sickness, disease, injury arising from their employment. But the steady improvement of workplace practices and declining rates of occupational disease and injuries in the global North has meant that the most dangerous and unregulated working conditions shifted towards cheap labour markets of the current garment producing countries.

Stress and Psychological Distress

The garment industry which employs a majority of women as workers has become most prominent where such employment has enabled them to assist their families, other concerns with regards to women in particular becoming the largest workforce in country's readymade garment industry. Apart from having to liven in often putrid conditions, women have often experienced terrible situations. It has been proclaimed that some are suffering from the consequences of stressful conditions. The ways in which psychological sufferings of women working in the garment industry are touched upon, in terms of consequences of stressful working conditions or physical ailments is problematic. It would be necessary to prescribe to a wide framework of psycho-social distress for the acknowledgement of the harm suffered by the women and for a better understanding of their situations. Although the definition of stress remain controversial, most research in the health field refer to stress as a response that arise when demands exceed the personal and social resources that an individual is able to mobilize (Avery & Baker, 1990). It is note that almost any distressing event may produce different response in two individuals or even in the same individual on different occasions. The response to stress involves psychological adjustments (aches, pains, high blood pressure etc.), reduction in emotional well-being (anxiety, depression, guilty, loneliness etc.), adjustment at the cognitive level (difficulty in concentrating, making decisions, forgetfulness etc.) and a range of behavioural responses (poor sleep, inactivity, substance use, and suicide).

The environmental approaches to stress focus on the environment conditions that promote stress. The work environment contributes to the physical and psychological well-being of workers. In addition to the physical work conditions (loud, noise, repetitive actions, toxic substances, and temperature extremes), there are non-physical work conditions (work overloaded, lack of autonomy, role ambiguity and job involvement) that might affect physical health and psychological well-being of the workers. High work pressure and physical conditions under which women workers have to work, among other things, can be stressful in a work environment. Given the specific tasks to do and are told exactly how to do that, they have little/no control over decisions involving their work. The stress that arise through isolation and the lack of recognition for using one's initiative may lead to difficulties in which they are able to cope with the demands of work and the challenges of life.

Stress can also arise from an individual's life outside work, family, community and equality of life etc. Everyday sources of stress can be both positive and negative. When people are exposed to more than one of negative stressors simultaneously, an individual will find coping much more difficult. Working in garment industry could be considered potentially harmful psychologically to women workers. The long hours of work, with very short breaks for meals – though they enable the increase of financial assistance brought to their families, but augment the vulnerability of women. Many women owing to the pressures of the quota system are forced to work till late. The unequal and meagre employment opportunities available to them as women, as well as frequently being the main source of income to their families, often make the job in the Free Trade Zone and other garment factories all more difficult, pressurising them to continue working in spite of unpleasant conditions. A majority of women workforce felt psychological hazards. Factors responsible for psychological illness are frustration due to type of work, risks involved in work, long working hours, lack of recognition, lack of job satisfaction, poor women management, lack of welfare activities and tensions at home and place of work. Work related stress is not an illness, but it can lead to physical effects such as heart disease and gastrointestinal disturbances leading to ulcers and psychological effects such as anxiety and depression.

Global Effects and Local Labour Practices

Safe working places are a cornerstone for enabling worker in factory settings. Occupational health and safety is perceived as most straightforward for implementation and where forward movement has been made under voluntary global governance regimes (Brown, 2009; Barrientos & Smith, 2007). Occupational health and safety is a disputed area as it essentially encapsulates the perennial conflict between state, capital and labour. The strength of labour movements, collective worker participation, dominance of bio-medical approaches and worker awareness all determine and shape the efficacy of occupational health and safety in factory settings (Brown, 2009, 2011; Elling, 1989; O'Rourke, 2000). They shed light on the varied ways workers experience factory settings, pointing to the continued work that needs to be done. Yet our awareness of the ways in which both management and workers interpret and implement occupational health and safety measures as they cross continents and countries is limited. Elling (1989) say that:

> This lacuna makes imperative the need for think description so as to expose the ways in which cultural hegemony operates to undercut and short change (occupational health and safety) and the workers exposure to occupational hazards (1989: 1179-1181).

Ethical codes are an important instrument of global governance in the garment trade where occupational health and safety issues have evolved rapidly because of their audible nature. However, growing evidence suggests that problems abound in occupational health and safety system in global supply chain. For example, factories generally lack on-site occupational health and safety professionals, and there have been significant challenges to the implementation and effectiveness of monitoring mechanisms. Consequently, factory fires and collapses with devastating and deadly consequences for workers continue to plaque the industry.

The ways in which global efforts take on a life of their own as they journey worldwide across uneven development spaces and through local settings in one area of ethical codes, that is, health and safety, is the focus. Examining how the global governance regimes take on situated meanings in the context of apparel production, a major labour problem in the realm of health and safety hazards occurs and calls for gathering detailed information for building alternative systems. Perhaps as a practical response to this challenge, the apparel industry has taken laudable steps to meet occupational health and safety requirements. The global capitalism governance regimes shape labour agency within the factory floor in messy complex ways. Pregnant workers effectively raise concerns to management and had unexpected success, but they also found that their disquiet does not necessarily yield desired results. Injured workers get the medical care and attention they need, but they are not able to get the unpaid leave for recuperation that they are entitled to and their injuries are not adequately recorded for auditing purpose. Existing management, labour power dynamics, gender relations and social hierarchies in the workplace suggest that the spaces of rupture in the implementation of ethical code are continuously constrained by wider social and material relations, in this case the increasing pressures on managers to meet production targets. Adopting an ethnographic approach to the study of health and safety allows us to recognize that codes are "always provisional — never stable, and never fixed" and as social products ... their meanings become realised in specific places (Prentice, 2010:10). This realisation of ethical trading codes, however, continues to be informed by political economy and global capitalism. As processes they are not simple unstable and continuously influx, but also implicated in social hierarchies and cultural mores of places which constrain labour agency. Despite extensive global legislation on occupational health and safety and other workers', rights, employers remain negligent and many do not comply with even the most basic regulations. These are often the very situations where the trade union rights are undermined; leaving workers exposed to the risk of occupational health and safety violations.

Conclusion

The emergence of a rapidly developing garment industry over the past decade has provided a large number of poor women with much needed work and enabled them to support their families. However, although wages in the industry are usually lower, average earnings are still too low to lift women and their families out of poverty. Large scale entry of women into the labour market has been one of the most striking features of recent industrialisation. The growth of readymade garment sector over the last decade, creation of employment opportunities, mainly for women constituting about eighty per cent of the sector workforce has been a striking feature of the rapid expansion of readymade garment industry. As the garment industries are found to have poor illumination, improper ventilation, excessive noise, congested work area, unhealthy working conditions. The workers are exposed to dust, chemicals in the form of solvents, ergonomic problems, psychological problems and so on. Due to lack of education, unawareness of hazards of their occupations, general backwardness in situation and poor nutrition aggravates their health hazards from wok environment. Hence measures towards improving the awareness of occupational health and safety, and thereby motivating the workers in use of personal protective equipment, would help in achieving a safe and healthy workplace environment.

The occupational health problems affecting workers of our country, in fact workers of any developing country are liable to be much more complicated and dangerous as compared to that of developing countries because of the reasons of—

(a) Poor health status due to poverty, overcrowding, illiteracy, malnutrition, higher prevalence of infections, parasites and other diseases, lack of adequate medical and health care facilities and a host of other factors.

(b) Non-industrial illness form a major part of the health problem of garment workers. In fact incidence of many common illnesses like respiratory ailments (flu, bronchitis, cough, and asthma), tuberculosis, peptic ulcer, dysentery etc. are higher among industrial workers as compared to the general population.

(c) Sickness absenteeism, the major contributory factor to absenteeism. The reason for this high sickness absenteeism is very much varied and complicated but there is no doubt that the prevalence of sickness is high among these workers. Effective health care measures taken at the place of employment to render immediate treatment at the early stage of many of these illnesses will cut short the course and will prevent the disablement due to sickness to a great extent.

(d) Lack of laboratory facilities to monitor, analyse and assessing the harmful contaminants in the work environment and their effect on health of women workers is causing health hazards.

The lack of effective legislation and punitive measures to confront the factories that violates occupational health and safety regulations, and the low levels of authority and manpower from factory inspection team and labour department, mean that appallingly low levels of health and safety compliance can go unnoticed and unpublished. Occupational health hazards generally remain invisible and underreported. Officially employers are required by law to provide health examination for workers exposed to hazardous working conditions, not only in the course of their duties, but also prior to the commencement of their employment as well as upon their departure. Medical surveillance is a valuable tool for assuring and maintaining a healthy workplace environment. Different sorts of morbidities with special reference to musculoskeletal problems among women workers are giving a warning signal. It is the periodic testing of employees exposed to potentially hazardous materials and other risks in the work place. It helps to detect early signs of work related illness so that appropriate action can be taken to eliminate the underlying exposures. Therefore, it is the actual need of the hour for right action for solving their job related health aspects so that they can have a better living. Proper counselling and health education can improve their condition on many aspects to make conscious about work related problems.

REFERENCES

Barrientos, S. and S. Smith (2007). "Do workers benefit from ethical trade? Assessing code of labour practices in global production system", *Third World Quarterly*, Vol. 28 (4) : 713-729.

Benjamin O. Alli. *Fundamental Principles of Occupational Health and Safety* (Geneva, ILO, 2001), p. 84.

Brown, G. (2011). "Corporate social responsibility, what is it good for? Factory fires in bangladesh: Again & again", *Industrial Safety and Hygiene News*, Vol. 45(5) : 34-35.

Brown, G. (2009). "Genuine worker participation — An indispensable key to effective global occupational health and safety", *New Solution*, Vol. 19 (3) : 315-333.

Elling, R.H. (1989). "The economy of worker's health and safety", *Social Science & Medicine*, Vol. 28(11) : 1171-1182.

International Labour Organization, Report of the Director General: Decent Work, International Labour Conference, 87th Session, Geneva, June 1999.

International Labour Organization (2009). *Health and Life at Work: A Basic Human Right*, World Day for Safety and Health at Work, 28 April, 2009, (Geneva, 2009), p. 5; ILO.

ILO Introductory Report: *Global Trends and Challenges on Occupational Safety and Health*, XIX World Congress on Safety and Health at Work, Istanbul, Turkey, September 2011(Geneva, 2011), p. 42.

"Seoul Declaration on Safety and Health at Work," adopted on 29 June, 2008 at the XVIII World Congress on Safety and Health at Work.

Kaila, H.L. (2000). "Occupational health of women", *Indian Journal of Occupational Health*, Vol. 43 : 109-16.

O'Rourke, D. (2000). "Monitoring the Monitors: A Critique of PWC Labour Monitoring", Unpublished Working Paper.

Prentice, R. (2010). "Ethnographic Approaches to Health and Development Research: The Contribution of Anthropology", In: I. Bowrgeault, R. Dingwell & R. Vries (eds.), *The Sage Handbook of Qualitative Methods in Health Research* (pp. 157-173). London: Sage Publications.

4

Urbanisation, Gender and Health

Vikas Saharan

Introduction

The world is becoming urban. The world's population has now shifted from predominantly rural to predominantly urban (Mike Davis, 2006). For the first time in history, the majority of people will live in cities and towns. This shift reflects the astonishing trend towards urbanisation that has occurred over the last several decades (UNFPA, 2007). In 1950, there were 86 cities in the world with a population of more than one million; today there are 400, and by 2015 there will be at least 550 (UN-HABITAT, 2002). In the future, cities will house virtually all additional population growth (UN-HABITAT, 2003). The UN predicts that the world's urban population will almost double from 3.3 billion in 2007 to 6.3 billion in 2050. Most of this increase will be in developing countries. Exponential urban growth is having a profound effect on global health, due to international travel and migration; cities are becoming important hubs for the transmission of infectious diseases, as shown by recent pandemics. By 2050, the world's urban population is expected to reach 6.3 billion, almost all of this growth will be in low income regions: in Africa the urban population is likely to triple, and in Asia it will more than double (UN, 2010). This worldwide increase in urban population results from a combination of factors including natural population growth, migration, government policies, infrastructure development and other major political and economic forces, including globalisation. At the most basic level, the growth of cities and towns is attributable to two main causes: migration from rural areas and natural population growth. In most low-income countries, urban expansion is due to natural population growth. However, migration of people from other urban centres or from rural areas contributes substantially to the growth of cities. A link between migration, urbanisation and health has been reported for different populations and locations (Scopus *et al.*, 2007). Migration affects the transmission of communicable diseases as cities might provide favourable conditions for the spread of germs that are imported by migrants, e.g. Schistosomiasis has established itself in urban areas most probably through infected migrants.

Different forces in different cities drive urban growth and the epidemiology of individual diseases might differ according to specific urban dynamics and contexts. In many low-income countries, economic growth does not keep pace with the rise in urban populations. Rapid urban growth affects urban housing, sanitation, transportation, and the environment. This transformation has profound implications for the general health and well-being of the population (G.W. Jones and P.M. Visaria, 1997). Important socio-economic disparities have emerged in urban centres mirrored by profound health inequalities (UN-HABITAT, 2006). Social and environmental changes have accompanied the on-going rapid urbanisation in a number of countries during recent decades. Urbaniser has reported worse socio-environmental conditions and worse working conditions than the other groups in many countries.

Urbanization of low-income countries raises new health challenges for the international community (Harpham and Tanner, 1995). Several rural pathogens have adapted to urban environments and others have emerged or re-emerged in urban areas. The heterogeneity in health of urban dwellers, increased rates of contact and mobility of people, results in a high risk of disease transmission in large urban populations. Cities become incubators where all the conditions are met for outbreaks to occur. In an interconnected world, cities become gateways for the worldwide spread of infections. These issues have substantial public health implications, reshaping the epidemiology of both chronic and infectious diseases, with consequences worldwide. The close proximity of people is a prominent urban factor. Population density affects diseases, particularly those transmitted *via* respiratory and faecal-oral routes. Because of high-population density, an increased amount of shared airspace increases exposure to Influenza, Measles and Mycobacterium tuberculosis.

Urban centres usually have higher rates of tuberculosis infection than do rural areas (Lienhardt, 2001). Some diseases, such as dengue, have become permanently established in urban areas and cause regular epidemics, while others might produce occasional, patchy outbreaks. Epidemic forms of certain diseases, such as chikungunya, might become restricted to the urban environment (Pialoux, Gaüzère, Jauréguiberry, and Strobel, 2007).

Many social determinants interact to define individual exposure and vulnerability to disease (Berkman, and Kawachi, 2000), socio-economic characteristics of neighbourhood also matter as slum dwellers and informal settlers are the most vulnerable groups. In urban settings, the most substantial factors include socio-economic status, place of residence, race, ethnicity, gender, and education (Ompad, Galea, Caiaffa and Vlahov, 2007). In most cities in low-income countries, high inequities in economic, social, and living conditions are often noted, which are often mirrored by inequalities in health (Brockerhoff and Brennan, 1998). The urban environment results in many changes in human behaviour that affect transmission risks, in particular, for sexually transmitted diseases. Decreased social cohesion, new family structures, and the relaxation of traditional cultural norms yield new patterns of behaviour, including changes in sexual activity and the use of drugs (Adler, Boyce, Chesney *et al.,* 1994). Differences in household structure have important implications for social support and health. Studies have shown the importance of social networks and family support, particularly elderly co-residence with an adult child and consequent intergenerational support in the household (Scopus *et al.,* 2007). A Chinese study, found that older parents living in three generation households had better psychological well-being than those living in single generation households (Scopus M. Silverstein, Cong, and Li, 2006). Urbanization is profoundly associated with the health-risk transition, For example, compared to those who remain in rural areas, the urban migrants generally have more income and assets, but worse diets, less physical and social activity, and more overweight and obesity. Many of these transitional phenomena noted above are linked to changes in the household social and physical environment (Scopus R. Kojima, 1996). An individual's place of residence and their status within that place are important determinants of health. Urbanisation is a dominant trend, with more people living in marginal conditions in cities. Urban populations have distinct vulnerabilities related to health hazards (Campbell, Lendrum and Corvalan, 2007). Urbanization contribute to ill health among dwellers due to poor access to sanitation and clean drinking water, even if it is available, access to safe water is often unaffordable for the urban poor. Slum dwellers and poor people especially women are particularly vulnerable to the negative health effects of rapid urbanisation and the rate of urbanisation makes it very challenging to manage. Findings of *New England Journal of Medicine* argued that urbanisation is a health hazard for certain vulnerable populations, and this demographic shift threatens to create a humanitarian disaster (Patel, Burke, 2009). Rapid urbanisation leads to lack of basic services (sanitation, potable water, and electricity), substandard housing, overcrowding, unhealthy and hazardous locations, insecure tenure and social exclusion (UNHSP, 2006). According to WHO, almost 137 million people in urban populations have no access to safe drinking water, and more than 600 million urban dwellers do not have adequate sanitation. Unsafe water sources and inadequate sanitation and hygiene are prime contributors to diarrhoeal infections and might lead to cholera endemicity. Urbanisation also creates an increasing problem for the management of solid waste.

Gender and Health

Women's and men's vulnerability is determined not only by biology, but also by differences in their social roles and responsibilities (Wisner *et al.*, 2004). Although they vary, these roles and responsibilities exist in all societies. The expectation that women fulfil their roles and responsibilities as career of their families often places extra burdens on them. The distinct roles and relations of men and women in a given culture, dictated by that culture's gender norms and values, give rise to gender differences. Gender norms, roles and relations also give rise to gender inequalities—that is, differences between men and women that systematically value one group often to the detriment of the other. Both gender differences and gender inequalities can give rise to inequities between men and women in health status and access to health care. Gender inequities may not always affect men and women in the same way, although women bear many disadvantages when it comes to access to and distribution of resources. Such inequities include differences in risk as well as in protective factors and an imbalance between needs and access to resources, which lead to the reduced impact of standard child and adolescent health policies and services. Gender profoundly influences an individual's way of living, seeking and receiving care. The failure to take gender into account in analysing the causal pathways of health and disease, as well as in developing health policies and programmes, leads to maintaining or even contributing to one of the most pervasive sources of health inequities. As far back as the 19th Century, differences in health status between different social groups have been studied with reference to socio-economic class differences (Farr, 1839). The idea of gender as a determinant in the health of women and men appears a century and a half later in research of the late 1980s and the 1990s (Sen *et al.*, 2002) when the debate around inequalities in health expanded beyond socio-economic class to include race and gender. Analysing their experiences with reference to the social, political and economic forces that shaped health, women explored the connections between race, class and gender based oppression as they affected the health of women. Between the decades of the 1970s and 1990s, the women's health movement in both developed and developing countries moved ahead (Correa, 1994) to establish that women's health was affected by the social context including unequal gender relationships.

The acceptance of gender as a health determinant emerged from the impact of the Fourth World Conference on Women, held in Beijing in September 1995. This provided an opportunity for the world community to focus attention on areas of vital concern for women worldwide; concerns that stem from social problems that embrace both men and women and that require solutions for both genders (Friedman, 2003). The WHO Commission on Social Determinants of Health acknowledged in its final report that Gender inequities damage the physical and mental health of millions of girls and women across the globe, and also of boys and men, despite the many tangible benefits it gives men through resources, power, authority and control (WHO, 2008). Thus, it raises awareness about the idea that gender is a relevant issue for both women and men. The women's health movement collectively identified the larger financial forces that were determining the availability and quality of health care for women. Among the poor, female-headed households are at a greater economic disadvantage because of the lower earnings of women and the dual nature of their work burden. This burden imposes severe time constraints, restricting such households' access to social and health services (Rosenhouse, 1989). Within male-headed households, the intra-household allocation of resources may have a gender bias, restricting women's access to adequate nutrition and health services. Power relations, sex and reproduction and the complex intersections of class and gender, profoundly affect women's health seeking behaviour and health outcomes. Gender, power and inequality are strongly interrelated with the spread of infectious diseases. In Pathologies of power, Paul Farmer stresses that gender is one of the explanations for why so many women die of AIDS. Besides global ideologies that view women as inferior to men, poverty is a potential determinant in women's lives, causing suffering and inequalities (Farmer, 2005).

Gender and urban development are intimately interrelated and the politics of space are never far from the picture. Recognition that space and the built environment are constituted by, as well as constitutive of gender, has long been established in feminist analyses of the city (Jarvis *et al.,* 2009). Urban transition offers scope for advancing gender equality, given the common association of urbanization with expanded economic, social and political opportunities for women, barriers to female 'empowerment' remain widespread, especially among the urban poor and in areas marked by one or more shelter deprivations in respect of services, tenure, overcrowding and so on. Gender-inequitable access to decent work and living standards, human capital acquisition, physical and financial assets, personal safety and security, and representation in formal structures of urban governance evidence this, *inter alia.* Limited access to land in rural areas, conflict, divorce and unemployment etc. force increasing numbers of women into living in marginalised urban and peri-urban areas and slums. These dwellings are often situated on ground with particular environmental risks, such as hillsides and low-lying plots. Poverty, exposure of dwelling, and managing on their own the disproportionate daily burden of infrastructural needs such as waste management, fuel, water and sanitation make urban female heads of households particularly vulnerable to natural disasters (Chant, 2007). As such, women living in peri-urban slums devoid of services and infrastructure, residing in low quality shelter, and constrained in their ability to connect with the rest of the city may be more challenged than their counterparts living in similarly marginalised, but more centrally-situated neighbourhoods (Khosla, 2009). One of the key demographic processes pertinent to the contemporary gender dynamics of cities is that women are increasingly forming considerable proportion of urban population. In urban Latin America, for example, households headed by women rose by a mean of 9.8 percentage points between the late 1980s and the end of the first decade of the 21st century (Chant, 2013). Other reasons commonly mooted for rising proportions of female-headed households in towns and cities include greater access by urban women to employment and independent earnings, and to land and property, and lessened control by patriarchal kinship systems (Chant, 1997). The rising rate of female-headed households in urban/peri-urban areas results in a shift of urban sex-ratios and feminization of urban poverty. UN-HABITAT's State of the World's Cities Report 2008-09 shows that in some countries, woman-headed households suffer disproportionately from inadequate housing in poor urban neighbourhoods. In Kenya and Nicaragua, for example, one-third of woman-headed households suffer from four shelter deprivations. These relate to the lack of durable housing, insufficient living space, poor access to clean water and inadequate sanitation or insecure tenure. Woman-headed households are becoming more common in urban areas, making up on average about 20 per cent of urban households in 160 countries surveyed (UN-HABITAT, 2008). Land and housing are economic resources that also bring social benefits and improved status to those who own, control or have access to them. Exclusion of women from land and property in rural areas has pushed many into the slums of urban areas, contributing to the rise in woman-headed households among the urban poor (UN-HABITAT, 2009). Even in cases where woman-headed households do not necessarily suffer worse conditions than other slum dwellers, shelter is a good place to start for empowering women. For women, the home is often not only a place to live, but where they raise their children and perhaps work to earn their living.

It is widely assumed that cities are far better places than rural areas for accessing safe and convenient water and sanitation services, but in developing countries, access to urban services often differs widely between the rich and the poor, and between men and women. Women tend to spend more time than men in the home and neighbourhood (UNESCO, 2003), they are also more directly exposed to environmental hazards of poor sanitation—such as diseases caused by poor drainage, contact with human faces and decomposing rubbish. Where dwellings lack domestic mains-supplied water, for instance, women have to collect it from public standpipes, wells, boreholes, rivers, or storage drums served by private tankers, a task which may be both arduous and time-consuming, especially where women have to compete with one another at communal sources (Thompson *et al.*, 2000). Where there is no electricity supply, time has to be spent collecting or buying fuel and making fires to cook and heat water, and to shop on a daily basis. Where there is no rubbish collection, women have to dispose of solid waste (Khosla, 2009) and in a number of South African cities, where waste management has been privatised, women now have to spend more time keeping streets clean in their communities (Samson, 2003). Lack of services not only impacts women's and girls' workloads, but their dignity and self-respect. Urbanisation has a distinctive gendered dimension. Although women make a crucial contribution to the prosperity of cities through their paid and unpaid labour, they remain at a disadvantage in terms of equitable access to work and living conditions, health and education, assets and representation in formal institutions and urban governance (Chant, 2011). Women's disadvantage stems from a wider set of factors that include their unequal position in the labour market, their limited ability to secure assets independently from male relatives, and their greater exposure to violence. Since, women hold primary responsibility for care and reproductive activities, they are especially affected by limited or lack of access to basic services. Similarly, limited access to essential infrastructure such as water and sanitation, inadequate shelter or poor housing conditions, distance from health services and schools, unsafe neighbourhoods and restricted mobility all put an additional burden on women's who, within households, are responsible for childcare, food preparation, cleaning and washing. This contributes to increase burden related to unpaid care work, and thus exacerbate gender-based disadvantage. Inadequate access to basic service makes women, more susceptible to a range of illnesses that overall compromise their immune system and make them more prone to HIV infection and accelerated progression to AIDS (Ambert, Jassey, and Thomas, 2007). Women's disadvantage is even more marked when reproductive health is taken into account. Reproductive health is a broad concept that refers to a state of complete physical, mental and social well-being and not merely the absence of disease or infirmity, in all matters relating to the reproductive system and its processes. In this sense, it encompasses family planning, conception and birth, but also imbalances in decision-making power in the context of sexual relations between women and men, including potential coercion and violence, and the related health risks (National Research Council, 2003). Women's access to different spaces in the city especially public space is generally more limited than that of men, not only due to the domestic-based time and resource constraints associated with reproductive labour, but because of strong symbolic dimensions surrounding the forbidden and permitted use of spaces governed by patriarchal power relations and norms of female propriety, which may require certain modes of dress and behaviour to render women invisible or unapproachable (Fenster, 2005). Restricted female mobility can seriously jeopardize women's prospects of availing basic facilities particularly health services.

Urban poor, especially women face health risks often as high and sometimes worse than those of rural residents, despite the proximity of modern health services (Montgomery, 2009). Residents of informal settlements suffer disproportionately from disease, injury and premature death, and the combination of ill-health and poverty entrenches disadvantage over time (Sverdlik, 2011). Household and neighbourhood physical hazards can have a significant health impact on large sections of the urban populations in low and middle-income countries. These include accidental burns and scalding, indoor air pollution due to inefficient cooking stoves, and the consequences of flooding and extreme weather events. In all cases, women and children are more likely to be affected (Sverdlik, 2011). In recent years, there is growing concern about detrimental effects of urbanisation on human health particularly on women's. Even if intra-urban health conditions are compared, conditions in slums are often so bad that the notion of an urban penalty in health has been widely discussed (Satterthwaite, 2011). Evidence from eight large Indian cities, for example, shows that slum dwellers suffer a disproportionate risk of communicable diseases such as tuberculosis, as well as health conditions attached to poor diet and inadequate healthcare, such as anaemia, with women and young children being particularly implicated (Gupta *et al.,* 2009). For women in slums, risks to physical and mental well-being are aggravated by a range of stressors attached to their routine household labour (WHO, 2009). For example, the use in cooking of solid fuels such as wood, coal and charcoal, are far more harmful to the environment (through deforestation) and to individuals (through lung- and atmosphere-polluting hydrocarbons and carcinogens) than 'cleaner', more expensive alternatives such as kerosene, liquid petroleum, gas and electricity. This is especially the case in cramped, poorly ventilated spaces, such that "indoor air pollution" has been termed a "quiet and neglected killer" of poor women and children (UN-HABITAT, 2008). Given the general observation that women and the poor worldwide are particularly prone to depression (Spitzer, 2005), evidence from São Paulo, Brazil, reveals that common mental diseases (CMDs) are almost twice as high (at 21%) in the poorest socio-economic district of the city than in the wealthiest (12%). Recent research on Cape Town, South Africa, reveals a higher prevalence of common mental diseases (CMDs) in peri-urban slums (35%) compared with rural areas (27%), and that being female, unemployed and/or engaging in substance abuse are the most common correlates (Harpham, 2009).

Urban women are at greatest risk of being victims of violence (CPRC, 2010). Now recognized as a major health issue-affecting women (WHO, 2009), gender-based violence (GBV) compounds a host of problems related to physical and mental well-being in cities and slums. In gender and health, violence against women is a major public health problem and human rights' violation throughout the world. It is violence directed against women or girls on the basis of their sex. It includes acts that inflict physical, mental or sexual harm and suffering, threats of such acts, coercion and other deprivations of liberty (WHO, 2002).

Gender-based violence along with unequal gender relations is also directly linked to inadequate basic infrastructure and access to services that increase women's vulnerability to attacks. There are direct costs of gender-based violence that affect women in particular in cities. As victims of violence, women experience physical and psychological health problems, and in some cases death. Health outcomes can include injuries and disabilities caused by violence, as well as sexually transmitted infections, unwanted pregnancies, abortions, AIDS-related deaths and illnesses, and chronic pain syndrome. However, the psychological trauma produced by victimisation or of witnessing violence is just as severe and can include post-traumatic stress disorder, rape trauma syndrome, depression, anxiety, and alcohol and drug abuse (Morrison, Ellsberg, and Bott, 2007). At the level of the city, gender-based violence undermines the economic productivity of the urban labour force. When women experience widespread and repeated violence, they will be unable to work or function effectively. In a study of Nagpur, India, 13 per cent of women had experienced incidents where they could not undertake paid work because of the health effects of abuse by a partner; they had to miss an average of seven work days per incidence of abuse (Krug *et al.*, 2002). One key aspect of widespread violence and fear is the spatial restrictions imposed on urban dwellers and especially on women. The fear of violence affects wider levels of social interaction, with women in particular being too afraid to leave their homes except for essential visits for work and education. Participation in community affairs is affected because of this, as most meetings take place in the evenings, and any spontaneous involvement with others will be married by suspicion (McIlwaine and Moser, 2007). These adverse health outcomes of gender-based violence put pressure on health facilities which are invariably concentrated in cities and which produce socio-economic costs at a national level in relation to lowering productivity and affecting the creation of human and social capital. The costs can be direct in relation to gender-based violence, in terms of expenditures on healthcare, and judicial and social services; indirect costs are linked with undermining productivity in the workplace as well as loss of earnings to an economy when someone dies (Morrison, Ellsberg, and Bott, 2007).

Conclusion

Women's are vulnerable to the negative health effects of rapid urbanisation. There is urgent need to understand the impacts of urbanisation on the health of poor women and to design appropriate adaptation policies. When planning public health interventions, there is need to consider the dynamic relationship between urbanisation and their impact on vulnerable urban populations. Women and girls should actualise their rights to city services, resources and facilities. These include rights to health services, schools and decent housing, and equal access to safe public transport, streets, sidewalks, parks, cultural centres and work spaces. Demographic transition has brought unequal access to health care services in urban areas, efforts should be made to improve the accessibility and affordability of primary health care services to poor urban women and children by increasing women's participation and employment in the urban health sector and providing preventive and curative services for women and children by improving their access to immunisations, reproductive health care, curative care, nutrition related services and health education, as well as assistance for women who are victims of violence. It is increasingly recognised that women and other vulnerable groups, lacking both a voice and equitable access to health care, should be involved at all policy and project levels. Many governments and city planners are now working with community groups, including women's networks, to improve safety and security through greater gender-sensitivity in urban design. For example, many local authorities involve groups of women in safety audits of cities. Some local authorities are also supporting campaigns to change attitudes condoning gender-based violence. Socially inclusive cities offer safety and security for all residents, despite age, race, gender or disability. Women bear the primary responsibility for domestic and care work, inadequate provision of basic services and unsafe environmental conditions so widespread in low-income urban settlements disproportionately affect women. Significant improvements in the health care of the urban poor, particularly women and children can be brought by adopting pro-poor targeting, public-private partnership (PPP) model, and gender action plan. Differences in health status for men and women are not merely biological, but fundamentally affected by the social, political and economic forces that shape their lives, including unequal gender relations. Equity and social justice cannot be achieved without recognizing the differences in vulnerability and strengths of women and men, and the various factors that contribute to vulnerability. Strategies need to take into account women's and men's relative and different capacities, power, social resilience, vulnerabilities and resources, because gender norms, roles and relations can either enable or constrain adaptive capacities. Recognizing these differences is a necessary and important component of any prospective attempts to address the gendered health consequences. The impact of gender inequalities on women's and men's health can take a number of forms, affecting not only health outcomes and health status, but also access to preventive and curative services. Moreover, the different health needs and opportunities available to men and women accompany them throughout their life course, from infancy to adolescence and adulthood. Gender inequity, combined with socio-economic inequality together forms a powerful explanatory *framework* for variations in women's and men's health. There is a need for the development of gender responsive and accessible health services that reach the poorest populations, thereby addressing particular health needs of women throughout their entire lifecycle. It is imperative to legitimize women's role in identifying and articulating their own needs, in planning, monitoring and evaluating health service provision. Policy solutions should focus on the more systemic transformation of larger social institutions to improve more equitable health outcomes. Individual agency needs to be contextualised within the larger political, social and economic framework and it should focus on decreased access to protective resources for health, including differential access to rights and resources, differential exposure to direct expressions of power such as violence and institutionalised disregard for women's biological needs and historical disadvantage.

REFERENCES

Adler, N.E., T. Boyceamd, M.A. Chesney (1994). "Socio-economic status and health: The challenge of the gradient", *American Psychology,* Vol. 49 : 15–24.

Ambert, Cecile, Jassey Katja and Liz Thomas (2007). *HIV, Aids and Urban Development Issues in sub-Saharan Africa,* Sida, Stockholm.

Berkman, L., Kawachi, I. (2000). *Social Epidemiology,* New York: Oxford University Press.

Brockerhoff, M. and E. Brennan (1998). "The poverty of cities in developing regions", *Population Development Review* : 24. pp. 75–114.

Campbell-Lendrum, D. and C. Corvalan (2007). "Climate change and developing-country cities: implications for environmental health and equity," *Journal of Urban Health,* Vol. 84 (Suppl.1) : 109.

Chant, Sylvia (1997). Women-headed Households: Diversity and Dynamics in the Developing World. Houndmills, Basingstoke: MacMillan.

Chant, Sylvia (2007). *Gender, Cities and the Millennium Development Goals in the Global south.* Working paper 21. London: London School of Economics.

Chant, Sylvia (2011). Introduction-UN-HABITAT, *State of Women in Cities,* 2012/13. UNHABITAT, Nairobi.

Chant, Sylvia (2013). "Cities Through a "Gender Lens": A Golden "Urban Age" for Women in the Global South?" *Environment and Urbanization,* 25 (1) : 9-29.

Commission on Social Determinants of Health (2008). *Closing the Gap in a Generation: Health Equity through Action on the Social Determinants of Health.* Geneva: World Health Organization.

Correa, S. (1994). *Population and Reproductive Rights: Feminist Perspectives from the South.* London: Zed Books.

CPRC (2010). *Stemming Girls' Chronic Poverty,* Chronic Poverty Research Centre, ODI, London.

Davis, Mike (2006). *Planet of Slums,* New York: Verso.

Fenster, Tovi (2005). "The right to the gendered city: Different formations of belonging in everyday life", *Journal of Gender Studies,* Vol. 14(3) : 217-31.

Farmer, Paul (2005). *Pathologies of Power: Health, Human Rights, and the New War on the Poor.* Berkeley, CA: University of California Press.

Farr, William (1839). First annual report to the Registrar General. London: Her Majesty's Statistical Office.

Friedman, E.J. (2003). "Gendering the Agenda: The Impact of the Transnational Women's Rights Movement at the UN conferences of the 1990s", *Women's Studies International Forum,* Vol. 26(4) : 313-331.

Harpham, T. and Tanner, M. (1995). "Features and Determinants of Urban Health Status," In: Harpham, T. and M. Tanner (eds.). *Urban Health in Developing Countries,* pp. 35–47. London: Earthscan Publications Limited.

Harpham, Trudy (2009). "Urban health in developing countries: What do we know and where do we Go?", *Health and Place,* Vol. 15 : 107-16.

Jones, G.W. and P.M. Visaria (1997). *Urbanization in Large Developing Countries,* Oxford, UK: Clarendon Press.

Khosla, Rena (2009). *Addressing Gender Concerns in India's Urban Renewal Mission,* New Delhi: UNDP.

Krug, E.G., L.L. Dahlberg, J.A. Mercy, A.B. Zwi and R. Lozano (2002). *World Report on Violence and Health,* World Health Organisation, Geneva.

Lienhardt, C. (2001). "From exposure to disease: The Role of environmental factors in susceptibility to and development of tuberculosis", *Epidemiology Review,* Vol. 23 : 288-301.

McIlwaine, C. and C. Moser (2007). "Living in fear: How the urban poor perceive violence, fear and insecurity", In: K. Koonings and D. Kruijt (eds.). *Fractured Cities: Social Exclusion, Urban Violence and Contested Spaces in Latin America,* pp. 117-137. London: Zed Press.

Montgomery, Mark R. (2009). "Urban poverty and health in developing countries", *Population Bulletin,* Population Reference Bureau.

Morrison, A., M. Ellsberg and S. Bott (2007). "Addressing Gender-based Violence: A Critical Review of Interventions", *The World Bank Observer,* Vol. 22 (1) : 25-51.

Ompad, D.C., S. Galea, W.T. Caiaffa and D. Vlahov (2007). "Social determinants of the health of urban populations: Methodological considerations", *Journal of Urban Health,* Vol. 84 (3 suppl) : 42–53.

Patel, R.B. and T. Burke (2009). Urbanization—An emerging humanitarian disaster, *New England Journal of Medicine,* 361: 741-43.

Pialoux, G.; B.A. Gaüzère; S. Jauréguiberry; S., Strobel and M. Chikungunya (2007). *An Epidemic Arbovirosis, Lancet Infection Disorder,* 7: 319–27.

Rosenhouse, Sandra (1989). "Identifying the poor: Is 'headship' a useful concept?" *Living Standards Measurement Study Working Paper no. 58.* World Bank: Washington, D.C.

Samson, Melanie (2003). *Dumping on Women: Gender and Privatisation of Waste Management,* Woodstock, Cape Town: Municipal Services Project and the South African Municipal Workers' Union.

Satterthwaite, David (2007). "The Transition to a Predominantly Urban World and its Underpinnings", *Human Settlements Discussion Papers Series—Urban Change*4. IIED, London.

Satterthwaite, David (2011). "Why is urban health so poor even in many successful cities?", *Environment and Urbanization,* Vol. 23(1) : 5-11.

Kojima, Scopus R. (1996). "Introduction: Population migration and urbanization in developing countries", *The Developing Economies,* Vol. 34 (4) : 349–369.

Scopus M. Silverstein; Z. Cong, and S. Li. (2006). "Intergenerational Transfers and Living Arrangements of Older People in Rural China: Consequences for Psychological Well-being", *Journal of Gerontology,* Vol. 61 (5) : S256–S266.

Scopus P. Pridmore, L. Thomas, K. Havemann, J. Sapag, and L. Wood (2007). "Social capital and healthy urbanization in a globalized world", *Journal of Urban Health,* Vol. 84 (1) : i130–i143.

Scopus, T. Kjellstrom, S. Mercado, M. Sami, K. Havemannand, S. Iwao (2007). "Achieving Health Equity in Urban Settings", *Journal of Urban Health,* Vol. 84 (1) : i1–i6.

Sen, G., A. George and P. Östlin (eds.) (2002). *Engendering International Health: the Challenge of Equity,* Cambridge, MA: MIT Press.

Spitzer, Denise L. (2005). "Engendering health disparities", *Revue Canadienne de Santé Publique,* Vol. 96(2) : 578-95.

Sverdlik, Alice (2011). "Ill-health and Poverty: A Literature review on Health in informal settlements", *Environment & Urbanization,* Vol. 23 (1) : 123-155.

Thompson, John; Porras, Ina; Wood, Elisabeth; Tumwine, Hames; Mujwahusi, Mark; Katui-Katua, Munguti, and Johnstone, Nick (2000). "Waiting at the Tap: Changes in urban water use in east africa over three decades", *Environment and Urbanization,* Vol. 12(2) : 37-52.

United Nations Fund for Population Activities (UNFPA) (2007). *State of the World's Population (2007): Unleashing the Potential of Urban Growth,* New York: UNFPA.

UN-HABITAT and UK Government for International Development (DFID) (2002). *Sustainable Urbanisation: Achieving Agenda 21,* Nairobi: UN-HABITAT.

UN-HABITAT (2006). The State of The World's Cities 2006/2007: The Millennium Development Goals and Urban Sustainability—*30 Years of Shaping the Habitat Agenda,* London: Earthscan.

United Nations Human Settlements Programme (2006). *State of the World's Cities 2006-07*. London: Earthscan Publications.

UN (2010). *World Urbanization Prospects: the 2009 revision.* (http://esa.un.org/ unpd/wup/index.html).

5

Medicalisation and Commodification of Women's Body through Assisted Reproductive Technology

A Feminist Review of Indian Infertility Trade

Sudeshna Mukherjee

Introduction

Reproductive technology covers a wide range of medical strategies for increasing the effectiveness of contraception, overcoming infertility and reducing the risk of genetically transmitted deformities. It includes abortion, contraception, amniocentesis, genetic screening, in-vitro fertilization (IVF) (test tube babies), artificial insemination by donor or spouse, development of sperm bank, storage of frozen sperm (cryopreservation), development of artificial womb, techniques for pre-determination of the sex of the foetus and specially designed nursery environment which makes it possible to maintain a foetus from the womb in the first trimester (Andrew Lori, 1984; McCormack, 1988). The present faith of the middle class in technology to deliver the planned goals of economic, social and environmental justice has provided a shield of absolutism to the ever growing domination of technologies (Qadeer, 2010). According to Andrew Feenberg, technological essentialism, is born out of a loss of distinction between analytical and ontological categories in the study of technology and society that has led to technology acquiring its independent existence and being seen as a distinct thing or practice interacting at its boundaries with society—what is generally referred to as interphase between technology and society (Feenberg, 1999: 1-19). With our ignorance and vulnerability on issues pertaining to health, growing faith with anything technical and societal premium on biological motherhood made us passive recipient of technological essentialism. In this light, my study following descriptive diagnostic research design and inputs (both primary and secondary) from various stake holders (medical practitioners, commissioning parents, surrogates, egg donors, social activists, legal practitioners etc.) would like to qualitatively trace how post-liberal, market friendly Indian state is promoting foreign revenue earning ART and surrogacy at the cost of commodification, objectification and medicalisation of impoverished Indian women.

Infertility Assisted Reproductive Technology and Medicalisation

Infertility/infecundity is mostly defined as failure of a sexually active couple to have a baby within one year of marriage without the use of contraceptives. It includes the term sterility. Sterility is primary when there is an inability to produce germ cells. It is absolute when there is inability to produce offspring's as a result of defects of the reproductive system (Qadeer, 2010). Gradually, the technology came to several developing countries with strong patriarchal structures where motherhood and male child attract strong social values (Qadeer, 2010). "In the Hindu normative order, the birth of a child—a son, in particular—marks the important shift in the man/woman; celibacy/marriage; father/mother axis" (Bharadwaj, 2002). The importance of this perceived son centred philosophy put extreme importance on reproduction and often, under the aegis of patriarchy, women carry the burden of reproduction as well as the stigma associated with infertility. The inability to have a child is seen as profoundly disturbing. Infertility requires continual decision-making about whether to continue treatment, try a new drug or procedure, or accept one's infertility and go on with other things in life. The development of new technologies offers at once both new hope and more difficult decisions (Strickler, 1992). The medical literature frames the problem of infertility in a narrow and clinical manner. The response to infertility is medical intervention with the goal of pregnancy. Physicians' response to infertility has become increasingly technological. Psychological factors are considered of minimal importance, and surgical intervention is emphasized. With the exception of references to psychological disturbance and stress (Keye, 1984), medical literature rarely discusses the non-biological context of infertility: the impact on a marriage, family relationships, career, or other aspects of everyday life. The goal of infertility specialists is to enable couples to have their own biological children. Patrick Steptoe, the techno-daddy of the world's first publicised test-tube baby announced blithely at a conference in Oxford in 1987 that motherhood is the natural goal of all "normal" women. "It is a fact that there is a biological drive to reproduce. Women who deny this drive or in whom it is frustrated, show disturbances in other ways."

There is an interesting difference in men's and women's responses to the experience of infertility. Men tend to withdraw; women are far more likely to want to talk about their problems but often try to comply with their husbands' wishes to keep their infertility a secret. If it is the husband who is infertile, women often feel guilty and uncomfortable about this shift in the balance of power. They are likely to cover up for their husbands and tell others that they themselves are the cause of the problem. (Those who use donor insemination rarely reveal this even to the child or the grandparents. Professionals often encourage such secrecy.) Women are far more inclined than men to see adoption as a solution to their fertility problems. When they resort to technological intervention instead, it is most often to satisfy a man's desire for a genetically related child (Strickler, 1992). Many women resort to IVF and other intrusive medical procedures to obey values of a male dominated society, a society which glorifies motherhood in order to motivate women to produce children for their husbands. Infertility could be primary or secondary. When there is inability to have babies after one or more initial births that is called secondary infertility. This is the more common cause of infertility in the Third World. Given the lower levels of primary sterility in the Indian context, the causes of secondary infertility become critical. The common obstetric and gynaecological morbidities that may led to infertility are complications of delivery, pelvic infections, STD, RTIs and endometriosis, repeated pregnancies associated with high infant mortality, inadequate facilities for dealing with difficult labour, lack of pre and post-partum care and the poor state of general health due to high rates of infectious diseases (Sciarre, 1994). Additional factors such as under nutrition, pollution, environmental degeneration, the stress of migration (Gupta, 2007) and complications born out of contraceptive use without proper guidance and care also contribute to secondary sterility as with quinacrine, IUD etc. most of these are preventable cause of infertility that call for social mobilization for changing the content of deprivation, poverty and lack of access to comprehensive primary health care rather than only specialised services for infertility. The social implications of infertility such as, isolation, denial of social status, contempt and abandonment, are well known in patriarchal societies (Widge, 2008) and demand attention towards the social context of the problem (Jejeebhoy, 1998). The desire for male children combined with the economic dependence of women and lack of social support systems for those who wish to opt of the cultural grove compels women to conform. It is this social reality that becomes easy to manipulate for the commercial forces that take advantage of women's disadvantage.

Feminist literature has criticized the increasing medicalisation of reproduction. To many feminist scholars, reproductive technologies are just a new form of medical interference with women's bodies. To feminists, the problem is not a woman's inability to bear children (which are seen as an individual, not social, problem) but the structure and institutions of society which reinforce the necessity of childbearing for women's fulfilment on one hand, and physicians' increasing power in managing procreation on the other (Strickler, 1992). Anti-reproductive technology feminists have recognised that motherhood is depicted increasingly as a need for women. Feminist opponents of the technologies have been extremely critical of the ways doctors and the media fit these technologies into their proposed vision of women's "natural motherhood," and the ways in which women are channelled into trying yet one more invasive and debilitating medical procedure in order to become pregnant (Raymond, 1989). Reproductive technologies not only increase the meaning of reproduction for physicians, but also increase the professional prestige of those medical specialties which control the new technologies. Obstetrics and gynaecology have traditionally been a low-status area of medicine (Summey and Hurst, 1986), and the world-wide coverage of 'miracle' babies has given obstetrics/gynaecology, a function more complex and prestigious than just 'baby-catching'. There is expressed concern about the potential 'routinisation' of in-vitro fertilization (IVF), following the examples of Caesarean section, ultrasound and foetal monitoring—all of which started out as responses to particular conditions and has become routine procedures (Rothman, 1984). It is becoming more common to use IVF (which involves surgery, drugs and a much higher financial cost) in the cases of male fertility impairment, in spite of the fact that the woman's reproductive system is unimpaired (Cohen *et al.*, 1988). The possibility of using reproductive technologies for selection of the sex or other characteristics of a child also concerns many feminists. While recognising that the infertile do suffer emotionally; feminists deny that medical intervention is the appropriate response :

> "The suffering infertility causes on women, is enormous and deserves to be treated seriously. I do not think that those who respond to the suffering by offering to probe, scan, puncture, suction and cut women in repeated experiments are taking that suffering more seriously that I. They are not asking how much of women's suffering has been socially structured and inflicted and is, therefore not, inevitable" (Corea, 1985 : 6).

In many cases medical treatment only exacerbates the suffering of infertile women, since treatment is lengthy, painful and generally ineffective. The justification of IVF because women 'need' or have a 'right' to bear children reinforces the attitude that motherhood is central to womanhood, and assumes biological determinism: the 'drive' to have children is seen as deeper than other desires (Strickler, 1992). The feminist perspective advocates enhancing women's control over their lives and broadening their choices of autonomy. While feminists may disagree about the centrality of motherhood there is general agreement that technologies which emphasise the importance of motherhood, define it very narrowly (genetic/gestational), and transfer control over the procreative process from the mother to the physician, are antithetical to feminist interests. ART procedures are extremely expensive; it caters to the need of the women belonging to the affluent section only. Thus, ARTs claim of reducing the sufferings of infertile women is self-defeating due to its inherent class bias. Assisted Reproductive Technology[1] and legality in the Indian context: On the issue of legality and ART, various countries all over the world take various stands. The Supreme Court legalised commercial surrogacy in 2008 in the case of baby Manji Yamada, daughter of Ikufumi Yamada and Yuki Yamada (the couple got divorced shortly before the child was born). The Indian Council for Medical Research has given Guidelines in the year 2005 regulating Assisted Reproductive Technology Procedures. The Law Commission of India submitted the 228th report on Assisted Reproductive Technology Procedures discussing the importance and need for surrogacy, and also the steps taken to control surrogacy arrangements. All these initiatives are culminated in The Union Cabinet's effort in the process of examining a Draft Assisted Reproductive Technology (ART) (Regulation) Bill, 2010. But still it has not been cleared by the parliament which shows governmental apathy towards women's issues. The salient features of the proposed ART legislation can be summarised as:

1. Either of the commissioning couple must be infertile and also, or, the commissioning mother must be incapable of carrying a baby to full term;
2. The commissioning couple should either be married heterosexual couples or in an unmarried heterosexual relationship. Individuals can also apply for surrogacy. However, homosexual couples living together and who are Indian citizens, are not recognised as commissioning couples when both apply together but individually they can.
3. 'Single' commissioning persons (male or female) must prove infertility or prove inability to carry a baby to full term (in case of single female) by the commissioning mother in case of a single woman or a couple.
4. The status of homosexual commissioning couples who are not citizens of India depends on their legal right to marry under the law of their country. The question whether they, as a couple, will be allowed to go for a surrogacy agreement in India is a matter of future legislative deliberations.

5. A couple or an individual shall not have the service of more than one surrogate at any given time.
6. A couple shall not have simultaneous transfer of embryos in the woman and in a surrogate.
7. A woman in the age-group of 21-35 can become a surrogate mother. She will be allowed five live births, including her own children. She will not be allowed to undergo embryo transfer more than three times in her life to the same couple. If implemented properly this provision will check the malpractice which compromise with the health of both mother and the child.
8. In case of a single man or woman, the baby will be his/her legitimate child. If the surrogate mother is married, consent of her spouse is mandatory. The commissioning parents will have to accept the child's custody irrespective of any congenital abnormality.
9. A child born to an unmarried couple using a surrogate mother and with the consent of both parties shall be the legitimate child of both of them.
10. During the gestation period, the couple will bear the surrogate's expenses and give monetary help to her. The couple may enter into an agreement with the surrogate. Clinics will have to keep surrogates identity strictly confidential.
11. Foreign couples must submit two certificates—one on their country's surrogacy policy and the other stating that the child born to the surrogate mother will get their country's citizenship. This provision is formulated keeping in mind a recent case of two twins born to a German couple in January 2008 to a surrogate mother in India who were rendered stateless as they did not get the citizenship of either India or Germany. After a two-year long legal battle, the Supreme Court got them exit permits in May 2010.
12. Foreign couples have to nominate a local guardian who will take care of the surrogate during gestation.
13. ART banks, accredited by the government, will maintain a database of prospective surrogates as well as storing semen and eggs and details of the donor. Any ART bank

or clinic cannot send Indian citizens abroad for surrogacy.

14. State boards will give accreditation to ART banks—private and government. The board will have a registration authority, which in turn, will maintain a list of all In-vitro Fertilization (IVF) centres and monitor their functioning.
15. The draft bill also entails provision for live in couples who can go for IVF only if the woman cannot biologically bear a child or if it is too risky for her. No ART clinic is allowed to carry a surrogacy for patients for whom it may normally be possible to conceive a baby. This provision also rules out the fear of use of commercial surrogacy by woman who opts for it due to their busy career life.
16. Introduction of "generational" clause in surrogacy which demands that in case of altruistic surrogacy where relative play the surrogate has to be from the same generation only and this discounts the role of 'mothers' to act as surrogate.
17. The Law Commission of India (2009) described ART industry as "Rs. 25,000 crore pot of gold". It recommended only altruistic surrogacy arrangements and not commercial ones. The report in its conclusion largely supports surrogacy, but its commercialisation is something that has been an issue in the mind of Law Commission. But the Draft Bill legalises commercial surrogacy as well.

The Draft Bill contains several landmark proposals to streamline surrogacy practices in the country since there were no rules earlier regarding the rights of the surrogate, minimum age, and details about the contracts, informed consent and adoption requirements. In these times of globalisation and market driven economies, there is a considerable demand for outsourced babies from India. The Bill is appropriate considering the exponential growth that commercial surrogacy is going to witness in India in the coming years. But this commercially motivated bill has its own lacunas.

Lacunas of ART Bill 2010

The Draft Bill in its present form focuses only on IVF clinics and semen banks, but ignores gynaecologists offering infertility 'treatments' and IUI procedure. The Draft Bill also does not take into consideration other consultancies, organisations, agents, private agencies and travel agencies involved in promoting IVF/ ART techniques, egg donation and surrogacy. The Draft Bill should ensure that the ART clinics provide all relevant and correct information to the individuals. All technical terms and details must be explained and all written information must be read out to non-literate persons in a language understood by them. The Draft Bill does not allow couples to advertise for surrogates without mentioning "details relating to the caste, ethnic identity or descent of any of the parties" and prohibits ART clinics from seeking surrogates for its clients. However, advertisements for egg donors or surrogates by advertisement agencies, tourism departments, surrogacy agents, women's magazines, medical tours and travel agencies are not covered in the Draft Bill at all. The Draft Bill does not adequately emphasize on adoption. Considering the fact that these technologies do not 'treat' or cure infertility, and keeping the potential risks for the mother and child in mind, a responsible legislation regarding infertility and ARTs must encourage adoption (Qadeer, 2010). Bill demands, "No woman shall donate oocytes more than six times in her life, with not less than a three-month interval between the oocyte pick-ups." However, the maximum number of cycles (which may be 6 or more) has not been mentioned. Also the mechanism to record and monitor the number of times a woman is making donations has not been mentioned. The three-month interval between the donations stipulated by the Draft Bill is very inadequate. This interval should be increased. Moreover, the potential of exploitation of women for their eggs is as great as for their wombs. Since the sourcing of both egg donors and surrogates is through semen banks, the risk of commercialization is similar. The flow of payment to the egg donor is not quite clear in the Draft Bill (SAMA, 2010). The Draft Bill advises a studied recommendation of foetal reduction for multiple gestations, it does not mention the morbid risks of foetal reduction which include: uterine bleeding, developing infection, premature labour and loss of all foetuses.

The Bill should emphasize on keeping the instance of foetal reduction to a minimum, for which the number of oocytes or embryos to be transferred must be restricted to irrespective of the age of the women, the nature of embryos/oocytes (fresh or frozen) etc. Risks associated with ectopic pregnancy include internal bleeding, pelvic and abdominal pain, scar tissue, shock and death and complications may occur during egg harvesting procedure were not discussed properly. The Draft Bill has left a substantial void in the regulation process by not specifying the maximum permissible age of women for undergoing ART procedures. Considering the serious health implications whose magnitude increases with the age of the women, this lacuna needs to be addressed. There have been cases where women as old as 60 years or above have been made to conceive through ARTs with serious implications to their health. Bill allows "monetary compensation" to be paid to the surrogate mother, apart from expenses relating to insurance and medical bills, by the commissioning parents. The decision relating to the amount of compensation to be paid for the surrogacy is left between the commissioning parent(s) and the surrogate mother. Thus, the amount of compensation to be received by her depends on the bargaining power of the surrogate as well as the support which she can garner from the ART Bank to which she belongs. A surrogacy agreement resonate exploitation of poor people and is prejudicial to public morality (Rahim, 2010). The clause also perpetuates existing inequality due to the lack of bargaining power of the surrogate who often hails from impoverished background. The Draft Bill prohibits the surrogate from being the egg donor. Success rates of pregnancy are generally higher for artificial insemination than for IVF, and therefore, by extension genetic surrogacy is generally more successful than gestational surrogacy (Qadeer, 2010). The Bill mentions that "No woman shall act as a surrogate for more than 5 successful live births", including of the number of earlier pregnancies although the medical risks of frequent child births without adequate spacing are well known. Restricting surrogacy in terms of successful live births is futile if the number of cycles is not specified. These, along with a lack of record keeping and subsequent failure to trace a woman's reproductive history may have hazardous consequences on her mental and physical (especially reproductive) health (Qadeer, 2010). The Draft Bill must ensure that intended parents understand and agree to the fact that the surrogate has a right to physical integrity and bodily autonomy, i.e. she cannot be forced to abort the foetus, go through foetal reduction or made to follow a certain diet. These decisions are for the surrogate, and no one else, to make. The Medical Termination of Pregnancy (MTP, 1971) Act guarantees women in India the right to abortion, while international human rights legislation guarantees her physical integrity. However, no sex-selection should be allowed even with the consent of the surrogate (SAMA, 2006). The most unaddressed person in this Bill is the surrogate child, who nothing but is a tailor made product of a successful business transaction mediated through technology. The Bill only ensures the child's legal rights but deprives him of his inalienable right to be breast fed by gestational mother. Under the aegis of patriarchy, medical industry undermines the interest of surrogate mother at all levels of ART and reduces her to a compensated reproductive worker devoid of integrity, autonomy and rights to maximize profit. Her early separation and anonymity from the child and commissioning parents kill the potential of ART to create space for new social relations (Qadeer, 2010). The proposed ART Draft Bill is in serious conflict with following State policies and International covenants where India is a signatory (Qadeer, 2010: 47-48).

(a) Two child policy of the State to ensure stable population and mother's health. It legally promotes ill health of surrogate mother.
(b) Although the Government. is committed under Millennium Developmental Goals to reduce maternal mortality, high risk ART procedures (multiple pregnancy, commissioned abortions, transplanting 3 or more embryos fertilized in-vitro) may add to mortality.
(c) Sale of children, human trafficking and sale of body parts are illegal in India, yet there is promotion of commercial surrogacy both nationally as well as internationally.
(d) Although India is a signatory to the UN convention on Child Rights and Their Protection, ART Bill inherently violative of Child Rights.

(e) In the absence of proper monitoring authority ART clinics in clandestine fashion may promote sex selective foetal survival.

Social and Ethical Issues Pertaining to Surrogacy

The presumably dubious moral nature of the surrogate agreement has been considered as exploitative. Surrogacy is criticized for its commodification, moral ambiguity and objectification. Ethical practice must take its cue from the experiences of surrogate mothers, who—motivated primarily by a shortage of personal income—often endure the social stigma associated with surrogacy. They may leave their homes, lie about the parentage and claim the death of the baby after it has been handed over. For example, in The Mother Machine, Gena Corea points to instances where women entered into surrogate arrangements under what may have constituted conditions of economic duress: one involved a penniless 18 year old widow, and another, the 23 year old wife of a terminally ill man. The danger is obvious: economic exigency may force some women to enter surrogate agreements when they might otherwise never have entertained the idea. The removal of a child from his birth mother—against her will and for profit—is even more heinous than the forced removal of a women's kidney. A birth mother (her body and her mind) is connected to and remembers her missing baby more vividly than she remembers her missing kidney. In this process a woman as a class is emerging as an exploiter of the reproductive labour of women of other. The decision to become a surrogate is essentially not a free decision; it is a product of the (male-dominated) social construction of the will of women. There is also an in-built bias against the newborn baby as the surrogate mother is constrained to underplay her bond with the growing baby from the beginning. Early separation is at the cost of the baby's immunological and psychological health. The baby is denied the right to breastfeed even for crucial first three months. This aspect is completely ignored with the burden of surrogacy being shifted to one who cannot protest. Every child born through ART, whether disabled or one of a multiple pregnancy must have the same rights of survival and care as any other child. The proposed right of social parents to ask for "pregnancy reduction" goes against this (Qadeer & John, 2008).

"Reproductive engineering" is liberating not only of women with fertility problems and losses, but also of other groups. For lesbians who utilise sperm banks and artificial insemination to achieve biological pregnancy without heterosexual sex, such technologies are a critical tool of reproductive freedom. The majority of poor and working class women in both developed and developing countries still have no access to amniocentesis, IVF and the rest although they have the highest rates of infertility and foetal impairments. Before attacking or supporting reproductive technology, we need to demand that all women must have access to the knowledge and resources to judge its uses and to use it wisely, in keeping with their own particular needs.

Today, ART markets as well as the State emphasise relationships of blood and the genetic basis of paternity, marginalising the essential social and biological contribution of nurturing children in an enabling environment. The amount of compensation given to the surrogate mother is another particularly difficult aspect when what is involved is the creation of life—a baby no less. It is telling that in the West up to 50 per cent of the total cost goes to the surrogate mother while in India sperm banks, ART clinics and lawyers appropriate most of the money (Qadeer & John, 2008). Commercial surrogacy in India, dubbed as the "surrogacy capital of the world", is projected to become a whopping US $ 2.3 billion Industry by 2012, according to the Confederation of Indian Industry. Surrogacy related fertility tourism has long been fraught with ethical and human rights concerns in the country. In India, major part of the payment (75%) paid to the surrogate is paid only after the "delivery"—delivery of the product. It has its inherent class bias in favouring the commissioning parents than the surrogate who risks her life. Surrogacy and ART also predict unforeseen genetic, social and moral catastrophes. The ART (draft) Bill, 2010 allows the sperm of a single donor for use up to seventy five times and any normal woman can donate oocytes not more than six times in her life. In all such cases, in general, confidentiality of donor's identity is strictly maintained and thus children born out of ART and Surrogacy generally have no access to their biological parents. Thus, a healthy sperm donor can sire many children (as depicted in the recent movie "Vicky donor") who are being oblivious of their biological origin may end up marrying each other. The following case studies will help to understand the anomalies, exploitations and moral impairment associated with ART and surrogacy practices.

Case Study – 1

"The Akanksha Clinic, situated in Anand, Gujarat, is at the forefront of India's booming trade in so-called reproductive tourism. Najima Vohra, immaculately dressed in an electric-blue tunic-and-pants set, arrives at the clinic an hour early for her meeting with Ordenes so they can bond a bit more before the procedure begins. Jessica Ordenes is a petite yoga-school proprietor from New Jersey. Unable to get pregnant but still ovulating, she spent years unsuccessfully trying to arrange for a surrogate in the States to carry her biological child. It is not the most intimate venue, but Vohra is uncomfortable being seen anywhere else—like most women here, she plans to keep her surrogacy a secret. Vohra says she's not ashamed of being a surrogate, but most locals are very traditional and do not understand. "They think it is dirty—that immoral acts take place to get pregnant," she whispers, explaining their disbelief that she could conceive a child without having sex. "They had shun my family if they knew." Vohra comes from a village 20 miles outside Anand, but she has temporarily moved to the town with her husband and two children, a 12 year old daughter and a 7 year old son, to hide what she is doing. "We told our neighbours we were coming here for work, which is not strictly a lie." Vohra has no job but helps her husband in his scrap-metal business, for which they earn Rs. 50 to 60 ($ 1.20 to $ 1.45) a day. If her pregnancy is successful, the $ 5,500 she receives will, as she puts it, "give my children a future." She plans to divide her surrogacy windfall three ways: buying a brick house, investing in her husband's business, and paying for her children's education. "My daughter wants to be a teacher," she says. "I will do anything to give her that opportunity." "I am fit and strong, and I have already given birth twice," she continues, scoffing at the idea of being nervous. And yes, she's mentally prepared to hand over the baby. "It would not even have the same skin colour as me, so it would not be hard to think of it as Jessica's." Of course, it is impossible for Vohra to know how she will feel after she gives birth. All surrogates at the clinic sign a contract agreeing to hand over the baby—which reassures prospective parents, but also supports arguments that the women, many of whom are illiterate, are being taken advantage of. (In the U.S., only a handful of states regard pre-signed contracts as legally binding.)" Abigail Haworth, Web MD Archive, http:// www.webmd.com/infertility.

Case Study – 2

Egg Donation and Exploitation of Young Women many a time results in Death. Sushma Pandey, a 17 year old young woman who died in 2010, two days after her third egg donation in an IVF clinic of Surat. Her death is being attributed to the procedures used to extract eggs from healthy, desirable young females like Ms. Pandey. These eggs are often resold to affluent Westerners for use in commercial production of their children. Her post-mortem report states she had "one abrasion, four contusions and a blood clot in the head, plus six injection marks" as well as "congestion in the ovaries and uterus." The possible cause of her death was listed as shock due to multiple injuries. This most recent exposure of the daily exploitation of females offers yet another wake up call to the truth of the real, repeat, and often lethal harms of invasive egg removal procedures, which masquerade under the lie of donation. These transactions are anything but "donations" as young females—nearly children themselves—all over the world, desperately fall prey to offers of money like those made to Ms. Pandey.

Case Study – 3

This is from a reputed infertility clinic of Bangalore. Shanthamma is a poor but happy home-maker with two children aged 2 and 4 years. Her husband works as driver. On her husband's insistence, to make an end to their abject poverty and give quality life to their children she agreed to become surrogate. Commissioning parents wanted her to have better nutrition and hygienic living conditions during pregnancy. So, she had to stay in the accommodation provided by the ART clinic, leaving the children with her mother-in-law and husband. Since, she was illiterate, all the transactions were between the party and her husband. An unsuspecting, Shanthamma dying to meet her children, when returned home after the completion of surrogacy contract, found to her dismay that her husband had remarried deserting the characterless wife and doing well in the business with the money he got from surrogacy.[2]

India and Fertility Tourism

In recent past, especially since 1990s the world economy is undergoing tumultuous changes. In the less developed or developing countries like India; economic transformation has been associated with the attempt to generate higher rates of economic growth. Following Chinese model, other Asian, Latin American and African developing nations, under the aegis of International Monetary Fund and World Bank driven "Structural Adjustment Programmes" abandoned import substitute strategies and attempted to integrate their economies into Global market place. The shift was perceptible from state planning to market driven decision-making in public policies (Aslanbeigui etc., 2013). Firstly, enforced reforms and world trade organisation agreements saw protective national policies as trade restrictive and tied member states to a trajectory that served the multinational corporations, undermining public services of health care, education, energy, water and sanitation (Sexton, 2001). Secondly, attention must be directed to the nature of the governments that willingly commercialise public resources to favour international and private actors (Qadeer, 2010).

Internet Advertisement on ART cost of an Indian Clinic.

Surrogacy with Indian Egg Donation Package
First transfer—made upon signing of contract— US$ 8,250.
Surrogate mother screening and administration fees—US $ 3,000.
ED selection and administration Charges— US$ 1,000 Surrogates medical examinations—US$ 500.
ED medical examinations— US$ 500
Sperm freezing fee— US$ 500
Surrogate's transportation expenses— US$ 200
Surrogate preparation and drugs before IVF— US$ 800
Drug for ED stimulation— US$ 1,500
Legal Consultation Fee— US$ 250
Second transfer—made before IVF— US$ 3,500
IVF with ICSI (one attempt)— US$ 2,500

Egg Donor compensation— US$ 1000 (may be less depending on egg donor)

Third transfer—After confirming the pregnancy— US$ 5,300
Cost of drugs and pregnancy care— US$ 3,500 Surrogate's monthly fee during 9 months— US$ 1,800

Fourth transfer—After Baby Delivery— US$ 8,450
Maternity house fee— US$ 3,000 (as per actual)
Surrogate mother compensation— US$ 5,200
Birth Certificate— US$ 250

Total Surrogacy Package fee— US$ 25,500
Caucasian Egg Donor Additional US$ 10,000.

Source: http://www.newlifeindia.com/Financial New Life India H32, Ring Road, Lajpat Nagar IV, New Delhi, India-110024. E-mail: *matuta@newlifeindia.com*

A diversion of global reproductive tourists was thus inevitable and its profits contributed to economic growth. Successive national governments pursued this policy of growth without equity, camouflaged in phrases like "security net", "targeting the poor" and "inclusive development" (Qadeer, 2010). With ambiguous health and population policy statements, the state actually drafted legislations such as the ART (Regulation) Bill, 2008 and the National Health Bill, 2009.

India is fast becoming a favoured destination for medical tourism. The above mentioned advertisement speaks a lot. It has become the Mecca for all treatment options for infertility and thereby opened new avenues for reproductive medical tourism or better known as the fertility tourism. India has emerged as the main surrogacy destination since it legalised commercial surrogacy in 2002. It is primarily for following reasons:

- Surrogacy in India is low cost.[3] The complete package costs just one-third of the total procedure cost in the United Kingdom and other developed countries.
- The legal environment here is favourable. In fact, there is no law as such to govern surrogacy in

India with the Artificial Reproductive Technique (ART) Bill, 2008, still pending with Parliament.
- Increasing number of infertility cases in the country due to myriad socio-cultural and environmental reasons like women's education, employment and subsequent delay in marriage and conception, sedimentary life style, environmental pollution and so on.
- Non-availability of legally adoptable children with stringent adoption practices The Indian society for Assisted Reproduction has a membership of more than 600. Though the number of experts competent to perform advanced procedures is still small, there are over 250 IVF clinics in India. In addition, smaller towns and rural areas have infertility centres that work with ART centres located in the tertiary care institutions of cities where specialties are available to perform IVF and ICSI (Intra-Cytoplasm Sperm Injection) procedures (SAMA, 2006).

Medical tourism has added ART to its list of attraction, as couples from abroad come seeking easy access to surrogate mothers, eggs and sperms to have their "own" babies. According to these private providers, first world comforts and quality is available at these Indian Institutions at the Third World prices. Often this is achieved by reducing to the bare minimum, the necessary tests and safety procedures. Also, the surrogate mothers are paid lesser here than in Western countries. Further on, benefits associated with fertility tourism are numerous. To name a few, fertility tourism brings in more income, creates jobs, improves lives and contributes to overall economic development. It has also showcased India as a progressive and developed nation erasing the Third World image.

Conclusion

Hilary Rose argues that "the IVF cat is out of the bag, and—whatever else IVF does—it meets real needs for (some) real women. Consequently, a feminism that accepts the diversity of women's needs, must now work to limit IVF's imperialistic claims over women's bodies, and its associated claim to consume even more of the health-care budget for high-tech, curative medicine" (Rose, 1987: 152). Surrogacy and donor egg IVF are transforming the moral and ethical dimension of the society. Women are pitched against women as commodities and consumers. The presumably dubious moral nature of the surrogate agreement has been considered as exploitative. Surrogacy is criticized for its commodification, morality and objectification. It reifies the notion of biological parenting over social parenting. Today, ART markets as well as the State emphasize relationships of blood and the genetic basis of paternity, marginalising the essential social and biological contribution of nurturing children in an enabling environment. Ethical practice must take its cue—from the experiences of surrogate mothers, who—motivated primarily by a shortage of personal income—often endure the social stigma associated with surrogacy. They may leave their homes, lie about the parentage and claim the death of the baby after it has been handed over. The danger is obvious: economic exigency may force some women to enter surrogate agreements when they might otherwise never have entertained the idea. "Reproductive engineering" is liberating not only of women with fertility problems but also of other groups. For lesbians who utilise sperm banks and artificial insemination to achieve biological pregnancy without heterosexual sex. Such technologies are a critical tool of reproductive freedom. The majority of poor and working class women in both developed and developing countries still have no access to amniocentesis, IVF and the rest although, they have the highest rates of infertility and foetal impairments. Along with constructive criticisms against reproductive technology, we need to demand that all women should have access to the knowledge and resources to judge its uses and to use it wisely, in keeping with their own particular needs. Thus to conclude, we can say ART and surrogacy as a concept has the potential to liberate as well as oppress women. ART and surrogacy debate oscillates between the complex question of women's bodily autonomy and exploitation mediated by male controlled technology and capitalism's inherent penchant for commodification. In spite of its limitations, a carefully drafted Act can expand the horizon of feminine liberty and minimize the potentially exploitative aspect to protect those who choose it as reproductive option.

Reproductive Technologies, fosters "enhanced decision-making" to assure that women make "informed, voluntary choices to use reproductive technologies," and "enhanced participation of women in the development and implementation of reproductive technologies ..." (Andrews, 1988: 14) will expand its horizon.

NOTES

1. Legal Position different countries on Surrogacy:
   North America: States that allow but regulate surrogacy are: California, Arkansas, Florida, Illinois, Nevada, New Hampshire, Texas, Utah and Virginia. Commercial surrogacy in Canada has been illegal since 2004, although altruistic surrogacy is allowed.
   Western Europe: Although surrogacy is legal in the United Kingdom, no commercial arrangements are allowed. Surrogacy is permitted for altruistic reasons. Only married couples can participate in a surrogacy agreement. Countries in the European Union who have banned all forms of surrogacy include Germany, Sweden, Norway and Italy.
   Eastern Europe: Russia and Ukraine are the only European countries where surrogacy is fully legalised. Foreign couples are allowed to pursue surrogacy arrangements in both countries.
   South Asia: Commercial surrogacy is legal in India.
   South-East Asia: Unclear laws regulating assisted reproductive services make Thailand, Malaysia and Philippines an ideal option for foreigners seeking surrogacy services in this part of the world. However, all forms of surrogacy are banned in Singapore.
   East Asia: In Japan, there is no law to regulate surrogate births. Gestational surrogacy is banned in China.
   Oceania: In Australia, the state of Queensland bans all forms of surrogacy. In the other Australian states such as Victoria, the Australian Capital Territory, Tasmania, and South Australia commercial surrogacy is prohibited, except altruistic surrogacy. Commercial surrogacy is banned in New Zealand (Centre for Social Research, Surrogate Motherhood—Ethical or Commercial, 2013).
2. This case study is collected during interaction in ART clinics.
3. According to the 228th report of the Law Commission of India, "the usual fee for surrogacy in India is $ 25,000 to $ 30,000, which is almost one third/one fourth to what it would cost in USA."

REFERENCES

Bharadwaj, Aditya (2002). "Why adoption is not an option in India: The visibility of infertility, the secrecy of donor insemination, and other cultural complexities", *Social Science and Medicine,* 56(9):1867-1880.

Birke, L.S. Himmelweit and G. Vines (1990). *Tomorrow's Child: Reproductive Technologies in the 90s.* Virago Press, London.

Boivin, J., L. Bunting and J. K. Collins (2007). "International estimates of infertility prevention and treatment seeking: potential need and demand for infertility Medical Care", *Human Reproduction,* 22 (6): 1506-12.

Centre for Social Research (2013). *Surrogate Motherhood—Ethical or Commercial,* New Delhi.

Cohen, J., M.J. Mayaux and M.L. Guihard-Moscato (1988). "Pregnancy outcomes after in-vitro fertilization", *Annals of the New York Academy of Sciences,* p. 541.

Corea, G., (1985). *The Mother Machine,* Harper and Row, New York.

Cornell Law Review (1994), 79(631): 637-644.

Dawn E. Johnsen (1995). The Creation of Foetal Rights: Conflicts with Women's Constitutional Rights to Liberty, Privacy, and Equal Protection, Yale, L.J., 599: 604-05.

Department of Health and Human Services (2005). "Centre for Disease Control (CDC): Full ART Report".

Feenberg Andrew (1999). *Questioning Technology,* Routledge Kegan Paul, London, pp. 1-9.

Fraser, N. (1989). "Struggle Over Needs: Outline of a Socialist-Feminist Critical Theory of Late Capitalist Political Culture", In: *Unruly Practices: Power, Discourse and Gender in Contemporary Social Theory,* Polity Press, Cambridge, pp. 161–87.

Gupta, Sadhana, Achala Sinha, and Pandey (2007). "Infertility Problems in couples with temporarily migrant male partners", *Journal of Obstetrics and Gynaecology India,* 57(1): 64-68.

Jejeebhoy, S. (1998). "Infertility in India: Levels, Patterns and Consequence Priorities for Social Science Research", *Journal of Family Welfare,* Vol. 44: 15-24.

Keye, W. (1984). "Psychosexual Responses to Infertility", *Clinical Obstetrics and Gynaecology,* 27:760-6.

Kurinczuk, J.J., M. Hansen and C. Bower (2004). "The risk of birth defects in children born after assisted reproductive technologies", *Curr. Opin. Obstet. Gynecol.,* 16 (3): 201- 9.

Law Commission of India (2009). "Need for Legislation to Regulate Assisted Reproductive Technology Clinics as well as Rights and Obligations of Parties to a Surrogacy," *228th Report.*

Lori, Andrew (1984). *New Conceptions: A Consumers Guide to the Newest Infertility Treatments,* Ballantine, New York.

Mallik, R. (2002). "Sex Selection: A Gender-Based Preference for a Pregnancy", *Reproductive Health Matters Elsevier Science,* 10(19): 189-90.

Menon, N. (1995). "The Impossibility of 'Justice': Female Foeticide and Feminist Discourse on Abortion", In: *Contributions to Indian Sociology,* 29(1 and 2): 369-92. New Delhi: Sage Publications.

Nahid, Aslanbeigui, Steven Ressnran and Summerfield (2013). *Women in the Age of Economic Transformation: Gender Impact of Reform in Post-Socialist Countries,* Routledge Kegan Paul.

Petchesky, R.P. (1980). "Reproductive Freedom: Beyond A Woman's Right to Choose", *Signs: Journal of Women in Culture and Society,* summer, 5, (66):1-85.

Qadeer, Imrana (2010). "New Reproductive Technologies and Health Care in Neo-Liberal India", *Monograph,* CWDS, New Delhi.

Qadeer, Imrana and Mary, E. John (2008) "The Business and Ethics of Surrogacy", *Economic and Political Weekly,* 44 (04):10-12.

Qadeer, Imrana and Mary, E. John (2008). *Surrogacy Politics,* KAFILA, December.

Raheem, Sapna (2010). "Freedom of Trade and Commerce and Reproductive Markets in India: Assisted Reproductive Technology Bill, 2010 and Its Challenges", *International Journal of Contemporary Laws.*

Raymond Janice G. (1989). "Reproductive Technologies, Radical Feminism", and "Socialist Liberalism, Reproductive and Genetic Engineering", *Journal of International Feminist Analysis,* 2(2).

Rose, Hilary (1987). "Victoria' values in the test tube: The politics of Reproductive Science and Technology," In: Stanworth, M. (Ed.). *Reproductive Technologies: Gender, Motherhood and Medicine,* Oxford: Polity Press, England, pp. 151-173.

Rowland, R. (1985). "A Child at Any Price? An Overview of Issues in the Use of the New Reproductive Technologies, and the Threat to Women", In: *Women's Studies International Forum,* 8(6): 539-46.

SAMA (2006). *ARTs and Women: Assistance in Reproduction or Subjugation?* SAMA Resource Group for Women and Health, New Delhi, p. 14.

Srinivasan, Sandhya (2010). "New reproductive technologies and India's transitional health system in making babies", pp. 1-21. *Zuban,* New Delhi.

Steinbock, B. (1998). "Rethinking the right to reproduce", *Harvard Working Paper Series,* Harvard School of Public Health, Cambridge.

Strickler, Jennifer (1999). "The new reproductive technology: Problem or solution", *Sociology of Health & Illness.*14(1): 111-32.

Summey, P. and M. Hurst (1986). "Ob/Gyn. on the rise: the evolution of professional ideology in the twentieth century", Part II. *Women and Health,* 11: 103-23.

Tong Rosemary (1997). *Feminist Thought: A Comprehensive Introduction,* Routledge Kegan Paul.

Widge, Anjali (2008). "Socio-cultural attitudes towards infertility and assisted reproduction in India".

Zhang, Y.; Y.L. Zhang and C. Feng (2008). "Comparative Proteomic Analysis of Human placenta derived from assisted reproductive Technology'. *Proteomics* (20): 4344–56.

WEBSITES

http://india.acrinews.com/catf.jsp?articleID

http://news.in.msn.com/national/article.aspx?

http://www.hfea.gov.uk/1424.html, accessed on 5/3/2010

http://www.renters.com/article/latestcrises/idUSDEL298-735

http://www.who.int/reproductive-health/infertility

http://www.searo.who.int/linkfilies/reproductive_health_Profile_infertility. pdf Accessed on 12/Nov/2007.

http://www.cdc.gov/art/ART2005/index.htmaccessed on 12/Jan/2008.

http://kafila.org.

http://www.hsph.harvard/HW papers/reproright.htm0l,

http:// www.womenleadership.in/Csr/SurrogacyReport.pdf

http://www.webmd.com/infertility-and-eproduction/features/womb-rent-surrogate-mothers-india

6

Reproductive Health Awareness Among Rural Women in Assam

A Sociological Study

Jyoti Prasad Saikia and *Rekhamoni Gogoi*

Introduction

Health is a concept which not only belongs to the field of medical science but also an integral part of socio-cultural phenomena alike. Each of these aspects are interrelated and interdependent, i.e. one aspect influences the other and *vice versa*. Health is also mainly resolved by the biological and cultural adaptation and evaluation of the society and the people. Every group of human society should realise the importance of their health. In this context, reproductive health is also very significant. The concept of reproductive health, according to the United Nation (UN, 1990), is a state of complete physical, mental and social well-being and not merely the absence of disease or infirmity, in all matters relating to the reproductive system and to its functions and processes. Women have to suffer different kinds of diseases at the reproductive age. Reproductive health includes, a satisfying and safe sex life which will be free from fear of disease. The ability to reproduce and the freedom to do so with the access to both infertility services and contraceptives is essential for ensuring reproductive choice for women and men. However, women and especially rural women are far from receiving such choices which make them more prone to such diseases. It was in the year 1994, the International Conference on Population and Development held in Cairo brought in the right to better sexual and reproductive health within the parameters of family planning. The

Cairo definition of reproductive health included sexual health which will enhance the life and personal relations of people and especially women. Reproductive health care, on the other hand, has been defined by this conference as the methods, techniques and services that contribute to reproductive health and well-being by preventing and solving reproductive health problems. The Cairo Conference also talked about gender equality and women's empowerment, bringing strong attention to young people's sexuality and health. Thus, Cairo Conference, for the first time, brought forward a completely new approach to women's reproductive health.

This study is primarily concerned with women's reproductive health. Hence, male reproductive health issues has been kept aside here. In the rural society women have been facing various problems of health, particularly the reproductive health. A good number of women are observed who have no adequate knowledge of the causes and consequences of their diseases. Even in certain situations, they are not aware of their health problems during pregnancy and or childbirth. But reproduction is considered as one of the fundamental features of all living creatures, in which females play a most important role. Women are not only to reproduce the children, but also to ensure proper upbringing and socialisation which makes good health of these women a prerequisite. Death and illnesses from reproductive causes are highest among poor women the world over. In developing countries the burden of reproductive problems are particularly severe for women since they are almost always illiterate, disproportionately poor and politically powerless. According to the World Bank, about one-third of the total disease burden among women aged 15 to 44 years in the developing countries is linked to health problems associated with pregnancy, childbirth, abortion, HIV, reproductive tract infections and among the diseases for which cost-effective interventions exist, reproductive health problems account for the majority of the disease burden in women of this age group (World Bank, 1993). The focus on women's health has gained impetus in recent time because of new knowledge and a deeper understanding of women's health problems. There is an increasing effort to view women's health issues in a more holistic manner, emphasizing the health needs and concern of women in every aspect of their lives—from birth to old age. A number of programmers and activities have been introduced along with interventions to address women's health issues in the country like the maternity benefits, equal pay for equal work, education in regard to reproductive health etc.

Review of Related Literature

A good number of social scientists have done their works on women reproductive health throughout the world. They have concerned with different kind of findings in their research activities. An anthropologist, Rose (2008) in his work, *"Reproductive Health Awareness among the Tribal Women in Manipur"* makes a comprehensive study of the reproductive health awareness among the tribal women in Manipur, with special reference to Churachandpur district. Ravendra K. Sharma and Manju Rani (2009) in their research work entitled *"Contraceptive use Among Tribal Women of Central India: Experiences among DLH8-RCH-11 Survey"* mention that the utilization of Reproduction and Child Health (RCH) services are comparatively low among Scheduled Tribes (ST) of this region. Krishna Bhomik (2006), in her work entitled *"Indian Women the Ushering of A New Dawn"* expresses her views that women's health is harmed by lack of access to and the poor quality of reproductive services because they are not aware of women health. Facts from NFSH-II highlights the dismal state of reproductive health of tribals in India. Rao (1985) in his work entitled *"Food Beliefs of Rural Women during the Reproductive year in Dharurad,"* Karnataka, reveals that the diet of a pregnant woman has a deficiency in all nutrients. A.R. Bang, A.T. Bang, M. Baitule, Y. Choudhury, S. Sarmukaddam and B. Tele (1989) in their study *"High Prevalence of Gynaecological Diseases in Rural Indian Women"* was carried out in two villages of Ghadiali district of Maharashtra. They observe that the prevalence of gynaecological or sexual diseases and the average number of such diseases per woman are remarkably high. It was observed in their study that iron deficiency, anaemia and vitamin 'A' deficiency are high due to poor economic condition of rural families. Reproductive tract diseases, gynaecological troubles caused by contraception are also high among them. K. Mitra and K. Basu (1998) anthropologists in their work *"Health Problems and Practices of Slum Women of Delhi"* have examined the various environments, socio-economic and cultural factors whose interplay determines the health of pregnant and nursing mothers in Bhumihun camp; a slum in Govindpuri. They have tried to understand the health problems and practices of slum women and the male of socio-economic and physical environment in influencing them. They have found that the most direct effects of poor health and nutrition among females in countries like India are high mortality rates among young children and women of child-bearing age and high morbidity rates throughout the life cycle. The effects of pervasive ill health extend beyond the woman herself. Women's health and nutritional status is bound up with social, cultural and economic factors that influence all aspects of their lives, and it has consequences not only for the women themselves, but also for the well-being of the family and functioning of households. For improving the health status of poor women, greater opportunities of schooling and employment as well as some changes in health system are needed, to increase the demand for health services and women's ability to use them. R.R. Prasad and A.K. Kapoor (1982) in their work people *"Obstetrical Practices Among the Bhotia Tribals"* expresses their views that the Bhotias use very simple and unhygienic method to expel the placenta, locally known as *'Phali'* from the mother's womb after childbirth. They said that the Bhotia women are also given a gentle abdominal massage and tea brewed from the *'Bodpa'* leaves, found in Tibet, to effect easy delivery of the child. Both Prasad and Kapoor observed the lapses of knowledge among Bhotia women towards their reproductive health. Even in their society people are not interested to follow the modern medical science. S.K. Basu and G.K. Kshatriya (1989) in their work entitled *"Fertility and Mortality in Tribal Population of Baster District, M.P."* observed that "maternal and child-care was largely neglected. Expectant mothers to a large extent are not inculcated against tetanus. They notice that more than 90 per cent of deliveries in their studies operated at home, attended by elderly ladies of the household. No specific precautions are observed at the time of conducting deliveries, which results in an increased susceptibility to various infections. Services of para-medical staff are secured only in difficult labour cases. They tell on the third day after delivery "the *Kasa-Pani* is provided to mother. *Kasa-Pani* is a herbal medicine which according to them gives soothing effect, helps in recovering the depleting energy and also acts as anti-infective." They also said that maternal mortality directly related to pregnancy and child birth has been found to be appreciably high among the tribal populations of Bastar district. In addition, a lot of families suffer from ill health due to pregnancy and child birth in the absence of well defined concept of health consciousness. P.S. Devarapalli (1996) in his work *"Maternal Care and Obstetric Practices among the Konda Gora Tribe"* expresses his views that, their women continued to work till the time of delivery. Dietary restrictions were also imposed on her during pregnancy. Beans were avoided, as they were believed to cause epileptic fats. Deliveries were conducted at home. Umbilical cord was cut with the help of sterilized knife. After delivery the woman remains completely at home for a minimum of one month. This process of delivery is no scientific and can make trouble for woman's health. So, he opined that lack of awareness among them towards their health condition trash themselves into lower status in the society. Pandey and Tiwary (1993) in their study *"Socio-Cultural Characteristics and Health Seeking Behaviour of Hill Korwas"* find out that the pregnant woman did not receive any special antenatal care or diet. There was no restriction on her daily work, including fetching of water and cutting of wood. The delivery was usually conducted by elderly woman and the ANM or trained *dai* was not called and in case of complication the pregnant woman was usually left at the mercy of God. The umbilical cord was usually cut with the help of sickle or old blade. In a report of research conducted by the World Bank entitled *"Improving Women's Health in India"* (1996), it was found that emphasis on women's reproductive health and the factors underlying excess female mortality at early ages. Other concerns, such as the diseases and conditions common to men and women and the health of older women, are given less attention then would be required in a comprehensive consideration of women's health issues. Gender based violence and occupational health issues for women are also noted, but many of the measures required to address these issues are beyond the scope of this report. The findings of this work also points our need of adequate awareness and knowledge is needed for rural women. Anupurna Rathor (2004) in her work *"Family Planning Practices in Third World Countries"* expresses her views that Asian countries have led the world in identifying problems related to rapid population growth and high fertility and in developing programmes to address those problems. Despite temporary economic problems in some of them, will continue to be leaders in development programmes in the twenty-first century as mankind continue to lead with the every challenging reproductive and family health problems of a world populated by more than 6 billion people. During the last quarter of the century the learning curve has shifted towards the increase prominence of issues such as population and family planning, primary health care, maternal and child health and most recently HIV/AIDS and other infectious diseases. Rajaram (2003) has conducted a very fruitful research work *"Adolescent and Adult Mother's Foetal Loss: Their Determinants and Policy Issues"* observed that reproductive health problems resulting from pre-marital sex and premature family formation patterns leading to induce abortion and foetal loss are found to be major and serious problems among adolescent mothers all over the world. He also found that the magnitude of foetal loss manifested among adolescent mothers (12 to 19 years) in comparison with their adult mothers (20 to 24 years). Their foetal loss is treated as a dependent variable and several independent variables like family type, age at menarche and marriage, anaemia, antenatal care, socio-economic status, weight of the mothers and foetus etc. are important in explaining the foetal loss of the mothers. Vatsala Samant (2000), a Gynaecologist, conducted a research work on awareness among women towards diseases of reproductive health in her work, entitled *"Health Awareness for Women"* expresses her views that due to lack of proper awareness more rapidly women are getting affected by diseases of reproductive health.

Field of the Study

Kekuri Borchapori village of Golaghat district of Assam has been considered as the field of this study. It covers an area of 6.30 square kilometres. It is 45 kilometres away from Golaghat town. To the east of the village there is Hurhuria and Chekaimora, to the west Dighali Majgaon, to the north Owguri Alichiga along with Dhanshiri river and to the south, there is Doyang river and to north-east railway line. The village is formed by adjoining two places, namely 'Kekuri' and 'Borchapori'. Earlier, when people illegally inhabited this forest area, they had come across the river Langkhang, which flows twisting near the village, so the village is called Kekuri. Again some of the people situated on another side of the Kekuri village on the bank of river Dhanshiri who inhabited from Bokakhat Borchapori village of Golaghat district, therefore, it is called Borchapori. There are no proper infrastructural facilities like electricity, water supply, health and hygienic atmosphere. Generally, most of the people live in *kuchcha* houses because they are economically very poor. The people also prefer nuclear family rather than joint family. Good health care facilities are not available in the Kekuri Borchapori village. Only one sub-centre is there near the adjoining village. The villagers depend on Borpathar Primary Hospital and Jamuguri Hospital for their primary health care. There are no sufficient educational institutions at different levels in this village. There are only two educational institutions, one is primary and other is secondary, namely Kekuri Janajati L.P. School and Kekuri Janajati M.E. School. No Higher Secondary School or College has been found in this village. According to 2011 Census; 694 persons are literate out of which 387 are male and 307 are female. Communication facilities of the village are very pathetic. There is no *pakka* road and no transportation facility in the village which makes communication difficult. The village has 203 households and 983 population. Out of this population, 509 are male and 474 female.

Objectives of the Study

This study concentrates primarily on three objectives. First, this study attempts to know the social background of the rural women as respondents. Secondly, this study has tried to understand the awareness of rural women towards reproductive health and finally, this study has attempted to explore and find out the knowledge of rural women about their diseases of reproductive health.

Theoretical Perspective

This study, as has been stated before, concentrates primarily upon the reproductive health awareness among women. When we talk about awareness, in its essence lays knowledge. Knowledge regarding any particular phenomenon, in this case reproductive health, may ultimately lead to awareness, which goes beyond just 'knowing' about something and reaching a certain level of consciousness regarding it. However, knowledge is not an isolated entity; it is influenced, moulded and shaped by various socio-cultural factors. In other words, knowledge is relative and not absolute. In India, reproduction is a subject which is hardly spoken about. It is, although not formally, tabooed to speak or discuss about it in the family. Under such condition, knowledge and awareness regarding reproductive health especially among women depends largely upon the socio-culturally produced and passed on knowledge, which is often influenced by misconceptions, stereotypes and stigma related to the issue. Under these conditions, the experience of reproductive health among women and their knowledge and awareness regarding it are affected by multiple variables. Interactionist Perspective of Health, drawn on the works of George Herbert Mead suggests that health and experiences of health and disease are formed in interaction with the individual and the society he/she lives in. This perspective suggests that, along with one's own understanding of health and disease, the views and opinions of other members of the society finally shapes the generally accepted idea of health and the personal experience, idea and awareness of health and disease as well. Following this perspective, this study has tried to explore various factors present in society that affects and influences the knowledge and in turn awareness of reproductive health among women. It is needless to say that woman in Indian society is usually the one who stands as the recipient. This is also true in terms of health. The gendered inequalities and the hierarchical social structure complement each other and shapes the lives and live experiences of women. Hence, it is imperative that we look at awareness of reproductive health among rural women in India from this point of view.

Application of Methodology

For the study the data were collected from both primary and secondary sources. In this study secondary data were collected from books, official documents, journals etc. After the collection of data, it was classified systematically question-wise. Since possible alternative answers were provided to each question the classification or responses had been done on the basis of the alternatively chosen by the respondents. Various responses were classified in homogeneous group, i.e. age group, caste group etc. The classified data ha been put into tables. Tabulation was done by employing the method of simple frequency tables. The collected data had been analysed statistically according to the table. In this study some specific questions had been asked to the respondents which were put under sociological investigation and analysis.

Social Background of the Respondents

The social background of the respondents is a very significant factor to understand any phenomena. Hence, social background of the respondents has also been analysed in this study. Here, maximum number of respondents of the village are from the age group of 25-31 years, i.e. 44 (44%). Only 1 (1%) belongs to the age group below 18 years. The highest number of respondents, i.e. 60 (60%) respondents belong to Other Backward Class (OBC). On the other hand, 37 (37%) respondents belong to Scheduled Tribes (ST). Again as many as 2 (2%) respondents belong to Scheduled Caste (SC) and only 1 (1%) respondent belongs to General category. Majority of the respondents, i.e. 90 (90%) belong to Hindu religion and only 10 (10%) respondents belong to Christian religion. Most of the families belong to nuclear family, i.e. 80 (80%). On the other hand only 20 (20%) respondents belong to joint family. It was observed that majority of the respondents got married at below 18 years, i.e. 52 (52%). Only 4 (4%) respondents belong to the age at marriage group 25-30 years. Regarding education, it was found that highest number of the respondents, i.e. 39 (39%) were illiterate and 37 (37%) respondents read up to Primary level. Further, it shows that 23 (23%) respondents passed Secondary School level, and only 1(1%) respondents have found who passed Higher Secondary (HS). In case of the level of education of the husbands. The highest number were read up to Primary level, i.e. 40 (40%). Again 38 (38%) number of the husbands passed Secondary School level. On the other hand 12 (12%) husband were totally illiterate, 7 (7%) husbands passed H.S.L.C. (Matric) Examination 2 (2%) completed Higher Secondary and only 1 (1%) husband were found who are Graduate. In context of income source the majority of the families depends upon agriculture, i.e. 75 (75%). Regarding income, it was found that maximum number of families belong to the income group of Rs. 5001 to 7000 per month, i.e. 54 (54%). The next families of the respondents arè from the income group of Rs. 3001 to 5000 per month, i.e. 36 (36%) and 6 (6%) families of the respondents are from income group Rs. 7001 to 9000 per month. On the other hand the lowest number of the families of the respondents, i.e. 2 (2%) are from the income group more than Rs. 9000 and below Rs. 3000 per month also.

Table 6.1: Respondent's Concept about Reproductive Health

Sl. No.	*Concept of Reproductive health*	*Number of respondents*	*Percentage*
1.	Safe motherhood	8	10.53
2.	Maternal well-being	2	2.64
3.	Child health	1	1.32
4.	Do not know	65	83.53
	Total	**76**	**100**

Source: Field Study (2011).

Reproductive Health and Awareness among Women

The right to health care is a fundamental right to each woman as an individual (Sinha, 2007). But unfortunately, it is clearly observed that still there are difference in factors determining health for men and women. It is depicted in the different research works on women health that women in our society suffer from inequality and discrimination based on sex in addition to poverty and injustice caused by the social, political and economic system (Sinha, 2007). Such realities have adverse impact on women as a whole and their reproductive health in particular. Therefore, women should always be concerned with and aware of their own reproductive health condition. In the study it was found that maximum respondents, i.e. 76 per cent had idea about reproductive health. Only 24 per cent respondents are not aware of it. Out of total 76 (76%) respondents majority of the respondents, i.e. 65 (65%) do not know what is Reproductive Health.

In this study only 10 (10%) respondents had idea about it, among them 8 (8%) respondents said that Reproductive Health is safe motherhood, and 2 (2%) respondents said that it is maternal well-being. On the other hand, only 1 (1%) respondent know Reproductive Health as a child health.

In this study maximum number of respondents pursued the idea of reproductive health from parents, i.e. 35 (46.06%), as many as 21 (27.64%) respondents are obtained the idea from pear groups and 15 (19.73%) respondents had punsued the idea about reproductive health from other relatives. Again 2 (3%) respondents got the idea about it from literature and same number of the respondent, i.e. 2 (2%) pursued from radio and only 1 (1%) respondent are obtained the idea about reproductive health from T.V. and other visual electronic media. Regarding Reproductive Health problem majority of the women, i.e. 72 (72%) are not aware about the reproductive health problems. Significantly, only 28 (28%) were aware of reproductive health problems. In this study 28 (100%) respondents suffered different reproductive health problems differently by nature. Among them 12 (42.86%) respondents suffered problem like Burning sensation while passing urine or abnormal frequent urination, 11 (39.29%) respondents suffered white and red discharge problem and 9 (32.15%) respondents suffered constant leakage of faecal matter. It was seen that due to white discharge 8 (28.58%) respondents faced bad odour and 7 (25%) had suffered irritation problem. Again 6 (21.43%) respondents suffered any other problems like vomiting, long time bleeding etc. On the other hand, abdominal pain are suffered by 5 (17.86%) respondents, 3 (10.72%) respondents suffered from mucopurulent (pus) discharge from vagina and only 2 (7.15%) respondents suffered reproductive health problem like pain during intercourse. In this study it was observed that 59 (59%) respondents faced problems during menstruation. Out of 59 respondents, majority of the respondents, i.e. 43 (72.89%) faced painful menstruation, 22 (37.29%) respondents faced any other problems like irregularity, irritation, lack of bleeding etc. It was seen that 19 (32.20%) respondents faced stomach problem during menstruation. Again 12 (20.34%) respondents faced over bleeding problem and only 7 (11.87%) respondents faced backache problem during menstruation. Regarding menstruation problem out of 59 (59%) respondents 39 (66.11%) respondents consult with others.

On the other hand, 20 (33.89%) respondents in this study never consult with anybody regarding their problem during menstruation period. Among 39 (66.11%) respondents, 14 (35.87%) respondents consulted with doctors of local dispensary, 10 (25.65%) respondents consulted with relative elder women regarding menstruation problem. Again 8 (20.53%) respondents consulted with mother as well as 6 (15.39%) respondents consulted with any others like husband, *Asha Karmi* etc., and only one (2.56%) respondents consulted with nursing stuff regarding menstruation problem. It was found that majority of the respondents i.e., 97 (97%) respondents were heard about contraceptives. On the other hand 3 (3%) respondents were not aware about it. In this study it was observed that out of the total respondents, 31 (31%) respondents had the experience of abortion. It was found that after doing abortion, a good number of respondents, i.e. 26 (83.88%) respondents faced health problem. Among 26 respondents, maximum number of respondents, i.e. 22 (84.61%), faced problem of weakness after abortion. It was found that out of 99 (99%) respondents those who become pregnant at least one time, 72 (72.73%) respondents were not aware of any problem during pregnancy period. Regarding the consciousness regarding the plight of reproductive health after delivery, maximum respondents i.e., 86 (86%) are not aware of it. In this study, it was found that maximum number of respondents, i.e. 82 (88.01%) involved in domestic activities after short distance from the time of delivery and due to this number of problems they faced. In this study out of the total respondents, only 25 respondents are aware of the Government Schemes.

Women and Knowledge of Reproductive Health Diseases

Women bear the important responsibility of reproduction in the family. More importantly she also ensures the sustenance and maintenance of the family which is a crucial task. In such a situation, a woman's role in terms of the reproductive activities and family maintenance affects the whole family, the society and consequently the whole nation. Hence, knowledge of reproductive health diseases among women is of utmost importance.

In this study, it was observed that maximum number of respondents, i.e. 96 had knowledge about puberty before the experience. Even they knew the appropriate puberty age. Only 4 (4%) respondents had no knowledge about it. In this study, 54 (54%) respondents did not suffer for menstruation. On the other hand 46 (46%) respondents suffered badly because of menstruation. In this study, out of total 46 (46%) respondents, majority of the respondents, i.e. 39 (84.78%) suffered from dysmenarrhea problem for menstruation, 5 (10.86%) respondents suffered from menorrhogia problem and only 1 (2.17%) respondents suffered from metrorrhogia problem for menstruation. It was found that majority of the respondents, i.e. 87 (87%) did not suffer from infertility; only 13 (13%) respondents suffered from it. It was found that out of total 13 (13%) respondents, majority of the respondents, i.e. 11 (84.61%) had no knowledge about the causes of infertility. On the other hand 2 (15.39%) respondents had knowledge about the causes of infertility. It was observed that out of 10 (76.92%) respondents, maximum number of respondents, i.e. 8 (80%) adopted any other measure like consulting with *'Beez'*, *'Dai'* etc. to improve fertility, 5 (50%) respondents offered *puja* to different temple, 4 (4%) respondents used traditional indigenous medicine and only 1 (10%) respondent consulted with medical practitioners. Again, out of total 3 (23.08%) respondents; all the respondents, i.e. 3 (100%) did not adopt any measure to improve fertility because of not accessibility of medical practitioners, 2 (66.67%) respondents did not adopt measure to improve fertility because of problems like communication or transportation etc. In this study, maximum number of the respondents, i.e. 90 (90%) did not get problem in their uterus and the rest, i.e. only 10 (10%) respondents suffered problem in their uterus. But unfortunately in this study only 11 respondents had knowledge about Fallopian tubes. Even 59 respondents of the total samples had no knowledge about puerperal. Significantly, 41 respondents suffered this problem during pregnancy period. In this study it was found that out of total 62 (62%) respondents, majority of the respondents, i.e., 44 (70.96%) did not consult with medical practitioners regarding diseases like puerperal infection, Fallopian tube and uterus problem. Only 18 (29.04%) respondents consulted with medical practitioners regarding all these diseases. It indicates the lack of knowledge about the problem of reproductive health. Maximum number of respondents, i.e. 10 (71.43%) had knowledge of HIV transmission at the time of breast-feeding from mother to child. Second highest number of respondents, i.e. 7 (50%) respondents knew that during pregnancy period HIV can be transmitted, and only 1 (7.15%) respondent had know during delivery period HIV/AIDS can be transmitted from mother to child. Hence, in this study it was tried to find out their knowledge towards whether they have know HIV/AIDS can be reduced from mother to child or not.

Conclusion

The findings of this study suggest that though the women have some knowledge about reproductive health, they are not sufficiently aware of it. Consciousness of the Reproductive Health among rural women. It is observed that awareness and the knowledge of Reproductive Health and its related diseases is highly absent due to poor socio-economic condition of the respondents. Even lack of proper education in both formal and informal ways is also standing as stumbling block for rural women to pursue adequate knowledge of reproductive health. Even they are still not away from such types of miss beliefs towards superstition and some other religious facts. They are being compelled to think more about their Reproductive Health by the so called values and expectations of male dominated society. Considering poor social environment, the rural women are failing to manage sufficient health care and nutritious foods. In this study, a good number of rural women have been found who suffered from various reproductive health diseases due to lack of proper social support and heavy workloads. At the same time it is also observed that attitude of women in this village towards sexual disease is not adequate. They have a negative attitude towards sex and any hidden Reproductive Health diseases. As the total process of reproduction system is a taboo in our society, social norms compel people, especially women, to keep it as an isolated and restricted subject for all. Therefore, discussion about reproductive health diseases openly are not acceptable for society. Especially, women never discuss it openly and they believe that subjects like menstruation, pregnancy, AIDS, sexual diseases and sexual intercourse are prohibited by social norms. Women even believe that any matter and object which is directly or indirectly related to diseases of Reproductive Health should not be discussed with others. According to them it should be hidden and confined with only spousal relationship. But it is very negative and unacceptable thinking for a civilised society. As women suffered mostly from the different diseases in Reproductive Health, they should have more knowledge and more aware of these diseases. Government and civil society also have responsibility to provide support service for creating awareness about Reproductive Health among women. If the women health is neglected, the entire reproduction systems will be collapsed, for which, society will have to face a big challenge to continue itself. Therefore, it is very essential to improve the Reproductive Health in true sense by providing complete support services from the all stackholders of the human society. Considering all these things, it may be concluded in very precise that Reproductive Health Awareness Among Rural Women is highly essential for the development of civilised human society.

REFERENCES

A Report on World Bank (1996). *Development in Practice Improving Women Health in India.*

Bang, A. R.; A.T. Bang; M. Baitule; Y. Choudhury; S. Sarmukaddam, and B. Tele. (1989). *High Prevelance of Gynaecological Diseases in Rural Indian Women,* Lancet, 14 January.

Barua, Alka and Kathleen Kurz (2001). "Reproductive health seeking by married adolescent girls in Maharashtra, India", *Reproductive Health Matters,* Vol. 9, No. 17: 53-62.

Basu, S.K. and G.K. Kshatriya (1989). "Fertility and mortality in tribal population of baster district, M. P.", *Biology and Society.*

Bhomik, Krishna (2006). *Indian Women the Ushering of a New Dawn,* Mittal Publications, New Delhi.

Chopra, Rakesh (ed.) (2005). *Academic Dictionary of Education,* Delhi: Isha Books.

Das, R. and J. Sharma (2004). "Antenatal natal and postnatal health care practice among the Idu-Mishim of Arunachal Pradesh", *South Asian Anthropologist.*

Dawn, C.S. (1987). *Textbook of Gynaecology and Contraception,* Outstanding Publication, p. 100.

Desai, N. and Krishnaraj (1987). *Women and Society in India,* New Delhi: Ajanta Publication.

Devarapali, P.S. (1996). "Maternal care and obstetric practice among the Konda Gora tribe", *Journal of Family Welfare.*

Ersheng, Gao (2003). *Reproductive Health Gender and Development,* New Delhi: B.R. Publishing Cooperation.

GAO Ershang and Iqbal Shah (1997). "Reproductive health research: Process and policy implication", In: *Progress of Social Science Research on Reproductive Health,* Shanghai, China: Population Publishing House, pp. 1-8.

Ghosh, B.N. (1992). *Scientific Method and Social Research,* New Delhi: Sterling Publishers.

Goode, W.J. and P.K. Hatt (1952). *Methods of Social Research,* New York: MacGraw Hill.

Irvine, Rod (1984). "Irregular vaginal bleeding: Postgraduate update, medicine update, *Jl of Cont. Edn. for Practicing Physician and Specialist",* August, Vol. 2, p. 307.

Jajeebhoy Shireen (1995). "What is reproductive health? Reproductive health needs in India", *Voices,* Vol. III, No. 2.

Johnston (2002). *"Abortion Practice in India: A Review of Literature",* CEHAT.

Junking, Wu., GAO. Ersheng, and Zbao (1997). "The Age at Mearche of the Reproductive Women in China", *National Demography and Reproductive Health Survey of China.*

Khongodier, R. (2002). "Fertility and Mortality Differentials among the War Kashi of Meghalaya, in *Tribal Studies in North East India* by (ed.) S. Sengupta, New Delhi: Mittal Publications.

Kolander, C.A., Danny, J., Ballard and C.K. Chandler (2005). *Contemporary Women's Health,* New York: McGraw Hill (2nd Revised Edition).

Kothari, C.R. (2004). *Research Methodology, Methods and Techniques,* New Delhi: New Age International Publishers.

M., Barton and Ozced (1996). "Why Sage Motherhood? How Paedeatricians Involved?", *International Child Health, A Digest Current Information.*

Mahadevan, K., G.A.O. Ersheng, Y.J.Yuan, Jayasree, Rajaram, Nabi Narun, Bourdier, Reddy, Kumar & Sandeep (2000). *Reproductive Health of Human kind in Asia and Africa: A Global Perspective,* Vol. 1, New Delhi: B.R. Publishing Corporation.

Mahadevan, K. (1982). "Early menopose and its determinants", In: *Journal of Biosocial Science,* Vol. 14: 473-479.

Mannheim, Karl (1936). *Ideology and Utopia,* London: Routledge and Kegan Paul, p. 50.

Mitra, K. and K. Basu (1998). "Health problems and practice of slum women of Delhi", *South Asian Anthropology.*

Murthy M.R.S.; N. Dhanalakshmi and S.J. Srivirajarani (2003). *Reproductive Health of Fisherman: A Case Study in East Godavari district of Andhra Pradesh,* New Delhi: B.R. Publishing Corportion, p.183.

Nembiakkim, Rose (2008). *Reproductive Health Awareness among the Tribal Women in Manipur*, New Delhi: Concept Publishing Company.

Padhi, S.R. and B. Padhy (2008). *Trends and Issues in Tribal Studies*, New Delhi: Abhijeet Publication.

Pandey, G.D. and R.S. Tiwary (1993). "Socio-cultural characteristics and health seeking behaviour of the hill Korwas", *Journal of Family Welfare.*

Pati, N.R. (2002). *Reproductive Child Health*, New Delhi: APH Publishing Corporation.

Pillai, V.K. and T.S. Sunil (2003). *Gender Inequality and Reproductive Decision Making: Identify the relationships between gender inequality and reproductive decision-making in Sub-Sahara Africa*, New Delhi: B.R. Publishing Corporation, p. 144.

Prasad, R.R. and A.K. Kapoor (1982). *Obstratical Practice Among the Bhotia Tribals*, Vanyojoti.

Prasad, J.H.; S. Abraham; K.M. Kurz; V. George; M.K. Lalitha; R. Jhon; Jayapaul, Shetty; and A. Joseph (2005). "Reproductive tract infection among young married women in rural Tamil Nadu, India", *International Family Planning Perspectives*, Vol. 31, No. 2. pp. 73-82.

Rajaram (2003). *Reproductive Health Gender and Development An International Perspective: A Festschrift for Prof. Kutton Mahadevan*, New Delhi: B.R. Publishing Coporation, p. 88.

Rajaram (2003). *Adolescent and Adult Mothers Foetal loss: Their Determinants and Policy Issues*, New Delhi: B.R. Publishing Corporation.

Rathar, Anupurna (2004). *Family Planning Practices in Third World Countries*, New Delhi: Adhyayan Publishers & Distributor.

Samant, Vatsala (2000). *Health Awareness for Women*, New Delhi: Gyan Puiblishing House, p. 28.

Saikia, J.P. (2017). *Gender: Themes and Issues*, Concept Publishing Company (P) Ltd., New Delhi.

7

Women and Health

A Study in Gulbarga District

Ashwini Jain

Introduction

A holistic approach to women health which includes both nutrition and health service will be adopted and special attention will be given to the needs of women hawkers and the girl at all stages of the life cycle. The reduction of infant mortality and maternal mortality, which are sensitive indicators of human development, is a priority concern. This policy reiterates the national demographic goals for Infant Mortality Rate (IMR), Maternal Mortality Rate (MMR) set out in the National Population Policy 2000. Women should have access to comprehensive, affordable and quality health care. Measures will be adopted that take into account the reproductive rights of women to enable them to exercise informed choices, their vulnerability to sexual and health problems together with endemic infectious and communicable diseases such as malaria, TB, and water borne diseases as well as hypertension and cardio-pulmonary diseases. The social, developmental and health consequences of HIV/AIDS and other sexually transmitted diseases will be tackled from a gender perspective. To effectively meet problems of infant and maternal mortality, and early marriage the availability of good and accurate data at micro-level on deaths, birth and marriages is required strict implementation of registration of births and deaths would be ensured and registration of marriages would be made compulsory. In accordance with the commitment of the National Population Policy (2000) to population stabilisation, this policy recognises the critical need of men and women to have access to safe, effective and affordable methods of family planning of their choice and the need to suitably address the issues of early marriages and spacing of children. Interventions such as spread of education, compulsory registration of marriage and special programmes like BSY should impact on delaying the age of marriage so that by 2010 child marriages are eliminated. Women traditional knowledge about health care and nutrition will be recognised through proper documentation and its use will be encouraged. The use of Indian and alternative systems of medicine will be enhanced within the framework of overall health.

Significance of the Study

A woman's health is her total well-being, not determined solely by biological factors and reproduction, but also by effects of work load, nutrition, stress, war and migration, among others. Women's health issues have attained higher international visibility and renewed political commitment in recent decades. While targeted policies and programmes have enabled women to lead healthier lives, significant gender-based health disparities remain in many countries. With limited access to education or employment, high illiteracy rates and increasing poverty levels are making health improvements for women exceedingly difficult. Health-related challenges continue. Many of the modest gains in women's health realised in recent decades are now threatened or have been reversed due to war, economic instability and the HIV/AIDS pandemic. Basic health care, family planning and obstetric services are essential for women? Yet they remain unavailable to millions. Gender-equitable approaches to health are needed to enable women's full participation in the planning and delivery of health services.

The healthcare industry changes quickly. With advances in medical technology, enhanced scientific research, improvement in treatments for women, and the ability to have so much information at our fingertips, the healthcare industry is an ever-evolving universe of numbers, research and changing practices. The fact is, because healthcare changes so rapidly, it often does not leave room for the basics in patient care, establishing intimate doctor-patient relationships, time for trials and testing, and sometimes even the development of confidence in the whole system. Healthcare has become a very big industry, focusing on profits before women patients' health, which leaves us all at risk.

Methodological Implication

In tune with the objectives mentioned above, a close study has been carried out by selecting the women, in Gulbarga district. The universe for data collection is restricted to the Gulbarga district only. The present study has been conducted with the help of both primary and secondary sources of data. The study is mainly based on the primary data. The primary data were collected through a questionnaire consisting both open and close ended questions. Before the actual collection of data, the questionnaires were pre-tested through a pilot study. Necessary modifications were made in the questionnaires on the basis of testing. The questionnaires were personal interview method. Some of the respondents were also contacted personally. An in-depth discussions/interviews were also held with women of Gulbarga district. Two hundred women were selected at random basis. The secondary data are drawn, classified, and studied from the Government Publications, monthly journals of the women health, including the annual reports of women health. Wherever, necessary reference was also made to different issues of bulletins viz., Healthcare Management Review, Women Health, Indian Journal of Public Health, Hospital and Health Service Administration, apart from this, different editions of daily newspapers such as *Economic Times, The Hindu, Indian Express, Business Line* etc. were also used for the purpose of collecting the information.

Analysis and Discussion

Health of women depends upon multiple factors. In this study a number of factors have been taken into account. It is hence logical that we begin our analysis with a careful analysis of those variables.

Table 7.1: Age Structure of Respondents

Age	*Respondents*	*Percentage*
20-40 years	49	49
41-60 years	28	28
61 and above years	23	23
Total	**100**	**100**

Source: Field Study.

Table 7.1 reveals that out of 49 respondents 49 per cent of the respondents belong to the age group of 20-40, followed by 28 per cent of the respondents, age group is between 41-60 and remaining 23 per cent are of the age group of 61 and above.

Table 7.2: Religion of the Respondents

Religion	*Respondents*	*Percentage*
Hindu	62	62
Muslim	18	18
Christian	4	4
Buddhist	11	11
Other	5	5
Total	**100**	**100**

Source: Field Study.

From Table 7.2 we can see that, the hawkers (62% of respondents) belong to Hindu religion, Muslim belongs to 18 per cent, followed by 11 per cent are from Buddhist, 4 per cent of the respondents are from Christian and remaining 5 per cent are from other castes.

Table 7.3: Family size of the Respondents

Size of the family	*Respondents*	*Percentage*
Joint	14	14
Nuclear	86	86
Total	**100**	**100**

Source: Field Study.

The distribution of respondents according to size of family is presented in Table 7.3. Table 7.3 reveals that, out of 100 respondents only 14 per cent of the respondents are staying in joint family and remaining 86 per cent of the respondents are Nuclear family. In order to know the economic background of the respondents, including boys and girls data were collected in the distribution of respondents according to family income which has been presented in Table 7.4.

Table 7.4 reveals an interesting fact that, from our field survey is found that lower the family income higher is the economic contribution of the women and others in the family. Six per cent of the family annual income is above Rs. 2,00,000—3,00,000, followed by 2 per cent is 3,00,000 and above, 36 per cent between

Table 7.4: The Family Annual Income of the Respondents

Particulars	*Respondents*	*Percentage*
Below Rs.1,00,000	56	56
Rs.1,00,000 to Rs. 2,00,000	36	36
Rs. 2,00,000 to Rs. 3,00,000	6	6
Rs. 3,00,000 and above	2	2
Total	**100**	**100**

Source: Field Survey.

Rs. 1,00,000—Rs. 2,00,000, 56 per cent are below Rs. 1,00,000. It is needless to state that the level of education and their life are usually correlated in a positive way. But, this contention may not be universally true.

Table 7.5: Educational Classification of the Respondents

Educational level	*Respondents*	*Percentage*
Illiterate	80	80
SSLC	13	13
PUC	7	7
Graduate	0	0
Total	**100**	**100**

Source: Field Study.

Table 7.5 indicates that, most of the sample size of Graduate is zero per cent of the respondents, followed by 7 per cent are from PUC and 13 per cent have SSLC and the remaining 80 per cent are illiterate. Leaving Gulbarga district which have relatively high penetration of health, general awareness about health was found to be low in rest of the Gulbarga. Though, women are familiar with the concept, the awareness on health was found to be very low.

Table 7.6: Poor Health of Respondents

Particulars	*Respondents*	*Percentage*
Yes	25	25
No	75	75
Total	**100**	**100**

Source: Field Study.

Table 7.6 demonstrates the factors of poor health of women shown by respondents in the study area of Gulbarga district. Twenty five respondents constituting 25 per cent universe have stated that poor health and another 75 (75%) respondents felt that did not know about poor health.

Limitation of the Study

The present research work was mainly based on the Primary data collected from the sample respondents. Many women have given poor responses to some of the questions due to lack of experience. Responses are in some cases, approximate. However, very cases have been taken to evaluate the evidence gathered from these interviews by final cross-checking to avoid the element of subjectivity in the responses. But, still the element of subjectivity could not be avoided altogether. The women are found very large in number all over the study area, but only limited number of women is selected for the present study because of time and resource constraints, conclusion is based on the researcher and experience gained during the fieldwork. Therefore, the personal limitation of the researcher is also needed special mention.

Findings and Conclusion

The important key areas of the health of women of the Gullbarga district, the facilities available for their health-care and their living condition are highlighted above. It is expected that the women as well as appropriate authorities (who are well aware about these facts) will use the said information and take necessary action to minimise the deficiencies. The appropriate measure against the shortcoming only can change the health scenario of the region because sound health of women and the basis for healthy manpower in future for the development of the district. The study reveals that, out of 100 respondents only 14 per cent of the respondents are staying in joint family and remaining 86 per cent of the respondents are Nuclear family. Six per cent of family's annual income is above Rs. 2,00,000–3,00,000, followed by 2 per cent is 3,00,000 and above, 36 per cent between Rs. 1,00,000–2,00,000, 56 per cent are below Rs. 1,00,000. Most of the sample size who possess Graduate is gero per cent of the respondents, followed by 7 per cent are from PUC and 13 per cent have SSLC and the remaining 80 per cent are illiterate. It is observed that 25 respondents constituting 25 per cent universe have stated that poor health and another 75 (75%) respondents felt that did not know about poor health. There is an urgent need to devise and implement comprehensive health awareness and educative programmes the increase in general level of understanding about health related issues. It is also admissible for policy-makers to initiate some drastic changes to impart good health to the masses. Such measures may include tobacco chewing. This is tough to achieve but nevertheless it should be aimed for. It is better to organise and demonstrate through road side dramas, about the dreaded diseases and in such drama sufficient information should be provided about such diseases, the way in which it spreads, the way in which it imparts and the way in which it can be cured. Thus, efforts should be made to develop health consciousness among the masses. The Government is spending lot of resources on Adult Education Programme. To reap the maximum benefit of it, it is better to educate to adults about various health issues also. Health resources will have to be increased to improve health systems, including a dramatic increase in hospital health care. Resources for health care should be raised by increasing the proportion of the overall health budget that is allocated to health promotion.

REFERENCES

Foster, C., L. Godkin, "Employment Selection in Healthcare for Structured Interviewing," *Healthcare*.

Jagannadhan, T., *Quality Healthcare through Patient Satisfaction,* Hospital Administration, September-October 1997.

Longest Beaufort B. (1990). "Inter organisational linkages in the health sector", *Healthcare Management Review,* Vol. 15 (1), Winter: 17-28.

Longest, B. (1978). "The contemporary hospital chief executive officer", *Healthcare Management Review,* Vol. 3 (2), Spring: 43-84.

Magnus, S.A. (1999). "Physicians Financial Incentives in Five Dimensions: A Conceptual Framework for HMO manager," *Healthcare Management Review,* Vol. 24(1): 57-72.

8

Decent Work is a Distant Dream

Study of Women in the Construction Sector, New Delhi

Ayushi Agrawal

Introduction

In India, construction sector is one of the biggest employers in informal sector after agriculture, for both male and female. Female worker participation in this industry is larger than their participation in any other industry; this shows that women participation is increasing in this male dominated industry which gives way to gender inequality. Construction industry is one of the industries which are characterized by very little unpaid labour and higher portions of migrant workers. Delhi is a place where huge construction is going on, and in a large number migrants are working. They migrated to have better living conditions, a better job opportunity, to have better standard of living which includes good health, three times meals and other basic necessities, but what is their experience in comparison to their expectations? Do they ever get what they want? Think about the woman who migrates to have a better future for themselves and their children but what they get is "inequality", a low paid unskilled job with no chance of upgradation. They are suffering from triple burden of work and poor health. Their days end up doing unequal wage work with equally tiring household work in order to fulfil the responsibilities of a wife, a mother and a worker. So, it is time to understand and analyse their expectation and experience after migration. Is the city succeed in fulfilling their expectation or the condition is something else? Decent work defined by ILO as "it involves opportunities for work, that is productive and delivers a fair income, security in the workplace and social protection for families, better prospects for personal development and social integration, freedom for people to express their concerns, organise and participate in the decisions that affect their lives and equality of opportunity and treatment for all women and men." The need for decent work is increasing with the increase in Informal sector. But due to the in formalisation of work introducing the components of Decent work seems like a distant dream. For example, if we talk about the construction work, where women neither getting the equal opportunity of work nor getting any chance of skill development or bargaining for their wages. They are just suppressed and downtrodden. As the composition of labour is changing and more and more women are participating in the labour force there is need that their work would provide them some social security. They should have the provisions for better health facilities at their work place especially in construction sector work, which opens them to many dangerous activities which have been discussed later in this chapter.

In India, there is a law for migrant construction workers, i.e. Inter-State Migrant Labour Act (Regulation of Employment and Condition of Work), 1976. According to this Act, Contractor must be registered if he is hiring 5 or more construction workers. Also, he has to pay the travelling cost and displacement allowance. Moreover, contractor has to arrange housing and food facility for them on site. In first National Commission on Labour 1969, there is some provisions for migrant labourers, like timely payment, payment of travelling allowance etc. But, unfortunately, these laws are remain on papers and futile to do any change in real condition. Not only this several gender related policies have been implemented by the government like policy related to sexual harassment, gender equality, empowerment, education, no discrimination in work, equal pay for equal work like this many other. The basic idea is to promote gender equality and bringing them at par with men. There are also various laws like Maternity Act, Equal Remuneration Act to provide them equality. But in actual, these policies and laws are not implemented properly. According to these policies women should not be discriminated on any ground whether it is related to pay, work or any other benefit. But, if we see, the actual condition of women is very poor. They are neither getting equal pay with men nor holding the skilled jobs. They even do not have the right to take decisions of their own. The condition of women becomes more vulnerable in informal sector and migration adds more reasons for their poor condition. The reason for discussing all these laws and policies is to analyse the implementation of these laws in the actual practice. Therefore, to highlight the facts from the construction industry a small study approximately for six months has been done. The sample size and study period was kept small due to resource constraint in terms of time and money.

The aim of this study is to conceptualise gender inequality both in terms of women participation at work and in terms of sharing household tasks, and then to discuss the specific issues and discriminations faced by the women workers at the migrated workplace. While working on the construction sector, it is very important to know about their pattern of migration, their living and working conditions.

Profile of the Area of Study

In Delhi, construction work is spread all over ranging from small construction to large construction sites. One of the common features of every construction site is that, the area is covered from all sides and on every gate security guard keeps a check and visitors are not welcome inside the working area. This gives more curiosity to know about what is going inside. Therefore, it became necessary to find a means to get enter into the area, so the best option was to seek permission from the higher authority and get entered. Though the permission was also not easily available but somehow it has been managed. During this research work many construction sites had been seen, but the site in Okhla, where construction of an Engineering College going on attracted the attention most. There were the large number of workers (both male and female) employed here. To add more curiosity to enter this site was a notice on entry gate stating "as per rule below the age of 18 year, workers are not allow to work on this construction site." Though by my first observation from the outside only, the condition seems to be as it is trying to say "that only below the 18 years of workers are allowed to work especially in case of women I am talking, who was my main target." This site on an average employed 3 to 4 thousand workers out of which approximately

1,000 were women. It is a deliberate choice to restrict this study to women so in this research mostly women voices is being covered, only few males have been interviewed to have a better and clear understanding of the facts.

In order to explore the experiences and struggle of women construction workers in the city, the structured questionnaire proved to be futile, it only make the discussion formal and one sided. Therefore, to facilitate discussion about their work and family, it is better to have unstructured interview. Sometimes when it became difficult to note down each and every detail, recorder proved to be a good method, which can also be used latter to clarify the facts. Also respondent feel free to communicate. Besides having these conversations, observations have been done to analyse many of the qualitative aspects which cannot be communicated easily. Based on these techniques many findings have been analysed and case studies have developed which make this study more enrich and focused. But only covering the women workers will not give answers of all the questions, therefore, it became necessary to include contractors and employer to know the pattern of migration, about the system of payment, reason for less women workers and doing some lower level work only and about their health, safety and welfare measure. To some extent these questions have been answered which appear throughout the text. The findings presented below are also includes participant observation. To some extent Time use survey method has been used to find out how women devote their time in different activities to get better understanding of their burden of work both wage work and household work. The sample size for the interview is 50, but many things like migration pattern, and place of migration, observation method had been used to cover large size.

Nature and Profile of the Workers

On this construction site mostly the migrant workers were working. They were from different states like Bihar, West Bengal, Rajasthan, Uttar Pradesh, Madhya Pradesh, Andhra Pradesh and others, the data is shown in Fig. 8.1. They were generally migrated in a group of male and female (Fig. 8.2). The migration pattern of these workers was on contract basis. The contractors hire them

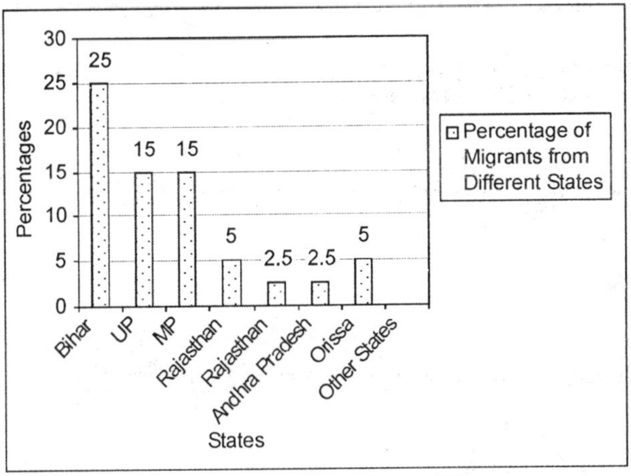

Fig. 8.1: Percentage of Migrant Workers from different states
Source: Field Studies.

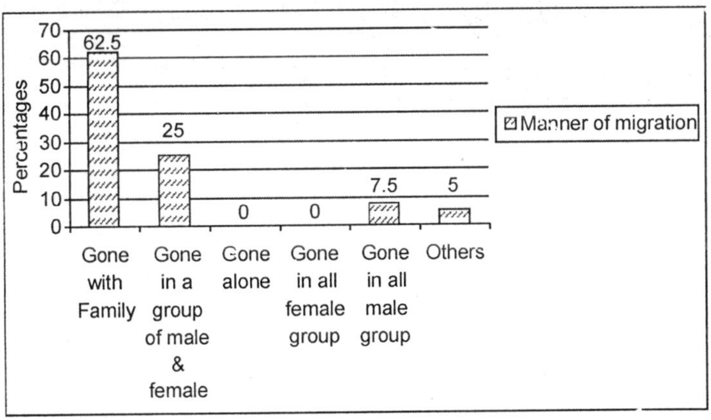

Fig. 8.2: Manner in which Workers Migrate
Source: Field Studies.

and these contractors are generally from their villages and they hired them against some nominal amount which partially covers their transport cost. Other way of recruitment was through the *thekedar*. Employer hired labour from the *thekedar* as per the requirement. From *thekedar* generally male labour was demanded not the female one. Because they think that female labour cannot do the construction work as they are meant for the soft jobs only. The labour was getting better wages when hired through *thekedar* rather than the contractor because Employer paid them better than the contractor. Contractors consume the cost of middle men and pays them very little amount even less than the minimum wages. Employer generally prefers to hire labour through contractors because it does not attract any burden as all the responsibility lies on the shoulder of contractors. Though, the contractors are also not fulfilling any responsibility. Following figure will more support the data.

Migration Pattern

Generally, men prefer to migrate alone. And if he is able to sustain himself in the new place he would not ask his family to join him in the new alien land. He wants his family including his wife and children, would remain in the village. Because, they are earning so less that it will be difficult for them to survive with family. But such cases were very few. What was more prominent there was men were living with their family. They need their wife's to cook food for them and to wash their clothes. But, as I mentioned that they have very less wages so they engaged his wife or other family member in the same work. In this way whole family got engaged in the construction work. This shows that women do not have any choice in decision of migration and they have to migrate with their husbands (CWDS, 2011). Also whether they like this work or not, does not matter, the only option they have is to join their husbands in their work. In this way women end up by working in the low paid unskilled job. They were generally working as a helper to their husbands and doing the work of head loading, stone crushing or collecting waste material (Fig. 8.3). Among all the women workers, women from West Bengal were in a more vulnerable condition because they did not know the local language of the place which makes them aloof from all. Too add more to their vulnerability, it was found that the name of the women workers have been changed while registering with the contractor in order to hide that these women are working somewhere. Because in their villages; they are not allowed to work outside home. In such miserable situations when women do not know the language of the place of destination or in situations where their identity are not recognised at new places they find themselves in extremely dreadful situations.

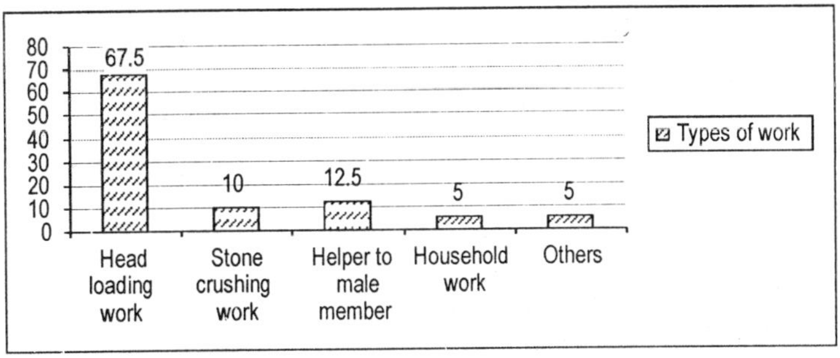

Source: Field Study.

Fig. 8.3: Types of works migrants perform

Figure 8.4 shows the age group of women employed in construction work. It was found that mostly the women were from age group 15-18 years, i.e. 24 women followed by the age group of 19-25 years, i.e. 12 women. In the age group of 26-30 only 2 women were employed and 30 onwards there were only 2 women.

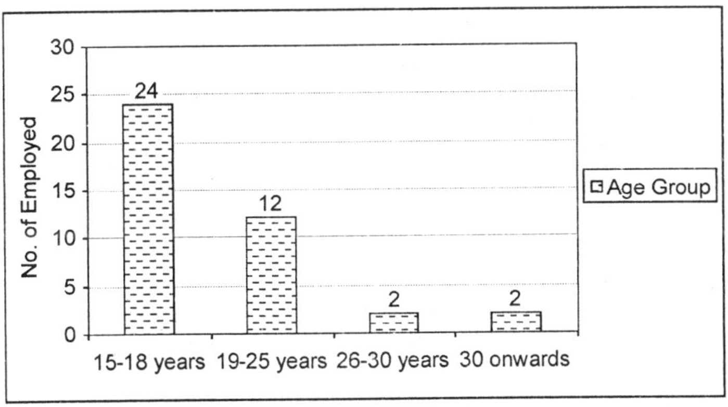

Source: Field Study.

Fig. 8.4: Age Group women employed in Construction work

Living Condition

Housing facilities have been provided by the employer on the construction site so that workers can live there and work even in odd times. The important reason to provide on site housing facility is to avoid wastage of time while coming for the work. For men these conditions are still fine but for women living on the work site it is very difficult. There was no toilet and washing facilities for women due to which everything they have to do in open which gives way to many accidents and health problems and from all worst was there sexual harassment from other male members. One of migrant women said that *"sexual harassment is very common on the site. Touching, using abusing language or starring used to happen every time. Now, we are used to it. We cannot complaint this to anyone even my husband did not notice it and quite reluctant for this. Therefore, in the end I left with one option to bear all these and do my work. I know women have to face all these problems and I have no escape from this neither I can leave the work nor I can go anywhere else of my own."* This was the women from Bihar named Priyanka. She migrated 5 years back with her husband and till now was working as a head loading worker. She has two small kids; means also has the responsibility to take care while working. She used to work from 8 a.m. to till 8 p.m. and was getting only Rs. 160. She is not getting overtime payment and used to get wages only after two months. Her wages are collected by her husband and also controlled by him only. She just has to come for the work finish it and again back to home. But her responsibility does not end here; she has household work also before coming and after leaving the work. She has to wake up at 4 a.m. in the morning and first has to go work toilet. She has to do it in the early morning before the male members wake up because they do not have any toilet or bathing facilities and this problem is common to all women working here. Do the women are born to face such inequalities. This is the biggest question which we have to ask from ourself.

Generally, the women are living in a double burden of work. They do not get time even to relax or for their recreation. It seems that this migration has increased their vulnerabilities and problems. They even do not have the proper drinking facilities. There was a common open pool from where they used to take water. It was so dirty and impure that it attracts many water borne diseases. But they have no choice but to drink water from there. They cannot go even outside to take water.

Existing Work Environment

The work environment is very tiring, especially for women. If we look at their time devoted to different activities, one can found that they have to wake up at 4 O'clock in the morning to complete their household work like collecting fire woods, preparing meal, feeding children and so on. After completing all these household works they have to reach on work site at 8 O'clock and continue till 9 p.m. They were working more than 8 hours but not getting any overtime payment and also cannot afford to get late for their work, if they get late even for 5 minutes, 4 hours pay has been deducted from their wages. Though in case of men, this condition did not apply. Even if they get late by half an hour only small amount of wages have been deducted. This is due to the reason because women are weak in bargaining and they will not oppose to any unnecessary deduction. Also they cannot leave their work whatever may be the conditions because they are dependent on their husband; in the sense if husband is working there they also have to do same work without having any other option. If we estimate the time of women and men work we can say that women are working more than men, combining both household and paid work but still they are weak and exploited (Antonopoulos, 2008).

Triple Burden of Work and Poor Health

Women are facing triple burden of work, i.e. reproduction, domestic work and paid work (Swaminathan, 2004). While working also they have to take care of their children due to which sometimes they were not able to focus on their work properly which cause decrease in their productivity and this leads to lower wages than men. To add wonders to the work it was found that the pregnant women were doing the work of stone crushing, the most difficult work and there were many cases of miscarriage. They have to work seven days a week and do not get any leave. Even if they are pregnant there is no leave or any other facility for them. One of the women told in this regard: *"I am 8 months pregnant but still I am working because I do not have any leave and I cannot afford to sit back at home. Earlier by working I had a miscarriage but still I did not get any leave and from very next day I started working. I used to wake up at 5 a.m. in the morning to do the entire household task. I have two daughters to look after. One is 10 years old who used to help me in my stone crushing and other is 7 years who used to stay back at home. My husband also doing the same work, the only difference is the size of the stone to be crushed. Being a male he used to crush big stone which has been further crushed by me. This also creates difference in our earnings. I work equally with my husband taking care of my family also. Not only this even to collect firewood for cooking I have to go. My husband believes he has only work responsibility and all the other responsibility should be accomplished by me. Under such exorbitant condition sometimes I feel exploited and depressed. Doing all the work by oneself that too in a new place is very difficult to manage".* This woman was from Madhya Pradesh named Jyoti. She migrated 20 years back and till now she is working as stone crushing worker and her whole family is engaged in the same work. She was getting only Rs. 230 per day. She has to manage all the work whether outside or inside home and also have to take care of her reproductive health without any help or support. Doing such hard work opens then many diseases like Severe Backpain, Headache, weak bodies, lack in nutrition value. Doing so many works simultaneously makes a very bad impact on their health. They do not get time to look after their health. Their family and work consume all their time. They do not even get Sunday to take rest. One can imagine how it badly affects their health. Though the women do not want to work here they want to do some domestic work as it is the extension of their housework. But this alien place does not allow them to make any other choice but to depend on their husbands.

System of Neo-Bondage

Construction sector can be seen as an example of neo-bondage. Many cases had been found where workers working in construction sector from last many years under the same contractor. The reason for engaging in this work and regular migrating was the fear of not getting any other work and holding of their wages by the contractor. Contractor never paid them full wages, he always hold more than half of their wages with a promise to pay after two months or in the next month due to which workers would not be able to leave their work. Contractor also threats them that if they will leave their work he will make sure that they would not get work anywhere else. Even there are examples of the workers who were earlier worked in Akshardham Temple[1], then at Common Wealth Games[2] site, and now working on this site of Okhala, there also they were in very poor condition (PUDR, 2009). The reason behind this is very exploiting. It is the contractor who does not allow them to go anywhere else. Once the work of one site got completed he transports them to the other site by packing their entire luggage. He does not give any chance to think of any other option to work on. Due to which if once the worker entered in construction he has to work throughout his life. Construction work is creating bondage for them. For men it is still fine but what about the women? They are the worst sufferer in the sense throughout their life they have to do such work. In their villages they are doing agricultural work which is still manageable for them but after migration doing construction work is a big problem for them. They are doing that work which requires lots of physical labour and in spite of doing that they are not getting their due share. They are always getting less than men and also not getting any other facility. Also their health is deteriorating day by day.

Hema from Madhya Pradesh said my parents are working as a construction workers from last 26 years I also joined them at the age of 15 as a head loading worker and now it is almost 10 years I am working in the construction sector as a head loading worker with a very less amount of Rs. 180. I want to leave this work and want to work as domestic labour. This construction work is very tiring and less paid with more hours of work. But, I cannot leave this worker because contractor would not allow me also as I am new to the place so I do not know where to go and what to do. I have no option but to stay here and suffer for the whole of my life. She used to migrate to different places like Bangalore, Madhya Pradesh and now in Delhi. Earlier she was working at Akshardham site and now working here under the same contractor. Her husband is also working on the same construction site as carpenter. She has four children and one of them is working with them and rests are in the village and getting education. She does not want that her children will also do the same work. She is under poor condition that she would not get time even to have breakfast or lunch. She said *"kitni baar aisa hota hai ghar ka kaam karte karte itna late ho jata hai ki bina khuch khaye piye hi kaam par jaana padta hai or pure din dhup mai kaam karte raho"*.

Trade Union and Existing Laws

Close to the site there was a Hind Kisan Mazdoor Sangh Trade Union Office. It was presumed that being so near to the site this trade union registered good amount of complaints of the workers. But the condition was something else the president of the Trade Union told that very few workers registered their complaints. They have the fear that if they register any complaint against contractor they will not get any work again after that, because contractors always threaten them for the same. In case of women he told that their ratio of complaint is almost zero. Sometimes, their husbands do not allow them to file any complaint and other time they do not know where to go and what to do. And if exceptionally there is any complaint from the women side than it is generally from the formal sector working women not from the informal sector in that case also they are accompany by some male member.

Government has implemented many laws for the protection and promotion of the labour welfare like The Building and Other Construction Workers (Regulation of Employment and Conditions of Services) Act, 1996, The Inter State Migrant Worker Act, 1979, The Minimum Wages Act, 1948 and like this many more Acts and all these talks about the welfare of the workers. The Building and other Construction Act is a Central Legislation and talks about the registration of workers and registered them under the benefit of welfare fund. The Migrant Workers Act talks about the payment of displacement allowance, payment of travelling allowance and more over the licensing of the contractor if more than 5 migrant workers are employed on the site. But, there implementation seems to be on paper only. In actual no worker is familiar with any of these laws. None of the women had any knowledge of these laws. They believe either their employer known this or their husbands; they were simply innocent to this fact. There was no registration of the workers provided nor has any identity card been issued to them. Even at the time of migration they are not provided with any amount and if they were provided than that amount would get deducted from their wages latter on. Even the Safety Officer appointed on the work site was not doing his work. His main work was just to see that work should go on, no matter workers are wearing any safety measure or not. No worker on the site was wearing any helmet, goggle or gloves. Even women were working without wearing their slippers on asking why they are doing so they answered, "We have only one pair of slippers and if they got break or something happen to it while working we will not get the new one because no one is ready to spend on us". Not only this every legislation guarantees compensation to the workers if any accident occurs on the site not always in terms of money, but also by way of medical aid, but these workers are not getting anything. If there is any accident occurs with the workers they are only responsible for that and all the expenses they have to bear by their own. And this condition again makes the women worst sufferer.

Conclusion

The women experience in construction work and migration to other city is full of difficulties and adjustments. Despite of doing everything like working on field, earning and taking care of family for whole day, they stand nowhere in the society. All these conditions make them overburdened and vulnerable. Employers do not want to recruit them because of the stereotype thinking that women can only do the soft jobs. Their husband would not notice their work because of the thinking that they are meant to do these works. Whether, it is outside or inside the home; no one is ready to recognize their potential and hard work. From century women are living under such condition and no idea till when these conditions will continue. Empowering of women seems like to be a distant dream. Moreover, in between all these inequalities, the issue of women health is mostly overlooked. No one is interested in consider their health problems. Even the women themselves are not interested in taking care of their health. They are more concern for their family members and their health. Series of laws have been implemented to make women empower and equal to men but all seems to be the futile efforts. Laws are so complicated and difficult that a poor and illiterate person cannot understand it. There is only one law which is related to women health, i.e. Maternity Act, 1961. But this is also of no use for the women in informal sector. This shows how much our government has overlooked this very important area.

Women work is always taken as granted and the gap between man and woman is kept on increasing. Many examples had been seen on the site where women for long engaged in only head loading work. Neither are they getting any skill upgradation opportunity nor any other work to move on. Though the government has implemented many policies but their implementation is very poor. There is a need to have a more focused implementation of policies. And policies like equal pay for same work, right of decision-making, more skilled jobs for women should be implemented in an easier and simpler way. And besides having implementing laws and policies there should be awareness in the society about gender equality. Nowhere women are allowed to be independent no matter they are at home or at work. Their income is treated as a supplementary income even when they are contributing equally like men. This vulnerable condition of women is everywhere more or less but example of construction sector was taken into account because here, gender inequality becomes more acute and blatant. Therefore, it becomes necessary to open our eyes towards this and some concrete steps should be taken, not only by the government, but also by the society, media, state and policy-makers. So, that women upliftment can be done and more generous and prosperous society can be created.

Above description clears the fact that in a developing country like India there is a total absence of decent work. As the composition of informal sector is increasing and more women are entering into work. There is more inequality and discrimination persists in terms of job opportunity and equal wages for equal work. Therefore, there is a high need to shift our focus on sustainable development where the condition of women and society as a whole can be improved. We can introduce Decent Work through social dialogue, where women workers get the chance to bargain for their wages as per their labour. Also they will get equal opportunity at work place and not get stuck with same type of work for years without any chance of skill development. No development will be possible until and unless we will not include women in the mainstreaming process. Gender inequality is still pervasive in the society which is needed to be rectified. Than only we can talk about the true development.

NOTES

1. Construction of Akshardham temple in Delhi was the biggest construction work which employed thousands of labour and most of the labour was migrant in nature. Here also the condition of labour was very poor.
2. Common Wealth Games take place in Delhi in 2010. Many countries have participated in this event. Large number of labour have been employed for creating the infrastructure like bridge, flyovers, parks, buildings and so on. The workers have not provided any safety measures which caused many accidents on the site.

REFERENCES

Agnihotri, Indu; Mazumdar, Indrani and Neetha (2012). *Gender and Migration: Negotiating Rights. A Women's Movement Perspective*. Centre for Women and Development Studies (CWDS).

Building and Other Construction Workers (Regulation of Employment and Conditions of Service) Act (1996). Accessed on 11th August, 2011 (http://vakilnol.com/bareacts/building&other Con.act/building Conact.html).

Chen, Martha (1995). "A matter of survival: Women's right to employment in India and Bangladesh", In: Nussbaum, Martha and Glover, Jonathan (eds.). *Women, Culture, and Development*, Oxford, U.K.: Oxford University Press.

PUDR Team (2009). "Violation of worker's right's at the common wealth games construction site", *EPW*, Vol. 44, No. 24, 19th June, 2009.

Swaminathan, Padmini (2004). "The Trauma of Wage Employment and the burden of work for Women in India: Evidences and Experiences", *Journal of Labour and Development*, Vol. 10, No. 2.

9

Health Status and Life Expectancy Among the Women of the Tai Khamyang Community in Assam

A Sociological Study

Kuki Boruah

Introduction

Health is a dynamic social phenomenon, affecting multiple aspects and being affected by multiple factors. As health is a determinant of various factors, so, it acts as the most important contributory source in regulating the life expectancy of an individual. Various socio-cultural aspects such as education, economy, health care practices, medical facilities, food habits, norms and values, regulate the health status of the women. According to the definition of World Health Organization, "Health is defined as a complete physical, mental and social well-being and not merely an absence of disease of infinity" (Cockerham *et al.*, 1997). Health encompasses the entire well-being of an individual and health status indicates the well-being of an individual and the society at large.

The value of adult female mortality rate (per 1,000 female adults) in India was 164.36 as of 2011 census. The value of female mortality rate was maximum 407.28 in 1960 and came down to a minimum value of 164.36 in 2011. Whereas the value of adult male mortality rate (per 1,000 male adults) in India was 251.13 as of 2011. Over the last 51 years, the male mortality rate has declined to a minimum value of 236.47 in 1990 from 397.94 in 1960. Adult mortality rate is the probability of dying between the ages of 15 and 60, that is, the probability of a 15 year old dying before reaching age 60, if subject to current age-specific mortality rates between those ages (United Nations, 2012). Statistics released by the Union Ministry of Health and Family Welfare shows that life expectancy in India has gone up to five years, from 62.3 years for males and 63.9 years for females in 2001–2005 to 67.3 years for males and 69.6 years for females in 2011–2015. This increase in life expectancy in both male and female is an outcome of better immunization and nutrition coupled with prevention and treatment of infectious diseases. The World Health Organization defines life expectancy as "the average number of years a person is expected to live on the basis of the current mortality rates and prevalence distribution of health states in a population." In India, average life expectancy which used to be around 42 in 1960, steadily climbed to around 48 in 1980, 58.5 in 1990 and around 62 in 2000 (*Times of India,* 2014). Thus, overall health status including the fertility rate, mortality rate and subsequently the life expectancy rate of the people in a particular society reflects the social structure of that society. Various societal elements act as a contributory source in either improving or degrading the health condition and facilitating the survival of the members of a society. In every society, there exists a set of beliefs and concepts with regard to the nature of diseases and its treatment which thereby determines the health condition and consequently the life expectancy of the people. Indeed in context of the tribal society, the maintenance of health does not remain just an individual factor but a community factor too. Even the acceptance and practice of a particular health care treatment largely depends on the social-cultural elements of the society. The tribal women being illiterate and economically unsound remain for most of the time ignorant of the various health facilities provided by the Government. In fact, it is seen that since long, the tribal people as a result of their interaction with nature, have been indulging in their traditional methods of curing any disease which has an impact on the health status and subsequently the life expectancy of an individual. Regulation of the fertility, mortality, and morbidity, rates being patterned by multiple societal aspects is widely associated in formulating the demographic structure of a particular society. Besides, the health scenario and its consequent demographic variation can also indicate the development rate of that society.

As health is a determinant of some other social aspects, the study could be analysed with the help of Talcott Parsons theoretical understanding of the interrelationship of the various subsystems of the wider social system responsible for the smooth functioning and survival of the society (Ritzer, 2007). The structural-functional perspective would help in understanding different dimensions of health and subsequently its regulation of life expectancy among the people. As women who are the producer of an individual and subsequently the nation at large, so, the health status which would regulate the life span of the whole community would thereby determine the development rate of a particular society. With this in concern, the health status and the life expectancy of the women in Tai Khamyang community, a sub group of the Tai Shyam clan inhabiting in Assam is attempted to be focused. Under the Tai Shyam clan, there are three sub-groups, namely the Tai Aiton, Tai Turung and Tai Khamyang. Thus, a brief history of the Tai Khamyang community is described below.

Tai Khamyangs: A Historical Insight

The 'Tai' is a generic name which connotes a great branch of the Mongoloid population of Asia. The Tai are mainly concentrated in the Indo-Chinese peninsula which extends from Assam in the west to Kwangsi and Hainan in the east and from the interior of Yun-nan in the north to the southern-most extremity of Thailand in the south. In the course of their journey from one place to the other, the Tai have acquired innumerable local appellations. They are known as the Shan, Siamese, Lao and Pai in the major areas of East Asia, namely Burma, Thailand, French Indo-China and Yun-nan respectively. But with whatever names they might be addressed, the members of this great race call themselves as the 'Tai' (Gogoi, 1990). In the mid-eighteenth century before engulfing the Shan kingdom of North Burma by the Maan king Alam Poyai, the Nongkheu Nong Nokjang area of Patkai range was under the Moungkong Kingdom. With the treaty being signed between the Ahom King Sudangpha and the Moungkong King Surungpha in 1401, the Nongkheu Nong Nokjang area came under the

Moungkong Kingdom. The Tai Khamyang community inhabited in the Nongkheu Nong Nokjang from the sixties of thirteenth century till the declaration of the treaty by the Ahom King and the Moungkong King who concluded the negotiations for peace that took place on the side of the Nongyang lake. Tne Tai Khamyangs had to cross the Patkai range and come to Kamrup[1] in search of the Moungmit Kingdom's King Sukanpha's younger brother Prince Sukapha. Prince Sukapha was the youngest son of Moungmit Kingdom's King Phutangkhang. After the death of the King, the throne was handed over to the eldest son Prince Sujatpha. But due to King Sujatpha's sudden death, the responsibility of the throne was handed over to the King's younger brother Sukhanpha. During his reign, King Sukhanpha once sent his younger brother Prince Sukapha along with a warrior troop to take over and conquer their lost kingdoms from the Chinese. But, Prince Sukapha lost the battle and came back and reached the entrance door to his Kingdom one midnight. But Prince Sukapha's brother, King Sujatpha according to the rules of the Royal Kingdom, without knowing the conditions and investigating in detail of the real identity of Prince Sukapha, did not permit to open the Kingdom's entrance door. After waiting for many days with a hope that the King's mind would change and the door would be let open for Prince Sukapha and his warrior troop to enter, things did not turn out as such. Finally, with anger and agony by this act of his brother, Prince Sukapha along with his troop went to Soumar land across the Patkai range and established the Ahom Kingdom in 1229. Coming to know about Prince Sukapha's desertion of the Moungmit Kingdom, King Sujatpha sent many investigating groups such as the Tai Aiton, Tai Phake, Tai Turung and many more in search of Prince Sukapha. But as these groups failed to found Prince Sukapha, King Sujatpha then organised a troop of nine Tai Khamyang Ministers each of them carrying large number of Tai Khamyang soldiers and sent the team in search of Prince Sukapha. During this period, the Tai Khamyang community inhabited Khamjang, the boundary area of Moungmit Kingdom and Moungkong Kingdom. Prince Sukapha after leaving his brother King Sujatpha's Kingdom, resided in Khamjang for a couple of years. As such, King Sujatpha thought the Tai Khamyangs inhabiting in Khamjang would prove to be the best investigating team to search Prince Sukapha and sent the troop of Tai Khamyang warriors under the leadership of nine Tai Khamyang Ministers from various clans such as Thoumoung, Chauhai, Pangyuk, Chaulu, Chaulik, Bailung, Tunkhang, Chauchang and Phalek. The Chief Minister of the troop was from the Chauhai clan named Hailikhi. This troop after crossing many hills and mountains finally reached Soumar. During their course of journey, the Tai Khamyang troop had to face many problems in different parts of the region. As such they had to shift from one place to the other. Further, with the increase in their population, the Tai Khamyangs established many villages such as Disangpani Gaon[2] in 1836, Chalapathar Gaon in 1868 and Rahanshyam Gaon in 1919 in Sivasagar District, Na-Shyam Gaon in 1885, Balijan Gaon in 1901 and Betbari Gaon in 1888 of Titabor area in Jorhat District, Nong Rajapukhuri Gaon of Golaghat District in 1919 and Payoimukh Gaon in Margherita of Tinsukia District in 1946. Some of them have also settled in various regions of Arunachal Pradesh (The Tai Khamyang Buranji Sampadana Samity 2008).

Significance and Objectives

Health is not a one-dimensional but a multi-dimensional aspect. In every society, the health status of an individual becomes a contributory factor of various social aspects and issues. Looking at the health scenario, the development rate and the demographic structure of a society can be formulated. The health condition of a particular community regulates the life expectancy of its members thereby highlighting the societal values and norms, education, economy, food habits, medical facilities, health care treatments, and gender issues. Indeed the development rate of a society largely depends on the health status of the women which has a direct bearing in the life expectancy. In almost every society, the health status of the women is seen to be either in a poor or in an average condition. In order to know about the health status and consequently the life expectancy of women, the demographic structure which includes fertility, mortality and morbidity rates comes into light. Whether a society has touched the pace of development largely depends upon the health condition of the women as women are the producers of children and subsequently the nation at large. But their life expectancy is at large a contributory factor of the societal values. Thus, this research work is an attempt to know about the health status and the determinants of the life expectancy among the women of the Tai Khamyang community in Assam.

Review of Related Literature

The Science News Letter (1948) has revealed that among the white girls in United States born during the period of late forties can expect to live till 70 while white boys till 65 in averages. A baby born in 1948 would live a whole year longer if he or she would have been born in 1945 and almost two years more if born in the pre-War years of 1939–1941. Considering the sex and race, a white boy of the age 10 and 20 would live another 58.3 years and 48 years respectively than a non-White young men of the age 10 who would live on average another 51.9 years. On the other hand, White girls of the age 10 would live another 63 years while non-White girls 54.8 years more. But on the contrary, the non-Whites at the age of 65 have a longer average lifetime left than the Whites. At the age of 75, White men expect to live another 7.7 years while non-white men 8.6 years. White women having the same number of years like the non-Whites men, non-White women expect another 10.5 years of life to live. Thus, the average life expectancy of both white and non-White women is higher than the White and non-White men. Miller and Gerstein (1983) in their study on the lifetime smoking habits of adults in Eric County, Pa. During the period of 1972-74 have found that the life expectancy difference between United States males and females has been increasing for many years. The average life expectancy among the non-smoking males falls under the age group of 80-84. Among the non-smoking women, the average life expectancy is above 85 years of age. This difference in the longevity statistics according to the vital statistics of the United States has been found as a result of the occurrence of traumatic deaths such as accidents, suicides and homicides among men in the age group of 20 to 55 years. Another reason in the differential life expectancy is due to ambiguous distinction between non-smokers and former smokers. A misrepresentation of the former smokers as non-smokers results in the classification of deceased former smokers as non-smokers thereby increasing the mortality rates attributed to non-smokers. Thus, in any discussion of the male-female longevity difference based on calculation of pension benefits or life insurance premium rates, these categorical differences should be taken into account along with the sex role behaviour which has an impact on health and morbidity and subsequently on longevity. Kar *et al.* in their work (1996) "*Health Culture and Tribal Life: A Case Study Among the Noctes of Arunachal Pradesh*" have discussed about the health status of the Noctes which is largely conditioned by multiple socio-economic elements and socio-biological norms such as marital alliances and age at marriage having a wide impact on the fertility and morbidity pattern. Besides unhygienic environment, maintenance of their cultural practices such as use of indigenous herbal remedies and supernatural powers for treating any disease acts as contributory factors in determining the health status of the Noctes. Jacobsen *et al.* (2002) in their study among the Danish women have found an increase in higher mortality rates which are associated with birth generation rather than calendar period. Although Danish men have a low life expectancy yet the women born between the two World Wars suffers a high mortality rate due to certain sex specific causes. With a substantial proportion of women smokers during the age period of 20s is a contributory factor. Besides women infected through sexually transmitted diseases in the mid-1940s and later entering in the Danish labour market in the 1960s have also an adverse effect on the health of the women. Thus, studies should be based on the differences in living conditions between the high and low risk generations. Singh in his work (2008) "*Tribal Health in North-East India*" has explored the complex interplay of socio-economic and political factors determining the health practices of the tribal population particularly the Karbis and Rabhas of Assam and the Khasis and Jayantias of Meghalaya inhabiting in North-East India. Intake of alcohol beverages, unhygienic living condition and lack of education and exposure to the Government schemes are highly responsible in determining high maternal mortality and child mortality rates thereby leading to a disproportionate sex-ratio.

Application of Methodology

In any social science research, methodology of data collection which is a systematic way of solving a research problem is the most significant process of carrying out the research work in a proper direction and to arrive at an accurate knowledge. As such in this study, besides the use of secondary sources, primary data has been collected with the help of interview schedule. Through survey method, the head woman from each household has been selected as the respondents for the study.

Field of the Study

With concern to the Study, which is based on the Health Status and Life expectancy among the women of the Tai Khamyang community, Balijan Shyam village situated in Titabor sub-division of Jorhat District, Assam has been taken as the field of Study. A brief description of the field is given below.

Assam is one of the North-Eastern States of India which extends from 89 degree 5 minute east to 96 degree 1 minute east longitude and 24 degree 3 minute north to 27 degree 58 minute north latitude. It has an area of 78,438 square kilometres and consists of 2,66,55,528 population. Towards the north and east, Assam is surrounded by the Kingdom of Bhutan. Along the south, lie Nagaland, Manipur, Tripura and Mizoram. Meghalaya lies to her south-west and Bengal and Bangladesh to her west. It has 27 districts. Assam is a temperate region and experiences heavy rain fall and humidity. Assam is mainly called the Land of ethnic diversity as the state is engulfed with diverse tribal groups such as Boro, Karbi, Mishing, Deori, Rabha and many more.[3]

Jorhat which is an administrative district of Assam is located in the central part of Brahmaputra Valley. Towards the north of Jorhat district, is the Lakhimpur district, towards the south lies the Nagaland state, on the east is Sivasagar district and on the west lies Golaghat. On the north of the district, the river Brahmaputra forms the largest river island of the world. The administrative seat is located in Jorhat town. Earlier Jorhat was a sub-division of undivided Sivasagar district. In 1983, Jorhat was carved out of Sivasagar district and was made a separate district. Jorhat district occupies an area of 2,851 square kilometres. There are six Assam Legislative Assembly constituencies in this district such as Dergaon, Jorhat, Titabor, Mariyani, Teok, and Majuli. According to the 2011 Census, Jorhat district has a population of 10,91,295. The district has a population density of 383 inhabitants per square kilometre. Jorhat has a sex-ratio of 956 females for every 1000 males, and a literacy rate of 83.42 per cent.[4]

Balijan Shyam Gaon

Balijan Shyam Gaon was established in the year 1901. The village covers a land area of around 1.5 square kilometres. It has total 219 population which consist of 102 male members and 117 female members. There are total 52 houses in the village. Towards the east the village is surrounded by Betbari Shyam Gaon, towards the west of the village is the Na Shyam Gaon, towards the north is the Adhalkatia Gaon and towards the south the village is surrounded by the Naga Mountains. There is also 1 Monastery in the village where the people unite to pray and celebrate all the religious functions. There is 1 lower primary school and 1 Anganwadi School. There is 1 sub-centre in the village which consists of only 1 compounder. There is 1 Primary Health Centre in the nearby village named Samuguri where there is 1 doctor, 2 nurses, 1 pharmacist, 1 laboratory technician and 2 asha workers. Distance from Jorhat to Titabor is 22 kilometres and from Titabor to Balijan Shyam Gaon is approximately 13 kilometres. Distance from Jorhat town to Balijan Shyam Gaon is around 35 kilometres.

In this Study, out of 219 population, 117 of them are female members. Out of these 117 female members, a total number of 52 women respondents have been selected from the Tai Khamyang community of Balijan Shyam village in Titabor sub-divison of Jorhat District, Assam.

Socio-Economic Conditions of the Tai Khamyang Women

Women's health which acts as a great force in developing a nation needs to be guarded from an early stage. Health status among the women of the Tai Khamyang community is a determinant condition of multi-socio-cultural issues. During the field visit, it is found that out of 52 respondents, all of them have followed Buddhism and believed in Lord Buddha. Out of 52 respondents, 2 (3.84%) of them have belonged to the age group of 25-30 years, 5 (9.61%) of them in the age group of 30-35, 9 (17.30%) of them in the age group of 35-40, 5 (9.61%) of them in the age group of 40-45, 2 (3.84%) of them in the age group of 45-50, 2 (3.84%) of them in the age group of 50-55, 5 (9.61%) of them in the age group of 55-60,

7 (13.46%) of them in the age group of 60-65, 2 (3.84%) of them in the age group of 65-70, 1 (1.92%) of them in the age group of 70-75, 8 (15.38%) of them in the age group of 75-80, and 4 (7.69%) of them have belonged to above 85 years of age. Out of 52 respondents, all of them who have once lived in a joint family have now settled in nuclear family as most of the family members have shifted to various industrial areas and other towns as a result of their employment in Governmental and Non-Governmental sectors. When enquired about their economic condition, it is found that 39 (75%) of the respondents have engaged themselves in weaving clothes for extra income apart from working in the agricultural land along with their husbands. Other 13 (25%) of the respondents falling above the age group of 70 who used to work earlier now do not either work in the agricultural field or weave. These 13 (25%) of the respondents who have worked as farmers along with their husbands now depend upon their children especially their sons to take care of them. When asked about their monthly income, it is found that 28 (53.84%) of the women who have indulged in weaving business besides farming earn around Rupees 7000 per month. Out of these 28 (53.84%) women, 7 (13.46%) of them also depends upon their husband's income who works as Government employees. Other 12 (23.07%) of the women who have neither engaged in farming nor weaving do not earn on their own, rather depends upon their son's income. Only 1 (1.92%) women who is a widow works as a cook in the Anganwadi School of the village. She also visits the house of the pregnant women and lactating mothers along with the Asha workers to provide instructions regarding baby care. In matter of decision-making process regarding the household expenditure to children's education and health, everything is being jointly taken between the women and their husbands. Only 39 (75%) of the women who engage in weaving have got the liberty to spend money on the materials required for weaving purpose. When asked about their educational qualification, out of 52 women, 4 (7.69%) of them are found to be illiterate, 3 (5.76%) of them are found to be matriculate and other 45 (86.53%) of the women have studied till lower primary level. Educationally, these women are found to be in a poor state as 14 (26.92%) of the women who are in their middle age and 22 (42.30%) who are in their old age, 50-60 years back were in such a condition where girls did not have any choice of

their own and were supposed to work inside the four walls and not to get highly educated or work in the public sector. Although, these Tai Khamyang women are not highly educated yet they are conscious of maintaining a proper health of their own and subsequently the whole community. Their social set up which provides equal status to both men and women has restricted the practice of negligence of a girl child which thereby has helped the women to develop well both physically and mentally since their childhood.

Regarding their religious principles, the people of the Tai Khamyang community follow certain principles such as Panchashil which consist of five principles, Astashil which consist of eight principles and Dashashil which consist of ten principles. The Panchashil such as not to take life without any reason, not to tell lie, not to steal other's property or take other's things without their permission, not to envy others or indulge in spreading any rumours of others and not to take any alcoholic products are to be followed by every Tai Khamyang people. Besides these five principles, there are three more principles in Astashil such as to have meal only once before noon and later can have light snacks like tea, milk and biscuits in the evening period, to stay away from all sorts of entertainment and to refrain oneself from applying all kinds of beautifying cosmetics are mainly followed by the aged people of the community. Apart from these eight principles, there are two more principles in the Dashashil such as not to sit or sleep on comfortable or luxurious seats on certain religious ceremonies being celebrated in the Monasteries and to practice *Brahmacharya* and stay away from all worldly desires and luxuries which are followed only by the Monks of the community. During festivals like *Sangkren*[5], *Poileng*[6] and in all the *Tithis*[7] being celebrated, 11 (21.15%) of the women who are Astashil holders along with the Monks who are Dashashil holders eat meal only once before noon and after that they keep fast till the next morning. This fast is followed weekly for a month. Apart from this, in other festivals being celebrated the whole year, this fast keeps on going. Many a times, keeping fast has made 9 (17.30%) of the women suffer from gastro-enteritis. To some extent, in the name of religious festivals, these women are deteriorating their own health but for which they are helpless. Even to a large extent, their economic condition and the social set up have regulated the choice of their treatments to cure any disease or ailment. Tai Khamyang people as a whole have a strong faith in the traditional healers and the medicinal plants that the healer uses to cure a disease. The practice of this herbal medicinal process of treatment by the healers has been in continuation since generations and is made a part of their culture. Besides economic and effective, this healing treatment is in practice among the Tai Khamyang people in order to keep intact their culture which can be signified as a mark of their identification. Indeed their economic condition, educational level, food habits, religious values, social norms, health care practices, availability and exposure to medical facilities and transportation and communication system all unite and works interdependently in regulating the health status of the women. Most importantly, their social set up which is based on equality among men and women has kept the women away from situations of negligence which has a great influence in conditioning the health structure of the women belonging to the Tai Khamyang community.

Health Status and Life Expectancy among the Tai Khamyang Women

Health status of an individual is largely determined by various socio-cultural elements. Improved health condition of women would result in low maternal and low child mortality rate which subsequently helps in leading a healthy life. During the field visit, when enquired about their knowledge of health, out of 52 respondents, 32 (61.53%) of the women have responded health as the state of remaining away from disease, 12 (23.07%) of the women have replied health as simply the physical existence of the body along with the maintenance of cleanliness, and other 8 (15.38%) of them have responded health as both physical and mental well-being of an individual. But majority of the women around 25 (48.07%) of them although are aware of maintaining a good health yet they could not explain the meaning of health in the proper sense. Only with further interrogation, they could express the idea of health properly. It is found that the health status of the Tai Khamyang women is largely determined by multiple socio-economic factors such as economy, norms, values, food habits, health facilities and many more. When asked about the maintenance of hygiene, all 52 of the women have responded that they know that they should keep their physical body and the surroundings clean and should have fresh cleaned water and food. But in reality, they are unable to follow everything. Although, these women drink fresh filtered water and eat clean foods they do not have the habit of washing their hands with hand sanitizer before and after meal. If required, they wash their hands with soap before preparing food and not before having the meal. Besides, 39 (75%) of the women who work in the paddy field along with their husbands used to have their packed lunch in the agricultural field itself without washing their hands with any soap or handwash. The rest 13 (25%) who used to work in the agricultural field earlier, have also stayed away from the habit of washing their hands which is still in continuation. Later, through observation it is found that all these women have engaged themselves in cattle and poultry farming in their homes itself. When enquired whether they are aware of the diseases being infected by staying along with the poultries and cattle, all the 52 women responded that they do not know about any such disease, but are simply aware of the fact that these animals should be kept in separate shelters and these animals and the area where they live should be cleaned regularly. Cow dung is stored and used as a fertilizer for vegetable cultivation. Although, these women are not been able to follow certain basic health maintenance requirements, yet because of their physical activities and fresh diet they are having a healthy life. As such, these women do not even fall easy prey to any disease. Only with some seasonal diseases like fever, cold and cough, these women are being infected for which they do not bother to be cared of. These women are even free from eyesight and hearing problems. But at times, these women have to suffer from back pain and knee joint pain as they used to work in the paddy field by bending the whole day and also have to cook food mostly in *saukas*[8], where again they have to sit and prepare the food. Out of the 52 women, only 2 (3.84%) of them have suffered from diabetes and other 3 (5.76%) of them have suffered from jaundice. Regarding the treatment of these diseases, it is found that basically 3 (5.76%) of the women suffering from jaundice have approached the local medicinal healer who cured the disease completely with the help of herbal medicinal plants and chanting of hymns. The other 2 (3.84%) of the women suffering from diabetes have consulted both allopathic doctors and also taken medicines from the medicine men. One of them have dealt with only herbal medicines but the other one has taken both the treatments being confused with which one could help her in curing diabetes.

Apart from this, when enquired whether the women have taken any vaccines during their childhood, all 52 of the women have responded that they have taken the only available vaccine during their time period that is popularly known as Chita.[9] When enquired about their age of attaining puberty, out of 52 respondents, 35 (67.30%) of the women have attained it at the age of 12-13, 11 (21.15%) of the women have attained it at the age of 14 and other 6 (11.53%) of the women have attained it at the age of 14-15. These women are not even aware of their actual age but have just mentioned about the age period. When asked about the regularity of their menstruation cycle, only 7 (13.46%) of the women who are under the age group of 35 have expressed that they have faced certain irregularity of menstrual cycle and have also suffered from lower abdominal pain. When enquired whether they have consulted any doctor, out of these 7 (13.46%) women, 3 (5.76%) of the women have consulted the modern allopathic doctors and other 4 (7.69%) of them have approached the local women healers who cure the patient with herbal medicines. When enquired about their age of getting married, it is found that 36 (69.23%) of the women have got married during the age period of 16-17, 6 (11.53%) of them have got married during the age period of 19-20 and other 10 (19.23%) of them have got married during the age period of 22-23. And soon within a year of their marriage, 13 (25%) of the women have delivered their first child, other 16 (30.76%) of them have delivered their first child after a year of their marriage, 16 (30.76%) of them have delivered their child after a couple of years and other 7 (13.46%) of them after three years and beyond. Out of these 52 women, 33 (63.46%) of them have given birth to their child at their homes with the help of some *dais* from the nearby tea garden community. Other 19 (36.53%) of the women have delivered their child at the Government hospitals and the private nursing homes. Within these 19 (36.53%) women who have delivered at the hospitals and nursing homes, 7 (13.46%) of them have given birth in the normal process and the other 12 (23.07%) have done caesarean. When asked about their number of children, 12 (23.07%) of the women have got only 1 child, 13 (25%) of them have got 2 children and other 27 (51.92%) of them have got more than 3 children. Besides, 2 (3.84%) of them have lost their first child as a result of being attacked by some evil spirits. One of them had a miscarriage which she believe has been killed by an evil spirit which came along with her husband who has visited one of his friend's death mourning. The moment the woman and her husband went to sleep at night, the former had a terrible pain and soon after that she found her foetus to be dead. The other believes that during her stay in Arunachal Pradesh of North-East India, her child was also being attacked by some evil spirit which according to the people of Arunachal Pradesh, resides in the nearby forest. This woman explained that when the child was at home, he used to cry for hours but once he steps out of home he is all fit and fine. Even the doctor they consulted could not detect any particular disease. These types of cases have made the woman to believe in all the supernatural forces leading them to approach the traditional healers or some magico-religious men. Later, when asked about the age difference between their children, out of 52 women, 40 (76.92%) of the women have got 2 and more than 2 children. Out of these 40 (76.92%) women, 3 (5.76%) of them have got three and a half year difference between their children, 9 (17.30%) of the women have got three to four years age difference between their children and other 28 (53.84%) of the women have got two and a half year age gap between their children. Women delivering not more than 1 and 2 children show their awareness regarding small family size owing to their economic condition. Delivering less number of children might also reflect the availability and usage of good medical facilities including the various health schemes. But this is not the fact. Indeed these women have preferred to bear not more than a couple of children because of their economic condition. Apart from their consciousness regarding the maintenance of a good health, they are also aware of their inability to provide a good life to their children as majority of the women's family income comes from their husband who happens to be a farmer. Although, these women are educationally not advanced yet they have quite a good exposure to the outer world and the modern know-how. The Tai Khamyang community is still holding the solidarity of their community. They try to reside under common norms and follow the same principles as far as possible. They have got a less number of population and as such try to stay united among the community members. Young married women have normally preferred to have only 1 child by looking at each other's family size. The Asha workers have contributed a lot to make the young women aware of the modern health facilities which the aged women lagged during their young age due to the unavailability of these Asha workers and other medical facilities. Regular visit of the Asha workers to the pregnant women have helped the women of the Tai Khamyang community to become conscious of the small family size and maintain proper health of themselves and their child by taking nutritious diet during pregnancy period and visiting the doctor for regular check-up both before and after the delivery. The Tai Khamyang women have maintained a good health by taking pure and fresh foods mostly cultivated in their own vegetable garden. When enquired about their food items being consumed during different periods of time, it is found that out of 52 women, 50 (96.15%) women used to have either rice or *jalpan*[10] taken with vegetables and non-vegetables at times and the other 2 (3.84%) of the women use to have *chapattis* with any kind of vegetables as they have suffered from diabetes and as such they are required to maintain their weight by not having too starch foods. During lunch, all 52 of the women have rice with either vegetables or non-vegetables with a boil item or fish chutney[11] most of the time. At night, except the 2 (3.84%) of the women suffering from diabetes, other 50 (96.15%) of the women used to have rice. The diabetic women used to eat *chapattis* or any other light food. Mostly, all 52 of the women prefer to have boil foods be it vegetables or non-vegetables as it is the traditional food item of their community. Although now-a-days, food cooked in oil is also being taken yet there is a preference for boil food and has a portion of it in every meal. These women have a good knowledge of various eatable plants which have got some medicinal value. These medicinal plants such as *nefafu*[12] which is good in controlling the blood pressure, *toragajoli*[13] which is good for diabetic patients, *mesaki*[14] and many more are being boiled and consumed. Interestingly, these women have got a good knowledge of some home remedies through which they try to get rid of stomach problem, headache, minor fever, cold-cough and menstrual pain. They use lemon pickle mixed with salt to cure stomach pain and juice of *tulsi* leaves mixed with ginger and honey in order to cure cough. These remedies have been prevalent in their society since generations through oral narration. Besides, these women also avoid certain kind of foods and beverages such as milk tea in empty stomach in the morning as they know that it is a source of gastric formation and also avoid bitter items like *titakarela*[15] and *bet-gaaz*[16] in dinner as they believe that these kind of foods could have sleeping disorder, hearing problem and gastric formation leading to stomach pain. Besides, during the summer season, they try to avoid eating*khar*.[17] And this knowledge of avoiding food during certain period of time has been gained by the elder members in their family. The elder members of these 52 women used to restrict these women during their childhood, to eat certain foods only as social norms or societal customs instead of giving a scientific cause. But today, these women have come to know about the real reasons of not having certain kind of foods during different periods of a day. As an individual's health is largely determined by the kind of food what is being consumed, so by having boil food in at least a meal per day, majority of the women are being able to achieve a good health. In fact the Tai Khamyang community people do not easily prefer to consult the modern allopathic doctors for any kind of diseases as they are not much concern about their diseases. Although physically they might become weak yet because of their mental strength they do not feel the illness or refrain themselves away from their daily activities. One of the striking features of this village named Balijan Shyam Gaon is the existence of more women than men. By going through in detail, it is found that 14 (26.92%) of the male members and 9 (17.30%) of the female members have died during the last 13 years mostly due to cancer. From 2001 to 2011, a total number of 12 Tai Kamyang people in the village Balijan have died. Out of these 12 people, 8 (66.66%) male members have died and 4 (33.33%) female members have died. Male members exceeded female members by 8:4 ratios respectively. From 2012 to 2014, a total number of 11 members died 6 (54.54%) being male and 5 (45.45%) female. Thus, a total number of 23 Tai Khamyang people have died during the time period of 2001 to 2014.

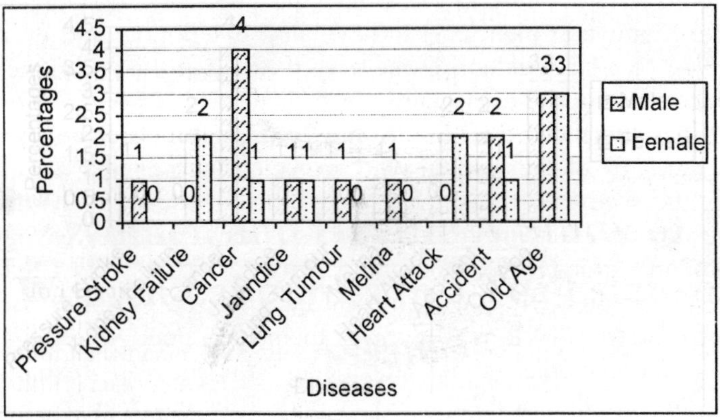

Source: Field Study.

Fig. 9.1: Causes of Death among Male and Female Respondents from 2001-2014

As shown in Fig. 9.1, out of these 23 dead people, 1 (1.92%) of the male members have died due to pressure stroke, 2 (3.84%) females have died due to kidney failure, 4 (7.96%) males and 1 (1.92%) female have died due to cancer, 1 (1.92%) male and 1 (1.92%) female have died because of jaundice, 1 (1.92%) of the males have suffered from lung tumour, 1 (1.92%) of the males have suffered from Melina, 1 (1.92%) male and 1 (1.92%) female have died as a result of heart attack, 2 (3.84%) males and 1 (1.92%) little girl of 15 months have died as a result of an accident and 3 (5.76%) males and 3 (5.76%) females have died due to their old age in the village. Thus, it can be said that the male members are more prone to diseases and also to any kind of accidents especially road ones than the females due to the former's exposure to the outer world. The average age of the males at the time of their death is under the age group of 70-80 and the females at the time of their death is under 75-85. The average female life expectancy since 2001 to 2014 has been 5 years more than the male. As a result, there is a chance for the female life expectancy to rise another 5 years till 2020. As most of the Tai Khamyang people do not have the habit of visiting the doctors or medicals for the treatment of any disease, so they cannot detect or come to know about their disease at an early stage. Normally, the people do not prefer to approach the modern doctors for minor problems. Therefore, the diseases they take to be lightly, later evolve as a serious problem taking the lives of lot of people. Unlike the Tai Khamyang women, the Tai Khamyang men used to have alcoholic liquors and even take *bidi*[18] to a large extent. These have resulted in the occurrence of cancer among the men mainly in their head and neck portion which has shortened their life leading to premature death. Apart from these, 52 of the women who are being investigated are all laborious women. They even help their husbands in the agricultural field apart from involving themselves in weaving clothes and doing other household activities. This proves that when the women who does physical labour have a regular and longer menstrual cycle which craves them for a good sexual life. And as these women attain late menopause, they are sexually active and indulge in it till a longer period thereby regulating a longer life cycle. Another factor leading to high life expectancy among women can be because of less earning pressure among these women as compared to the men folk. Out of these 52 women, the ones whose husbands are alive practice farming and they earn only for their livelihood rather than huge production for market economy. As a result, these farmers have a responsibility of running the whole family whereas their wives mostly have the burden of all the household activities. So, there is a pressure among the male folk which at times has made them suffer from high blood pressure. It is a significant fact that the age gap between the husband and wife is minimum 10-15 years among majority of the couples. Only the young generation couples have an age difference of 4 to 5 years. As there is a huge age difference between the husband and wife, so the male members die soon leaving their female counterparts alone. Besides having aged husbands, the female members also have a longer life expectancy than male members which acts as an added factor in the increase in female population among the Tai Khamyang community. Earlier due to lack of medical facilities there were more maternal deaths. Women used to get married at a lower age and as such give birth to many children without much age gap among the children, thereby resulting in the deterioration of their health. But, today due to the availability of medical facilities, there is a decrease in the maternal mortality rates. Exposure to formal education and to the outer world at large, age at marriage among the women has also decreased. Even with the help of the health workers being recruited by the Government in every village, primary health centres have worked hard towards the maintenance of the health of both the pregnant women and their children. The Tai Khamyang women have become much conscious of their health than the women in earlier days.

It is a significant fact that a psychological dependency has crept the minds of the Tai Khamyang people that the act of following their custom of tying up the whole surrounding of their homes with white threads for thrice a time in the name of Lord has helped in protecting their home and the family members from evil spirits and in the maintenance of a good health. Apart from the socio-economic factors that have contributed to the development of the health status thereby leading to long life expectancy among the Tai Khamyang women, one of the significant factors is that of the initiatives taken by the Government in providing modern medical facilities in the village. Government has taken initiative in providing health related schemes like the *mamoni* scheme and *majoni* scheme in the primary health centre. Some vaccines for eradicating encephalitis and hepatitis B have been provided for all the villagers at the only lower primary school in Balijan Shyam village. The Government has provided a group of health workers to go to the villages for regular health check up in every month. But, this health workers' group in Balijan Shyam village is not regular and the villagers are not being satisfied with their performance. The medicines that these health workers provide are not strong or effective. As such, the health workers could not attract the villagers to come to the sub-centre for regular check-up of their health. Generally, the Tai Khamyang people have the practice of following their traditional healing system to a large extent. There are some specialised local healers in the village who have gained the knowledge of these herbal medicines by the elder members of the family or by some other medicinal men. The Tai Khamyang women normally approach the traditional healers in case of problems like menstrual problem and jaundice. In presence of both the traditional healing system and the modern medical system, there are no such ambiguous views among the older and younger generation people regarding the selection of health treatments. Indeed they do not find any problem in choosing the appropriate treatment for some particular diseases such as menstrual problem and jaundice. They also do believe in some evil spirits attacking especially the children which undoubtedly can be cured only by the traditional healers. For such kind of diseases, one is sure to approach only the traditional healers and not the modern doctors because the traditional healing system has been followed since past and is effective and economic. The healers do not charge any cost to their patients. For curing women's menstrual problem there are specially women healers available in the village. It is found that out of 52 women respondents, 2 (3.84%) of them are themselves healers for curing problems related to menstrual cycle, headache, stomach problem and *alokhoni*.[19] Normally, the medicine men present in the village deals in curing various diseases and ailments such as fever, headache, joint pain, *sahoni*[20], dog's bitten area, snake bitten patients and many more. The Tai Khamyang women have also been following the traditional healing system as a part of their culture. They want to maintain their unique identity as tribal people. As the Tai Khamyang people have been associated with nature for various purposes, so their knowledge of the different medicinal plants and animals could not restrict them in keeping themselves away from utilising these medicinal flora and fauna. Indeed there is a sense of keeping intact the knowledge of various medicinal herbs. These medicinal herbs do not have any side effects and thereby are beneficial in the maintenance of the health condition among the Tai Khamyang women. Although modern medical system has started providing its facilities to the villagers yet the Tai Khamyang people as a whole do not refrain themselves from indulging in dealing with the traditional healing system, because of its effectiveness. Even the choice of treatment do not just remain an individual factor rather at times with various views, advices and discussions among the villagers, it becomes a community factor. The community maintains unity and provides helping hand to each other at times of need. Thus, apart from the food habits and other cultural elements, social values which keeps the Tai Khamyang women at equal level with men is a contributory factor in improving the health status of the women.

Concluding Remarks

It has to be noted that the Tai Khamyang women although educationally and economically not sound, yet they are aware of the fact that their health is an important asset of their life. Their religious principles are a great contributory factor in regulating their life style including their health status. The fact that the Tai Khamyang women should not take any alcoholic products according to their religious principles has helped the women more than men in maintaining a good health condition. The Tai Khamyang community men are more prone to diseases like cancer which has led to the death of many male members during the last 15 to 20 years. In comparison to men, women of the Tai Khamyang community in Balijan Shyam village have more life expectancy. Various socio-economic factors such as education, economy, culture, norms and values influence the people to choose the type of health care treatment which has an impact on the health status of the women. Basically, their food habit has made the women healthy. These women are poorly educated and as such they are not exactly aware of the term hygiene. But without knowing it properly, these women are indirectly maintaining quiet a good health by maintaining the basic cleanliness like keeping the house clean and drinking fresh water and eating fresh clean foods. With the help of the Asha workers in the village, the women have come to know about the family planning and have become conscious about their own health and their children's. The medical facilities being provided by the Government has also attracted the women to avail it. Apart from availing these medical facilities, the women have also indulged in approaching the traditional healers who mainly use medicinal herbs for curing any disease. These medicinal herbs which have been followed since years can give an effective result without any side effects and thereby helping in the growth and development of the women's health. Apart from the sense of conserving the culture of practising herbal medicines, their economic condition and lack of education has forced them to keep intact the traditional healing system which is both economic and effective. Besides, the recognition of women as equal to men has made the women enjoy liberty without feeling the sense of any negligence unlike many Indian societies. As there is no such negligence of a girl child, so the women since their childhood could have equal attention like a boy child which has helped in the proper growth of their body without any deficiency. Basically their physical activities, food habits, health care practices and the social values and norms have contributed towards the development of the women's health which has resulted in the enjoyment of a longer life among the women than men. Although, the Government has taken initiative to provide health related schemes, programmes and other medical facilities in the villages yet there is a need on the part of the Government's role to be improvised. Government should also develop the transportation and communication system and try to provide more improved medical facilities along with sufficient doctors, nurses and good quality medicines in order to make it convenient for the people to avail the modern health facilities.

NOTES

1. It is the old name of Assam.
2. Gaon means village which is mostly used in Indian society.
3. Description of Assam has been abstracted from Wikipedia. URL: http://en.wikipedia.org/wiki/Assam
4. Description of Jorhat has been abstracted from Wikipedia. URL: www.en.wikipedia.org/wiki/jorhat.
5. *Sangkren* is a festival being observed from the last day of March till the first two days of the month of April where the idol of Lord Buddha on the last day of March is brought from its place inside the Budha-Bihar or temple and is placed in the centre of an wooden pledge under the shelter of a tomb like structure where the area around the pledge is full of water. The idol is then washed with water and then it is placed in its original place.
   All the young boys and girls play with mud and apply it on each other's face. They also use water and throw it on one another. Adult members also get involved in the game. The other two days, all the people enjoy by engaging in different entertaining and playful activities and arranging feast inside the temple compound.
6. In *poileng,* the dead body of the senior most Monk or the ash of the dead body, is being placed in a chariot and is pulled together by all the young boys and girls in an exciting mood with all their energy. All the villagers indulge in merry making process. After that they burn the dead body and dump the ash of the burnt body by making a shelter for it with bricks and cement.
7. *Tithi* is a religious day or religious moment which might fall for many times in the same month or is observed after a certain period of time. This *tithi* is celebrated in the temple where everybody gathers in the morning and pray to Lord Buddha. During these *tithis,* the aged people who are the *Astashil* holders and the Monks who are the *Dashashil* holders eat only one meal before noon and take light snacks in the evening. They spend the

night by singing prayers and then sleep on mats and not on any other comfortable seats.

8. *Sauka* is a means which is used to cook food in absence or in substitute of a burner gas. This *sauka* is made of mud in a triangular shape which is broadened at the base and little pointed towards the top. There are three triangular shaped tower like these things and are placed in a triangle shape where in the middle of these, the cooking utensil can be placed.
9. It is a kind of vaccine which was stamped in the hand beneath the shoulder area of a person.
10. It is sticky type rice normally taken with milk and sugar or jaggery. It can also be taken with vegetables and non-vegetables. Other than this sticky rice, *jalpan* also includes puffed rice which can be taken with milk mixed with sugar or jaggery.
11. Fish *chutney* is a delicious item made with boil fish, raw onion, coriander leaves, mustard oil, a pinch of salt and some chillies. All these items are mixed together to make a *chutney*.
12. It is a medicinal plant which is almost round in shape and little pointed towards its tip.
13. It is a long stick like thing. The outer cover is dark green in colour and inside it is the *toragajoli* which is white in colour. It is soft and elongated. Out of these only the white thing is edible one.
14. Its leaf is long and the side of the leaf is sharp. It is boiled and then fried with potato or pork.
15. It is the local term for bitter gourd.
16. It is a stick of a bamboo tree. The inner portion, which is white in colour, is being eaten. The outer layer is dark green in colour and is thrown away. It tastes bitter and is good for diabetic patients.
17. It is a dish prepared with cabbage or papaya mixed with dried pulp of banana and is boiled in water.
18. It is like a cigarette. In *bidi,* tobacco is grated and wrapped in a leaf.
19. It is a symptom of being attacked by any evil spirit particularly among the children. A child who is being attacked by *alokhoni* cries non-stop until he or she gets fainted. This problem is being solved by the aged women of the village. In the evening, these women goes to a nearby paddy field cut water and tie a thread around the bamboo sticks that they put in the field. By taking the name of Lord, they request the evil spirit to leave the body of the child and make him or her fit. With this, the women come back with the thread and tie it up on the hand or waist of the child.
20. It is basically seen among the children. It is a disease where cough gets stuck in the child's throat.

REFERENCES

Cockerham, W.C. and F.J. Ritchey (1997). *Dictionary of Medical Sociological.* Westport: Greenwood Press.

Gogoi, P. (1990). "The Tai: Their origin and branches", In: Gogoi, L. (ed.). *The Tai Khamtis of the North-East,* Delhi: Omsons Publications.

Goode, W.J. and P.K. Hatt (1952). *Methods in Social Research,* Delhi: Surjeet Publications.

Grut, M. (1998). "Why do Women live longer than Men?" *European Journal of Epidemiology,* Vol. 14, No. 3. Netherlands. Springer. URL: http://www.jstor.org/stable/3582425. Accessed: 07:03 PM. 29/07/2014.

Jacobsen, R., N. Keiding and E. Lynge (1979). "Long Term Mortality Trends behind Low Life Expectancy of Danish Women", *Journal of Epidemiology and Community Health,* Vol. 56. No. 3. Denmark. BMJ.URL: http://www.jstor.org/stable/25569658. Accessed: 07:01 PM. 29/07/2014.

Kar, R.K. and J. Gogoi (1996). "Health culture and tribal life: A case study among the Noctes of Arunachal Pradesh", In Das., F.H. and I. Barua. *Communities of North-East India,* New Delhi: Mittal Publications.

Miller, G.H. and D.R. Gerstein (1983). "The life expectancy of non-smoking men and women. public health reports (1974)", *Association of Schools of Public Health,* Vol. 98. No. 4. URL: http://www.jstor.org/stable/4627451. Accessed. 07:05 PM. 29/07/2014.

Ritzer, G. (2007). *Modern Sociological Theory.* United States: McGraw Hill International Edition.

Singh, U.P. (2008). *Tribal Health in North-East India—A Study of Socio-Cultural Dimensions of Health Care Practices,* New Delhi: Serials Publications.

Thai Khamyang Buranji Sampadana Samity (2004). *Thai Khamyang Buranji – A Brief History of the Thai Khamyang Community of North-East India,* Sivasagar: Thai Khamyang Pranayan Samity.

Times of India (2014). URL: http://timesofindia.indiatimes.com/india/Life-expectancy-in-India-goes-up-by-5-years-in-a-decade/articleshow/29513964.cms. Accessed: 01:58 PM 18/10/2014.

10

Political Economy of Population Control and Women's Reproductive Health

Rabin Deka

I

To answer to the question "What is a woman?" Simone de Beauvoir, in her celebrated book *The Second Sex* referred to a French phrase: "*Tota mulier in utero*", which means: "woman is a womb" (Beauvoir, 1997:13). "Woman? …she is womb, an ovary; she is a female–this word is sufficient to define her", Beauvoir, in the same book, further explained to define a woman (p. 35). The womb and the uterus inside the body have given the woman a distinct identity different from a man.

Do women actually have control over their wombs? There is a popular belief that reproductive technologies with the attendant choices facilitate women's control over their own reproductive processes. But the reality is far away from this popular conception. The modern male controlled, technology dominated and market oriented medical system has made the womb its target (Riessman, 2010). Increasing medical intervention in the area of birth has actually led women to experience a lack of control of their bodies. The woman has been alienated from her own body, from her womb. The occurrences of sterilization deaths in India in the recent years have shown how women, especially from the socio-economically marginalized section, have become victims of coercive family planning policies of the government supported by the global male dominated medical system.

II

In a significant study "Population Target: The Political Economy of Population Control in Latin America"—E. Bonnie Mass (1970) described how Third World Women living in such areas as Latin America have had birth control measures forced upon them at the whim of government policy. Rather than birth control decisions being left to the people involved, birth control in Latin America had become population control, an aspect of economic policy linked to development. While poor women in population target zones were once considered vital to the supply of a "cheap labour force", their children in the modern era have been seen as obstacles to economic growth and political stability. To achieve these economic and political objectives, women have been forced to participate in birth control programmes (Elliott, 1978).

The book suggests that behind the proliferation of population studies in aid of population controls in Third World countries lay the capitalist profit motive. The inter-connections of the population control campaign with private institutions and business conglomerates like the Ford and Rockfeller Foundations, Hugh Moore Fund, and Planned Parenthood Fund are obvious (Sukedo, 1979).

The views of Thomas Mathus (1766-1834) that human reproduction always outturns available resources and that human population growth invariably leads to famine and poverty gave rise to genesis of various misconceptions regarding population growth among intellectuals and political leaders in the twentieth and twenty-first centuries. Ecologist Paul R. Ehrich's best selling book *The Population Bomb* (first published in 1968) is the best example of legacy of Malthusian doctrine. *The Population Bomb* had tremendous impact on population polities throughout the world and ultimately on women's reproductive health. Paul argued that overpopulation is the main cause of mass starvation. In the opening chapter of the book "To Many People" Ehrlich, he predicted that a minimum ten million poor people will starve to death during each year of the 1970s (Ehrlich, 1968: 3). As remedies what Ehrlich suggested was alarming: "We must rapidly bring the world population under control, reducing the growth rate to zero or making it negative." He suggested some measures to control population such as: (a) tax scheme in which additional children would add to a family's tax burden at increasing rates for more children; and (b) incentives for men who agree to go for permanent sterilization before they have two children. He advocated that the American government adopt stringent population control measures, both domestically and for the Third World countries that received American foreign aid. In the mid-sixties, in response to the views of the overpopulation ideologues, U.S.A. Congress finally appropriated federal funds to carry out first domestic and then foreign population control programmes. As a result, there billions of dollars available to fund global campaigns of mass abortion and forced sterilization that eventually led to human catastrophe on a worldwide scale (Zubrin, 2012).

III

India has for centuries a rich intellectual tradition concerning both the quantitative and qualitative aspects of population, as well as practical experience in controlling fertility since time immemorial (Raina cited in Connelly, 2006). But Westerners preferred to make an example of India when developing their own theories and deriving lessons for policy. T.R. Malthus taught colonial administrators at Haileybury[1] that alleviating famines in India would only compound the evils of overpopulation. Similarly, Annie Besant, one of the first neo-Malthusians, cited the same famines as proving that poor people everywhere should practice contraception (Ambirajan cited in Connelly, 2006). The Malthusian paradigm started influencing the economists, planners and social activists in India right from the pre-Independent days and consequently, the debates concerning India's population size started in the earliest days of independence (Guha, 2007: 514). Family Planning Association of India was set-up in 1949 by social workers. The Planning Commission too had urged for the importance of family planning since its inception in 1950-51. In the meantime, in the line of Malthusian framework, of the sterilisation of women has been the main method used in India's population control policies. Even today, the Emergency period remains one episode in the history of Family Planning in India. Even before the proclamation of emergency, idea of family planning received urgent attention of professionals, administrators and of the political leaders in India.

Government of India has been coercive while implementing family planning policies. The financial incentives which became part of India's family planning, to use Gunnar Myrdal's terminology, in a soft state. It is not to be confused here that, to Myrdal, the style of government and the degree of personal freedom were not the foremost criteria of a "soft state". According to Myrdal, both democratic and authoritarian regimes could be "soft states," because the essence of such state was that it lacked internal social discipline and the political desire to bring about basic reforms in the interests of the whole. Today the "soft state" is confused with "voluntarism" about which Myrdal also talked (Vicziany, 1982). What Myrdal could not recognize was that the financial incentives which became a part of India's family planning programme in the mid-1960s constituted coercion.

The decision-makers' assumption that there was a mass demand for contraception in the rural India was erroneous. Moreover, their (policy-makers) view of the good life as a function of small families was not universal; it was just the reflection of their class perceptions. These led to the fact that with regard to family planning the Government of India did not adopt the "extension education approach" as it does not produce a quick result. Instead, Government of India went for a bureaucratic and merchandizing approach. The family planning workers were assigned targets and the family planning was to be promoted through financial incentives to people who agreed to be sterilized or have an Intra-Uterine Contraceptive Device (IUCD)[2] insertion.

During the 21 month emergency period (1975-77), Sanjay Gandhi's five-point programme[3] to complement his mother's (Indira Gandhi) twenty-point one facilitated India's family planning programme to attain a momentum. In the *Illustrated Weekly of India,* 15 August, 1976, Sanjay Gandhi claimed that if Family Planning Programme was implemented, "50 per cent of our problems will be solved". He expressed himself in favour of compulsory sterilization and for which facilities should be provided. Sanjay Gandhi catalysed a competition between the states of Indian Union in attaining targets. The officers, who met the targets, were rewarded and transferred otherwise. The drive led to widespread coercion. Truck drivers would not have their licensees renewed if they could not produce a sterilization certificate. Similarly, slum dwellers would not be allotted a plot for resettlement unless they did the same (Gandhi, 2007: 515-16).

The Government of India in its Reproductive and Child Health Programme (Phase II) launched in 2005 declared sterilization to be the most common method of family planning. The irony lies in the fact that while the Government was instrumental in keeping the 'targets', the procedures of sterilization remained unscientific leading to several deaths of women beneficiaries. To popularize the scheme Family Planning Linked Insurance Scheme was introduced with effect from 29th November, 2005 to take care of the cases of failure of Sterilization, medical complications for death resulting from sterilization, and also provide indemnity cover[4] to the doctor. As a measure to encourage people to adopt permanent method of family planning, the Ministry of Health and Family Welfare, Government of India, has been implementing a Centrally Sponsored Scheme since 1981 to compensate the acceptors of sterilization for the loss of wages for the day on which he/she attended the medical facility for undergoing sterilization.

Table 10.1: Compensation for Acceptors of Sterilization

	Public facilities		*Accredited Private/NGO Facilities*	
	Vasectomy	*Tubectomy*	*Vasectomy*	*Tubectomy*
High Focus States	1500	1000	1500	1500
Non-high Focus States	1500	1000 (BPL/SC/ST) 650 (APL)	1500	1500 (BPL/SC/ST)

Source: Family Welfare Statistics of India, 2011 (Statistics Division, Ministry of Health and Family Welfare, Government of India).

The Twelfth Five Year Plan (2012-2017) of the Government of India set three health outcome goals in the line of the millennium development goals: (a) Reduction of Infant Mortality Rate (IMR) to 25 per 1,000 live births by 2017 (b) Reduction in Maternal Mortality Ratio (MMR) to 100 per 10,00,000 live births by 2017; and (c) Reduction in Total Fertility Rate (TFR) to 2.1. In tune with these goals the Government of India launched Reproductive

Maternal Neonatal Child Health plus Adolescent (RMNCH+A) approach in 2013 which essentially looked to address the major causes of mortality among women and children.

On October 20, 2014, the Ministry of Health and Family Welfare, Government of India, strategically announced an "Enhanced Compensation Scheme" for sterilization services in 11 states having high Total Fertility Rates (TFR)—Uttar Pradesh, Bihar, Madhya Pradesh, Rajasthan, Chhattisgarh, Jharkhand, Uttarakhand, Odisha, Assam, Haryana and Gujarat. More than 13 women lost their lives after going through surgeries in a sterilization camp in Bilaspur district of Chhattisgarh. It also added a new component of Post-Partum Sterilization (PPS) done soon after delivery or within seven days to the package for which an extra amount of Rs. 3,000 would be given, of which the woman (the acceptor of sterilization) would get Rs. 2,200. This was in addition to the hiked compensation of Rs. 1,400 from the earlier Rs. 600. For vasectomy[5], it hiked from Rs. 1,100 to Rs. 2,000.[6] The other components of the Compensation against each PPS were: Rs. 300 for Motivator/ASHA, Rs. 250 for Surgeon, Rs. 50 for anaesthetist, Rs. 50 for staff nurse/ANM, Rs. 50 for OT technician/helper etc.

In less than after the announcement of the scheme there were shocking news covered by all leading national dailies about deaths of several women for undergoing sterilization related surgeries. The news headline published in *The Hindu*, November 14, 2014, that read "Targets that endanger lives" narrated how the sterilization procedures (laparoscopic tubectomy) carried out on 83 women at a camp in Pendari village under the Bilaspur district of Chhattisgarh ended up killing eleven women and leaving 69 others ill, some of them critically. In another such sterilization camp, as per the same news item, held in Guarella in the same district on November 10, one of the 56 women sterilized has died and 12 others remained in critical condition.

IV

What was evident from the media reports was that violation of standard operating procedures was the main cause behind the deaths of the women. It was observed that a single doctor and a health worker carried out the procedures on all the women in both the camps. According to an official document on standard procedures for sterilization services in camps published by Family Planning Division of Ministry of Health and Family Welfare, Government of India (March 2008) it was stated that for maintaining quality service, each surgeon should restrict to conducting a maximum of 30 laparoscopic tubectomy (for one team with 3 laparoscopes) or 30 vasectomy or 30 minilap tubectomy cases. The document also stated that even with additional surgeons, support staff, instruments, equipment and supplies, the number of procedures performed by a team should not exceed 50.

In response to a public interest case filed by activist Devika Biswas who highlighted the horrors of January 7, 2012 mass sterilization procedure done on 53 women at a school compound in Araria district of Bihar, the Supreme Court of India in September 2016 passed a significant judgement on mass sterilization camps. The Apex Court blamed the Centre Government for the increasing number of sterilization deaths in mass camps. The Court directed the Central Government to end mass sterilization camps on the ground that they infringe on the "reproductive freedoms of the most groups of society whose economic and social conditions make them easy targets to coercion." The poor and tribal men and women can not be reduced to mere statistics in the country's population control campaigns. The Court expressed its concern on the fact that the National Policy has continued to remain a draft on the website of the Ministry of Health and Family Welfare for over the past one and a half years. The Court directed the Ministry to finalise the National Health Policy by December 31.[7]

V

The government is accountable to every death of women due to the family planning surgery during the recent years. Henceforth, ensuring the safety of women who undergo a tubectomy is of immediate concern. The civil society can effectively monitor the sterilization activity if the detail is provided by the government in the internet. The Central Government should address the issues raised by the Supreme Court. In 2015, the Population Division of the UN took note of the extraordinary levels of sterilization resorted to in India and pointed out a huge mismatch between what is being offered and what women would like with regard to birth control.[8] The larger question remains is that of the fairness of promoting permanent contraception, often for young women, who are unable to exercise their reproductive rights due to social and economic factors. The judgement has acted as an eye opener for all concerned, especially for the Government of India. In fact, the Court's order, if followed up, will be a road map to formulate a people friendly policy of population control.

The population control measures should not be imposed coercively on the young married couples having children. Hence, offering financial incentives and subjecting women to permanent contraceptives is questionable. Empowerment of women through education and employment and access to all contraceptive options and right to choose any of them (contraceptive measures) should be central to national policy for reproductive health. A holistic national policy has, therefore, become the need of the hour.

NOTES

1. Haileybury was the training establishment founded in 1806 for administrators of the East India Company.
2. An IUCD (also known as the IUD or loop) is a small, 'T-shaped' contraceptive device placed in a women's uterus. It prevents sperm reaching an egg (womb) and thereby fertility of a woman.
3. Sanjay Gandhi's Five Point programme includes family planning, afforestation, abolition of dowry, the removal of illiteracy and slum clearance.
4. Indemnity insurance is an insurance policy designed to protect professionals and business owners when they are found to be at fault for a specific event.
5. Vasectomy is a surgical procedure for male sterilization which prevents sperm from entering into the ejaculate and thereby fertilization.
6. *The Hindu,* January 1, 2015.
7. *Ibid.,* September 15, 2016.
8. *Ibid.,* September 17, 2016 (Editorial: "Towards a National Health Policy").

REFERENCES

Beauvoir, Simone de (1997). The Second Sex. London: Vintage.

Connelly, Matthew (2006). "Population control in India: Prologue to the emergency period", Population and Development Review, Vol. 32, No. 4 (Dec., 2006), pp. 629-667.

Elliott, Jean Leonard (1978). "Population target: The Political Economy of Population Control in Latin America" (Book Review). Atlantas, Vol. 3, No. 2., pp. 167-169.

Ehrich, Paul R. (1968). The Population Bomb. New York: Buccaneer Books, Inc.

Guha, Ramachandra (2007). India After Gandhi. London: MacMillan.

Mass, Bonnie (1978). Population Target: The Political Economy of Population Control in Latin America. London: Zed Press.

Riesssman, Catherine Kohler (2010). "Women and medicalization: A new perspective". The Politics of Women's Bodies. (Ed.) Rose Weitz. New York: Oxford University Press, pp. 50-51.

Sukedo, Iris D. (1979). "Population target: The political economy of population control in Latin" (Book Review), Third World Quarterly, Vol. 1, No. 2 (April, 1979), pp. 151-153.

Vicziany, Marika (1982). "Coercion in a soft state: The family-planning programme of India: Part I: The myth of voluntarism", Pacific Affairs, Vol. 55, No. 3 (Autumn, 1982), pp. 373-402.

Zubrin, Robert (2012). "The population control holocaust", The New Atlantas. No. 35 (Spring 2012), pp. 33-54.

11

Gender Discrimination in Terms of Healthcare Spending on Female Child in the Household Level with Special Reference to Purba Medinipur District of West Bengal

Labani Dey

Introduction

Gender discrimination is the consequence of persistent inequality between men and women in all spheres of life. The dimension and degree of discrimination against women manifests itself in different cultures, politics, races, regions, countries, and economies differently. However, gender discrimination is considered as a tremendous constraint towards the development process and it is found as a causal factor of violence against women (Jannatul Ferdaush, K.M. Mustafizur Rahman, 2011).

Gender equality is the current subject of concern among the policy-makers of the world because of enhancing economic growth and maintaining continuity of the development process as well (CPD-UNFPA, 2002). The present concern for gender equality in order to forward the development process is established on a long historical background. Gender issue, in particularly, bringing equality between men and women, has been become a common goal for the International Community since it had been set out in the preamble to the Charter of the United Nations (UN) in 1945.

However, different approaches or strategies had been adopted in the past few decades with a view to promoting the advancement of women and gender equality as a whole but in course of time, it was found that the successive approaches failed to address gender issue in a proper manner and could not improve the status of women as it was expected. Thus, at present time, some significant changes have been noticed in the efforts to promote gender issue at national and international level.

During that time, attention was given on women's reproductive health, especially women's access to food, contraceptives, nutrition and health care. However, by the early 1970s different feminist groups, social workers, policy-makers and networks had created tremendous pressure on their governments for policy reform and pursuing better strategies to address the gender issue (Farida Faisal, 2011).

In this backdrop, the present chapter tries to analyse the gender discrimination in terms of in terms of Healthcare Spending on Female Child in The Household-level with Special Reference to Purba Medinipur District of West Bengal.

Literature Review

A wide range of empirical studies are available on investment in healthcare spending at household level. Most of the studies of this kind have been conducted with a view to determining gender biasness in healthcare expenditure and suggested some policy implications how to reduce gender gap from the health sector. It also provided with some valuable recommendations how to improve women's health status and integrate them into the mainstreaming economic activities in order to empower women as a whole. We have reviewed some of the research papers which focused on women's health situation and determined the factors that cause gender discrimination against women.

Abay Asfaw, Stephen Klasen, Francesca, Lamanna (2007) have investigated whether there is gender discriminations in the health care financing behaviour of household for the infants and children of age below nine years old, in India. The findings of the study reveal that no discrimination among boys and girls is found, while the households use current income to finance in patient health care expenses.

Miller (1989), Murthi, Anne and Dreze (1995), Gupta and Bhat (1997), George (1998), Bhat and Zavier (2003), Mishra, Roy and Rutherford (2004), Dyson and Moore (1983), Krishnaji (1987), Siddhanta, Nandy and Agnihotri (2003), Pandey (2003), Hill and

Upchurch (1995) and Acharya & Kumar (2004) explained the extent of gender differences in infant and child mortality in terms of gender differences in health status, disease incidence, preventive and curative treatment and social status.

Sudha, Rajan (1999), George (2002), Rutherford and Roy (2003), Bose (2007), Visaria (2007) examined the causes for eliminating the girl child. It indicates that they are rooted in rituals and perceptions that go back centuries: the fear of having to pay for a girl's dowry, the belief that for true salvation a son should perform the last rites, the conviction that lineage and inheritance run through the male line and that a son will look after his parents in their old age, whereas the daughters will belong to another family. Tied up to all this is the old perception of seeing only men as the bread earners.

Aims and Objectives of the Study

Gender situation in India has been changing over last two decades due to considerable economic transition and social change. Low literacy rate among the women of age group (15-49) enhance the ratio of child marriage and adolescent motherhood. In the long run, it is found that high maternal mortality ratio in the country is attributed to early marriage, women's malnutrition, lacking of access to and use of medical services and lacking of knowledge and information. There is a huge impact of socio-cultural settings of India on gender disparity. It is, therefore, mentioned worthy that multi-dimensional religious norms exist in the society of India which affects the gender relation in different ways. Statistical evidence shows that women's opportunity and public involvement, particularly in labour force and in economic activities, has been gradually increasing in the recent decades. A significant progress is found in reducing gender gap in school enrollment for some effective public interventions in the education sector.

Sexual abuse of children and adolescent girls is a significant problem in the country. The situation of children and women of marginalized groups, vulnerable and disadvantaged groups, including urban slum dwellers, refugees, tribal groups, river gypsies and those living in remote and inaccessible areas deserve special attention. However, issues of gender equality, equity, and the empowerment of women are increasingly recognized as essential to the process of sustainable development. Gender issues today are not merely special concerns but are considered crucial elements in policies, plans and strategies. Women's and men's contributions to society, their partnership and full participation, their different needs and different access to resources are essential components towards the development process. Thus, it is a dire need to address the gender issues properly and effectively. This chapter, therefore, would be an effective endeavour towards addressing the gender issues in terms of healthcare spending in Purba Medinipur district of West Bengal.

Now, the major objectives of our study are:

(i) To examine gender biasness in healthcare spending for the children the household; and

(ii) To find the determinants that causes gender gap in the household as well as in the society. Now, rest of the study can be summarized as: Section 2 deals with the methodological issues. Section 3 analyses the results obtained. Lastly, Section 4 deals with summary and conclusion of our study.

Methodology

To assess gender disparity of woman child in terms of health care spending, cross-sectional sampling survey method is used through scheduled questionnaire. We also used District Level Family and Health Survey (DLHS) data in enriching the study. In drawing of samples, the simple random sampling without replacement technique has been used in our study.

A simple random sample from finite population is a sample selected such that each possible sample combination has equal probability of being chosen. It is also called unrestricted random sampling. Now, in simple random sampling without replacement technique the population elements can enter the sample only once, i.e. the units once selected is not returned to the population before the next draw.

In this backdrop, total 400 households are surveyed through our scheduled questionnaire from the Purba Medinipur district of West Bengal.

Results and Discussion

In India most of the women are still not receiving health facilities. Poor condition of women can be seen in availing nutritious food, prevalence of anaemia and nutritional status of women. Women's autonomy has been determined by three areas—control over finance, decision-making power and freedom of movement. Women with greater freedom of movement obtained higher level of antenatal care and were more likely to use safe delivery care. The influence of women's autonomy on the use of health care appears to be as important as other determinant such as education.

According to NFHS 3 almost one out of every five women in India did not receive any antenatal care for their last birth in the five years preceding the survey.

In this backdrop, the healthcare spending on female child can be explained by the following way:

(i) ***Nutritional Status of female child:*** For women, weight and height measurement can be used to access health risks. A widely used indicator of nutritional status is the body mass index (BMI), which is defined as the weight in kilograms divide by height in square metres (kg/m^2). This indicator is used to assess both thinness and obesity. It is helpful in detecting the risk of health or nutritional disorders. A BMI of less than 18.5 indicates chronic energy deficiency (CED). At the other end of the spectrum, women with a BMI of 25.0-29.9 are considered to be overweight and those with a BMI of 30.0 or above are identified as obese. According to DLHS there are 42 per cent women in Purba Medinipur district have chronic energy deficiency and 17 per cent women are overweight. CED is particularly pronounced for rural women, illiterate women, and women living in households with a low standard of living and among those women who do not consumes proper nutritious food.

(ii) ***Bias in the Intra-Household Distribution of Food and Nutritive Elements:*** In Purba Medinipur district, sex preference is mainly manifested in the form of excessive mortality of female child. The poor health status of female child relatively to male child is found to be due to the discrimination against females in the allocation of food and health care within household. There is gender discrimination in childhood feeding, immunization coverage, treatment seeking and nutritional status. According to our survey, women consume less nutritious food than man. In this regard, Tables 11.1 and 11.2 disclose some vital facts.

Table 11.1: Percentage distribution of female child and male child age 1-10 consuming specific foods at least once a week

Types of food	*Female child*	*Male child*
Milk or Curd	56.5	68.8
Pulses or Beans	90.5	92.8
Dark Green Leafy Vegetables	93.9	94.0
Fruits	38.8	49.2
Eggs	30.2	45.0
Fish	26.2	32.9
Chicken or Meat	20.8	30.0
Fish or Chicken/Meat	33.4	43.9

Source: Author's own findings.

The pattern of food consumption, Tables 11.1 and 11.2 show that male child is more likely than female child to consume milk or curd regularly. Men are less likely than women to completely abstain from eating chicken, meat, fish, or eggs. The last row of each panel shows the frequency of consumption of fish, chicken, or meat. Overall, 33 per cent of female children and 24 per cent of male children are vegetarians according to this measure.

Table 11.2: Food consumption for female child and male child in Purba Medinipur District of West Bengal

Types of Food	*Frequency of Consumption*			
	Daily		*Never*	
	Female Child	*Male Child*	*Female child*	*Male Child*
(1)	(2)	(3)	(4)	(5)
Milk or Curd	39.8	46.7	11.4	7.0
Pulses or Beans	52.7	52.1	0.9	0.9
Dark Green Leafy Vegetables	64.2	59.1	0.3	0.4
Fruits	12.7	13.1	3.5	2.6

(Contd.)

(1)	(2)	(3)	(4)	(5)
Eggs	3.5	5.2	34.8	23.3
Fish	6.3	6.2	37.5	30.5
Chicken or Meat	0.9	1.2	35.1	25.6
Fish or Chicken/ Meat	6.8	6.9	32.6	23.9

Source: Author's own findings.

(iii) ***Anaemia among Women and Men in India:*** Anaemia is a major health problem in India, especially among women and children and it can result in maternal mortality, weakness, and diminished physical and mental capacity, increased morbidity from infectious diseases, prenatal mortality, premature delivery and low birth weight.

From DLHS data, we found that gender differential in anaemia levels for female child and male child. Around 48 per cent of female children and 22.2 per cent of male children, whose haemoglobin level was tested were found to be anaemic. Thirty two per cent of female children are mildly anaemic, 14 per cent are moderately anaemic and 2 per cent are severely anaemic.

Therefore, we can say that there is gender differentials in terms of healthcare spending in Purba Medinipur district of West Bengal.

Now, when we tried to find out the basic determinants of this kind of gender differentials, we found the following reasons:

Women in India find themselves in subordinate position comparing to men. Women have very limited access to resources in the country and they are socially, culturally, and economically dependent on men throughout their whole lives.

The major causes of women's powerlessness and dependency on men are illiteracy, lack of awareness, poor knowledge and skills. Besides this, they are lacking of self-esteem and confidence. Moreover, like many other developing countries, patriarchal system of social structure exists in India where women hold the lower hierarchical position compared to men and have a little control over the household decision-making process. The major reasons may be written as follows:

(i) ***Hierarchical Family Settings:*** Historically, hierarchical family settings still remain in this district in which men hold the controlling position (in terms of resource allocation and domestic decision-making process) in the household and women as a whole hold relatively lower hierarchy which largely discriminate women from birth to adulthood (even in whole life).

(ii) ***Learning at the Childhood:*** Conditioning (differentiation) of girls and boys starts immediately after a child is born at home; at the same time, different roles and attitudes of the family are observed based on gender (sex) of the new born baby which demonstrates the social norms and values. These social norms reveal, whether girls and boys get equal access to early childhood education. For example, socialization goals and child-rearing practices of the parents in the society differ substantially for boys and girls. In the early age, a girl is taught how to achieve pain bearing capability, hardships, and modesty which favours the boy of that family. More likely, a girl of tender age is taught to earn domestic skills such as cooking, sewing, caring and cleaning. Emphasis is given to prepare her to take the responsibility of child bearing and rearing in future. On the other hand, a boy is taught how to achieve skills for income generating activities and he is sent to school on the priority basis. Family tries to prepare him as the future leader of the family, more widely as the future leader of the society (UNESCO, Bangkok, 2007, A.M. Sultana, 2010).

(iii) ***Negligence (Girls are Neglected) since Birth:*** Female children are often neglected in the household in India. It happens even in the well-developed higher class people. A common practice based on religion in the Muslim community that '*Azan* (a call for prayer at mosque)' is given immediately after a male child is born.

(iv) ***Women's Access to Education and Gender Gap:*** Lack of education is one of the root causes of gender gap which prevent women from equal participation in socio-economic activities along with men and it enhances the degree of discrimination against women. According to the human development report (HDR) 2002, UNDP, the literacy rate among male and female are 52.3 per cent and 35 per cent respectively. Though the school enrollment rate of female children at primary and secondary level is much more higher than boys in recent years. Yet, the status of women does not change accordingly. It happens because parents are much more concern about the safety for their daughters than sons (Haider, 2012). There are a wide range of factors such as poverty, low status in the family and community, backwardness in education, traditional social practices and lacking of social safety net which enhance the dropout (from school) rate among the adolescent girls. As a result, they (adolescent girls) fail to continue study towards higher education, rather in most cases, family arranges marriage for these adolescent girls. In Bangladesh, one-third of the population is estimated living under poverty (HIES-2010). Thus, poverty, negligence and discouraged by family, lack of security and opportunities are the basic constraints towards the female education particularly higher secondary and above. According to the report of UNICEF, the school attending rate of adolescent girls is 53 per cent at secondary level and for tertiary level, the figure is more shocking. It is six girls for every ten boys which is well below the MDG target of full equality (UNICEF, 2010).

(v) ***Women and Poverty:*** Women are the direct victim of the curse of poverty. It is seen that among the poor, women seldom can have basic needs like the health care services, education. One of a consequence of poverty is child marriage which is embedded so deeply in the social and cultural setting that it could be a leading cause of women discrimination and deprivation of access to all opportunities and benefits in family and societal life. Though there is a existing law in order to protect the child marriage, yet the proportion of child marriage is quite high in Bangladesh. The chart shows the prevalence of child marriage.

(vi) ***Religious Influence on Women Lives:*** Religion belief and rules puts significant impact on the lives of her people. In the Hindu community, it is mandatory that sons are responsible to perform the last rites at their parents' funeral and it is strictly maintained in the society which influences the parents to have a male child. A local belief, based on Islam, is that heaven lies under the feet of husband which affects the lives of women, especially the lives of rural women (Haider, 2012).

(vii) ***Labour Force Participation:*** Women in India are mainly engaged in household chores such as child rearing, cooking, cleaning and caring of others. A little number of women are engaged in paid work. As a result women's access to resources in India is very limited which results into less women's access to decision-making process in the household.

(viii) ***Health Situation of Women:*** The common picture of women's health situation in India, is high maternal mortality, high fertility rate, malnutrition and ill health. In patriarchal social setting where women are often dominated by men, the status of women is always lower than men. Thus, the lower social status, poverty, and illiteracy cause women's deprivation of necessary healthcare and malnutrition (Haider, 2012). Moreover, as caring of other family members is a women's traditional responsibilities, they (women) are to wait for meal until all the family members finish their meals. Though women needs to have more nutritious diet due to menstruation and pregnancy, particularly for reproductive health, they seldom get it. Consequently, they suffer from anaemia, malnutrition, and so many physical complicacy (Srivastava, Goswami, 2011). Women are also susceptible to diarrhoea and communicable diseases because of poor sanitation (unhealthy/ non-improved) system.

Conclusion and Recommendations

The principal aim of this study is to assess gender gap in medical investment for children within the household and to identify the fundamental determinants of gender discrimination against women exist in the society. The study reveals that there is a clear gap between male and female children in healthcare spending within the household in Purba Medinipur district of West Bengal.

Furthermore, the study pays attention in determining the root causes of pervasive gender discrimination against women in the community. It has been revealed in many empirical studies that in spite of remarkable progress in some socio-economic indicators for instance substantial reduction of poverty rate, increase in enrollment rate (both male and female) in primary and secondary level schools, increase in women's participation in labour forces etc. over last two decades, still higher degree of gender gap persists in India almost all sectors like health, education, participation in labour force, and access to and control over resources etc. It is found that socio-cultural norms, religious beliefs, patriarchal family setting and dominance of male counterparts of women contribute to the regular forms of discrimination against women. The study highlights some basic causes of gender disparity against women includes patriarchal family settings, ignorance of female children at birth, lacking of opportunities for education, poverty among women, less investment for women's health care in the household and so forth. As it has been proven that at household level, the investment in health care for female children is significantly lower than that of male children, the study suggests to invest more for women's healthcare as a whole (at both household and government level) and it also emphasizes for special measures on the social, economic and environment (improve sanitation, access to drinking water, logistic supports etc.) determinants of health. It is perceived that a comprehensive health care policy including institutional and programme levels might help to improve the health situation of women which would result in reduction of gender gap prevails in health sector.

However, women are often discriminated at home, at work places, and overall in the community. This study, therefore, also reveals the root causes of pervasive gender gap in the society which should be reflected in the policy formulation in reducing gender gap. The promotion of gender and empowerment of women is a burning issue for achieving MDGs and sustainable economic development. The Government of India expressed strong commitment to improve gender situation by adopting policy reforms and development programmes which comply with the Convention on Elimination of All Forms of Discrimination Against Women (CEDAW) and Fourth World Conference on

Women: Equality, Development and Peace was held in Beijing in 1995. In addition to it, many national and international NGOs also have been working towards the reduction of gender gap by improving the status of women. Though some progress has been made on this issue, the government still has been facing tremendous challenges in achieving expected equality between men and women. Some policy implications (both short term and long term), therefore, are recommended on the basis of this study in order to achieve substantive gender equality.

I. It is essential to ease the health care budget of the household so that all the family members can get better health care services. At the same time, everybody should have some specific health insurance policy;

II. To promote advocacy and comprehensive gender analysis on health financing and health insurance proposal in order to address women's health and family planning needs effectively;

III. Government should ensure equal and easy access to gender responsive health and education services more widely;

IV. Law and order enforcing agencies along with both marriage registrars and birth registrars should be more efficient and sincere in order to end violence against women and girls at home and in the communities;

V. Early marriage and dowry, which are two root causes of gender discrimination, are deeply embedded in the improvised and traditional cultural settings in India. No single solution is available to prevent and protect such kind of social diseases. The following study, therefore, suggests that women need to have easy access to education, particularly to the higher study and comprehensive social awareness programmes need to be undertaken by the government in collaboration with NGOs of national and international level;

VI. Mass media like electronic media, print media even social media like Facebook, YouTube, Twitter etc. should come forward in order to build mass awareness against dowry, early marriage, son preference, and violence against women. They should also take pragmatic steps in raising voice for women regarding women's legal rights, better education, nutrition, reproductive health, participation in labour market and above all for their access to better opportunity.

REFERENCES

Ansley J. Coale (1991). "Excess female mortality and the balance of the sexes in the population: An estimate of the number of 'Missing Females'", *Population and Development Review*, 17(3), Population Council.

Bhat, P.N. Mari and A.J. Francis Zavier (2003). "Fertility decline and gender bias in Northern India", *Demography*, 40(4), Population Association of America Northern India, pp. 637-657.

Census of India (2011). Office of the Registrar General & Census Commissioner, India.

K.B. Pathak, Griffith F. and Norman Luther (1998). "Alternative contraceptive methods and fertility decline in India", *National Family Health Survey Subject Reports*, 7, International Institute for Population Sciences, Mumbai.

K.S. Sugathan, Vinod Mishra, and Robert D. Retherford (2001). "Promoting institutional deliveries in rural India: The role of antenatal-care services", *National Family Health Survey Subject Reports*, 20, International Institute for Population Sciences, Mumbai.

P.N. Bhat, Mari, K. Navaneetham, and S. Irudaya Rajan (1995). "Maternal mortality in India: Estimates from a regression model", *Studies in Family Planning*, 26(4), Population Council of India.

Rohini P. Pandey (2003). "Selective gender differences in childhood nutrition and immunization in rural India: The role of siblings", *Demography*, 40(3), Population Association of America, 2003.

Sen, A. (2001). "Many faces of gender inequality", *Frontline*, 18 (22), October 27-November 09.

Shelah S. Bloom, David Wypij, Monica Das Gupta (2001). "Dimensions of women's autonomy and the influence on maternal health care utilization in a North Indian city", *Demography*, 38(1), Population Association of America.

SRS Bulletin, 45(1), Sample Registration System, Office of the Registrar General; India, 2011.

12

Reflections on Social Structure and Women's Health in Assam

Gargee Gayan

India is a vast country which is blessed with enormous natural resources that is essential for a nation's prosperity. However, the most significant of the resources in India which still remains untapped and poorly developed is none other than the human resource. Today development is the prime target of our nation which is clearly spelt out by different visionaries as well as policy-makers. But, a nation can develop only with the progress and well-being of all its citizens. In order to effectively contribute towards the nation's prosperity every individual must possess a sound body and mind. As rightly pointed by Professor Amartya Sen (2003) the key aspects which indicate the level of development of a nation are expansion in capabilities of the citizens and improvement of the 'quality' of life of all. Most importantly this approach stresses on ensuring availability of choice for all. Since women constitute half of the population in any nation availability of choice for them is an imperative to ensure their active participation in the development process according to their choice. This is because the availability of choice generates bargaining power and also provides an avenue for self-expression which lends freedom to an individual. But this is critical in Indian context because the notion of 'choice' of woman (in particular) in India has been shaped and constrained by the social structure. The following lines reflect the idea,

> "The very notion of entitlement—whether to membership of a family, to access to strategic resources, to food and nutrition, to health care, to education, or to authority and

> decision-making—cannot be understood without accepting that the kinship system to a large degree provides the language for it and give it legitimacy" (Dubey, 1997: 5).

The idea of who is entitled for what, finds expression through customs and traditions which functions through various social systems like caste, class, kinship.[1] These social systems provide the organising principles which administer enrolment of individuals to different social groups and also determine the roles and responsibilities of the individuals within it. Most of the parts of the Indian society is rooted in patrilineal and patrilocal kinship ties which grants limited (though variations exists) choices to woman. Differential entitlements as well as limited or lack of choice in life also have had a profound impact on the health status of woman in India. The social systems also generate different ideologies. The ideologies are used to socialise individuals regarding one another's entitlements, role and status. Ideologies are also used as a mechanism to exercise control over the bodies and the resources of woman. Therefore, locating the complex link between health status of woman and the social structure has become critical at this juncture because despite investments in the form of different health policies for woman, the health status of woman in India and particularly in the state of Assam continues to be a murky[2] picture.

Impact of Socio-economic Factors on the Health of Woman

Irrespective of gender proper nutrition and a balanced diet is essential for leading a healthy life. According to World Health Organization (WHO), "Health is the state of complete physical, mental and social well-being and not merely the absence of disease or infirmity (WHO, 1946). Health of an individual is influenced by several factors like the social and the physical environment throughout his/her life cycle and most importantly the health of the mother itself. Therefore, nutrition of a woman requires additional significance due to its complex association with their well-being as well as the well-being of the subsequent generations. Health of a child starts taking shape from a mother's womb itself. As mentioned above, along with other antecedent factors social environment plays a significant role in shaping the health of a person. India being a patrilineal society, considers the sons as the sole breadwinners/producers for the family as well as the reproducers[3] (despite women's contribution in both the productive and the reproductive process) and therefore, a strong preference for sons prevails. In its extreme form this preference leads to sheer hatred for female child leading to foeticide and infanticide.

Differential treatment meted to a child on the basis of gender impacts the health status of a child.[4] Several researchers have elicited that even the child rearing process differs on the basis of gender. The differences may range from subtle unconscious neglect to different forms of abuse. Prothro (1967) through his findings argued that male children are generally treated with more warmth than female children. He also pointed that male children are breast-fed for longer duration than female. Similar studies have been conducted in India which reveal that male children are breast-fed for 25.3 months and on the other hand female children are breast-fed for 23.6 months (IIPS, 1995). One of reasons for this difference in time-span of breast-feeding between male and female child is often due to the fact that after giving birth to female child women are under pressure to give birth to a male child as soon as possible. Accordingly, they try to become pregnant as soon as possible. On the other hand when a woman gives birth to a male child, they tend to avoid pregnancy at least for a certain time period in order to ensure maximum attention to the newly born male child (Das, 1982; Khan, 1989; IIPS, 1995).

Along with inadequate nutritional intake, inadequate care and treatment received during different incidences of illness leaves a profound impact on the growth and overall health of a child. This also has an impact on one's health in the latter stages of life. In case of woman malnutrition possesses serious implication which increases the risk of maternal mortality. Maternal malnutrition may lead to anaemia, intrauterine growth retardation, child malnutrition causing vulnerability to chronic disease etc. (Jose *et al.*, 2008). It is also noticed that due to inadequate nutrition girl/woman takes longer to recover from illness. Thus, apart from issues related to reproductive health, malnutrition[5] or under nutrition is alarming among women in India.

Assam is one of the States where maternal mortality continues to be a grave concern. According to the recent research conducted by the Planning and Development Department of Assam, the maternal mortality rate (MMR) in Assam is found to be 328 which is even higher than the national average. Early marriage and teenage pregnancy among significant number of girls in the State is gauged to be one of the reasons for maternal mortality apart from inadequate nutrition. However, with the increasing institutional deliveries under the schemes like *Janani Suraksha Yojana* MMR has declined in the State in comparison to the previous years. Apart from maternal mortality, it also found that the prevalence of other short term ailments is higher among the female (Assam Human Development Report, 2014) population of the State which is again attributed deficient nutrition. These issues require immediate intervention, because persistence of illness acts as a hindrance in full expression of one's capability.

Apart from gender inequality in distribution of food, poverty is one of the major reasons for persistence of malnutrition. The Human Development framework perceives poverty as a multi-dimensional deprivation. In context of Assam multi-dimensional deprivation is associated with someone when he or she lacks accessibility to certain basic requirements like at least six years of schooling, access to proper sanitation facility, housing and improved fuel for cooking etc. (Human Development Report, 2014). In Assam 30 per cent of the population is found to be multi-dimensionally poor and 17 per cent are susceptible to become multi-dimensionally poor. In other words many people are living a life of hand-to-mouth existence. In such a situation it becomes difficult for many people to meet the specific needs as required during the reproductive stages of a woman.

Ideology and Health of Woman

In the previous section one has pointed that inadequate nutrition is one of the reasons for the persistence of maternal mortality and infant mortality. However, the issue of women's nutrition in India often assumes a secondary position under the guise of family welfare (Jose and Navaneetham, 2008). In this context ideologies play a vital role in defining family welfare very often at the cost of woman's health. The idea of 'what one is entitled for', is shaped by one's idea of 'self'. This idea of self develops both consciously and unconsciously out of the interaction process. From childhood itself through the interaction processes people are exposed to different ideologies in the form of narrative or normative literatures. These ideologies provide the individuals with the guidelines to develop their personhood. For the woman in India religious ideologies play a vital role in shaping the desired *strisvabhava* (Chakravarti, 2009). Once the woman internalise these ideologies they themselves keep a check on their conduct and even try their best to meet the standards created by the society. The following lines from *Lakhi Pasali*[6] reveal the fact:

> *"Swami-putrake banchia jitu nije khai, Xuna Provu eru moi tair thai.* (One who have food before her husband, O Lord, I leave her place)
> *Kayamone baikke jei kore swamiro pujon, xei naarir ghore bandha thake muro mon.* (My heart remains bonded to the household where the ladyworships her husband with all her soul and heart).
> *Swami esto, swamitotusto, Swamihe poromo dewota, Ei vab thoka jonike nasare moi e xoitto kotha".* (Husband is god, one should remain contented with her husband and Husband is the god of all the gods, I shall not leave a woman who possesses such thinking).
> *Xokol dewota ke puji ji fol pai, Swami xewa totadhik fol xomuday"*(whatever blessings one can get after praying all the gods, is less that what one can get after providing services one's husband)
> *Swamito vokoti xoda jitu naari koroyo, jeba xei banche muto xorbob xidhi hoi.* (One who worships her husband, even gets everything from me).
> *Xukhi Romoni Xitu Jaro Anodito Mon, Aaharo Koreyo Jitu Oti Olpo khyon"* (A lady remains happy when she has cheerful mind and who does not take much longer to eat).

Since birth family is the primary agency which socialises its members regarding the ideas—health, hygiene as well the intake of food.[7] Traditionally, a man in India is expected to earn for the family by working outside and the woman is expected to look after the household. It is generally assumed that the work of man or work that is done outside the household is more strenuous than the household chores.[8] Even, in the production process woman play an active part especially during the transplanting and harvesting season. But, often the work done by women in the fields is not recognised as an economic activity and therefore, women are considered as dependants (Cited in Assam Human Development Report, 2014). Therefore, proper diet and adequate rest only for men in the household is given more prerogative. Even in the well-to-do families, it is the male members who are fed first followed by the older woman. The young woman who cooks food is supposed to eat at the last and very often they are left with less than the required food. Again, virtue of woman lies in her ability to satisfy the hunger of all (*Annapurna*) and her ability to ensure less wastage food.[9] Thus, as rightly pointed by Simone de Beauvoir (1949) "One is not born, but rather becomes, a woman." In other words woman is created and the normative and narrative literature acts as the tool for the creation of a woman 'desired' by Society.

The period of pregnancy and lactation places demand for special nutritional and other associated care. However in many instances, it is seen that women are bound to work until late pregnancy and resume work after child birth as soon as possible. In absence of proper rest and the required amount of nutrition leads to, "cycle of maternal depletion that can have devastating consequence for a woman's health and undermine her capability to carry out her responsibilities" (World Bank, 1996: 57).

In case of a married couple the man is considered to be the custodian (which reflected through the common usage of the word *swami* or *malik* to refer husbands) of the household and therefore, all the decisions pertaining to production and reproduction is taken by the male members. Thus, even though a substantial number of women of the state of Assam is engaged in different kinds of work; it is seen that their share in the decision-making process continues to be negligible both at the macro as well as at the micro level. At the micro (household) level this has an impact over the fertility issues. It is found that 13 per cent of women in the State undergoes sterilization against just 0.2 per cent of males. Again only 3.0 per cent males use condoms, whereas 18.3 per cent of women consume pills to check unwanted pregnancy and 1.3 percentage use IUDs (Intra Uterine Devices) (Assam Human Development Report, 2014). Many women are not even aware of the existence of contraceptives that can be used by the males.

Health and Education

On the eve of Independence, the policy-makers recognised the significance of education towards the social transformation of the nation. Thus, expansion of education at all the levels was one of the prime targets. In this direction the efforts by government culminated into the enactment of the Right to Education Act. As a result of this Act huge rate of enrolment in the primary schools is evident but conversely higher rate of drop-outs at the middle and high school level is also seen. This has become a matter of grave concern in recent times since education has been recognised as critical for capability building as well as to ensure availability of 'choice'. However, it is also found that the impact of primary education (many times even secondary education as seen in case study-I) to enable women to take decision has been negligible (Thapan, 1997). Thus, it calls for a need for a different 'kind' of education which will enable woman to take independent decisions rationally.

It is also found that the matters relating to the reproductive health of woman like the kind of food that one needs to eat during puberty, pregnancy, what one needs to do when experiencing specific problems during these stages still remains to be widely discussed in the existing school curriculum. In absence of an institutional system of socialisation regarding various aspects of health, the traditional practices and beliefs continue to be the source of knowledge and guideline for young woman. Several evidences reveal traditional medical practices served as effective healers. But, many times it is seen due to the lack of proper knowledge about the procedures as well as required quantity of medicine[10] had led to repercussions.

Narratives of Woman Regarding their Social Practices during Pregnancy

Assam is a state in which resides a number of communities. Every community has their own principles of social organisation. Every social organisation determines the social practices of its group that needs to be followed during the life cycle events, like birth, death and marriage. In this section one has tried to present narratives by four women from different communities residing in Guwahati. The interviews were intended to gain insights regarding their lives and some of the values (in particular the ones that necessary before and after child birth) held by them. One has employed convenient, purposive and snowball sampling to select the women for interview.

1. *Name:* Rita Das
   Age: 28 (approx.)
   Community: Assamese
   Educational qualification: Matric Pass
   Occupation: Homemaker
   Occupation of husband: He works as a watchman apart from other occasional works like selling vegetables, cooking food at different social functions etc.
   "After a year of attending higher secondary college I got married. My son was born after a year who is eight years old and my daughter one year nine months old. During my pregnancy I did regular test in Gauhati Medical College. There the check up and medicines are free. But when the prescribed medicines are not available we bought it from outside. When I was expecting my son I did not had much problem with regard to food. I had fruits, *xingi, magur*[11] fish (fish is fetched by her husband from the sewer adjacent to her house) during his time. But during my daughter's time there was monetary constraint so the situation was little tight. After they were born I was prescribed to have plain boiled rice and mashed potato for a month. It is said that just after birth it is not good to have stomach full food so though food was served to me all the three times a day it was less than my appetite. It is said that full stomach food enlarges the belly after delivery. After the birth of my son I started to take contraceptive pills. I got to know about the pills[12] from other woman, my sister-in-law". My son was fine at birth. No one said anything. We were little tensed when he could not stand even after a year but people said it is okay boys usually take little more time. But then he was 3 years old but still could not walk properly. After that we started consulting several doctors, both allopathic and homoeopathic, we did physiotherapies but still there was no positive result. Doctors said he had nerve

problem. We had spared no stone unturned and had spent a lot. At last we came to know that there is good doctor who had cured many such children. We went to him. Now, though he walks slowly and differently at least he can do things by himself.

2. *Name:* Afruja Begum
Age: 24 years old,
Community: Bengali Muslim
Occupation: Works as domestic help
Occupation of husband: Worked as wage labour, died in ethnic clash 3 years ago.

"I have an eight year old son and a six year old daughter. I delivered both my children at hospital. During pregnancy my husband took me to the nearby doctor. I never remained empty stomach. There were days when I did not feel like eating at all but then I would think if I do not have this rice, the one inside the stomach will also remain hungry. You people will buy a dozen bananas but for us we think, one banana is 20 rupees so instead of that I will get 1 kg of rice. But, after birth my son had breathing problem. We cried a lot. But the doctors were nice. He was kept in a glass box. Those were very difficult days. We had to stay there day and night and spent Rs. 70,000. But, then he was fine after that. After delivery one cannot digest much so for week puffed rice served for a week in little quantity at different times. Then on the seventh day seven different kinds of black fish are brought by the relatives and we keep a paper above the head of the child. It is because on that day the soul enters and his or her journey is determined. Like you and me have the similar soul, blood but journeys are determined differently. I am destined to work. I work for you people (meaning Assamese people). There is an *ojaha* (black magician) belonging to your community. We used to go to her place often during my pregnancy. During pregnancy bad *hawa* catches the lady easily. One feels dizzy, head keeps spinning, anytime you feel *deeshtup-deeshtup*, means one comes to know when she is caught by *hawa*."

3. *Name:* Rupa Rabha
   Age: 32 years old
   Community: Rabha
   Educational Qualification: Matric pass
   Occupation: Homemaker
   Occupation of husband: Husband works as a clerk, owns landed property in Guwahati which is rented out for different business purpose.

   "I am mixed. I was Bodo[13] before marriage, now married to a Rabha.[14] Again my grandmother was Assamese. I have two daughters. One is 14 years and the other one is 6 years. I got married at 18 years of age. He (referring to her husband) would come to my house regularly and finally, I got married. But, just after marriage I had to face a lot of misery but I survived because I was strong. It was foretold during my birth nothing bad will be able destroy me, I am fortunate. Just after few days of my marriage my husband left. I came to know some one has done *elani* (blackmagic). I would cry the whole day and would not do anything. My mother-in-law cooked and did everything. I just sat in a corner and cried. Even during the time of delivery I got admitted myself. I was the patient and I was the guardian. They took so much time, I was angry. Then they told I cannot have normal delivery and said have I have to do caesarean because my child was in upside down position. Maybe because I did not do anything just ate and cried. But, I ate nicely getting admitted to hospital (she laughs). I even ate meat because getting admitted means I would not be able to eat the next day. I did not feel much pain because I already had much pain of not having my husband by my side. Then at night sister told I had delivered a girl and asked if I want to see her? I said *dhuiii*....girl! I will see her tomorrow, I will sleep now (she laughs). I though if the child would have been a boy, there would be no need to think for another child. I was still weeping, the doctors and nurses told me why are you sad all your in-laws are here. But, how would they know my pain. Then they said me, "you are so young, we had a tough time saving you." Now, do one thing either do not get pregnant or still if you want take a longer duration." What would happen to me *Shiv baba* and *manosamaa* is always with me. After delivery I was given boiled rice, I refused to have it. I said I have suffered so much, lost so much blood and on top of that I am already sad. You all cannot understand it I had operation you all had normal delivery. I asked them to bring fried fish for me. They said if the bones of fish get contact with your stitches you will get septic. I said oho....I will chew even the bones, now go and bring (laughs). In the meantime I met several *ojas* to bring my husband back. After two months he came back. During my second daughter's birth he was with me. Second delivery was also caesarean. After delivery I was given loose boiled rice and my husband was there having chicken curry. I asked him to give me too. He said it is too spicy for me. I asked him wash few pieces with water and give me (laughs again). So, I had everything and there was no problem at all."

4. *Name:* Sangita Paul
   Age: 22 years
   Community: Bengali Hindu
   Education: Higher Secondary Pass
   Occupation: Works in Beauty Parlour
   Husband's occupation: Business

"A pregnant woman should think good and do good when she is expecting. This is because the baby which inside you is learning everything from you. So she should get up early, pray, offer *bhog* to *Thakur* (god). After offering *bhog* to Thakur, one should serve fresh food first to her husband. This is because husband is *Promeshor* (god). So, since he is god you cannot serve him without bathing. If husband is not there an elder can be served. Look, I stay here along with my husband, brother-in-law and sister-in-law. I can even wake up at 8 O'clock. My husband won't say anything. But, still I have a responsibility as the daughter-in-law of the family. Certain behaviour does not suit a daughter-in-law so I get

> up at 5 O'clock. According to our tradition a pregnant woman should not have banana flower because it reduces her milk. Again, too much sour things are also not prescribed. Moderate ones like orange can be eaten. Pineapple and raw banana is also prohibited. After child for three days puffed rice, *sira* is given. After that slowly boiled rice is given because food will be difficult for the woman to digest. Accordingly spicy food is also restricted.

Conclusion

Multiple factors shape as well as affect the health of woman. In India ideology plays a major role in the process and its influence can be seen across class division (however variations exist). Within the household nutrition of male members is given more attention. The ideology of *Stree Dharma* and *Pativrata Dharma* justifies this practice. Again, economic constraints too place lot of hurdles in the lives of women. Many women had/have to unwilling drop-out of the school either to look after their younger siblings, to financially help the parents or get married in order to reduce economic pressure of their parents. Thus, they remain ignorant about many things including their physical requirements and many times they are unable to incur the cost of the required diet.

It is seen women are oriented towards female contraception and more often towards oral contraceptive pills. However, they remain ignorant about side effects of oral pills. There also lies a lot of dependence on traditional hear say knowledge in absence of an adequate medical support system. It is seen that various medical schemes along with different forms of mass media is concentrating to reach pregnant women even remote corners of Assam to suggest and motivate women regarding the proper nutrition. However, the period after child birth and the lactation period too require adequate supervision in relation to the specific nutrition particularly when a woman experience lot of blood loss after complications during the delivery process.

The reproductive life of women begins after puberty. Many times menstrual period is characterised bodily discomforts (many times in form of abdominal pain) and it is seen women resort to pain killers without doctor's prescription to get relief from pain in order to continue with their other activities. However, there lies a possibility of repercussions due to continued consumption of pain killers. Therefore, a change in the school curriculum is an imperative so that women are able to understand their bodies as well as its requirements.

NOTES

1. Martha Nausbaum argued, "Custom decrees who gets access to education that would open job opportunities and make political rights meaningful. Custom decrees who can go where in what clothing and with whom. Custom decrees who gets to make what sorts of protests against ill-treatment both inside and outside the family, and whose voice of protest is likely to be heard... Customs, in short, are important causes of women's misery and death" (1996:3).
2. Assam recorded the highest cases of maternal mortality in the country in the year 2011 (*The Hindu*, March 5, 2010).
3. This notion is reflected in the widely accepted idea of masculine seed and the feminine earth (Leela Dubey, 2001:128).
4. In rural Assam female infant mortality rate is found to be much higher than the male infant mortality rate (Assam Human Development Report, 2014).
5. Facts related to nutritional intake in South Asia reveal that in comparison to men, girls and women are worse off (Sheshadri, 1994). Further in context of Assam lack of proper nutrition and care is linked to the high level of anaemia among girls/women which is attributed to increased number of maternal mortality rate.
6. *Lakhi Pasali* is an important religious text in Assamese for Hindu families. Women are expected to read this text at least during *Lakhi* (Goddess of Wealth) *puja*. The text contain verses which describe the nature of an ideal woman whose conduct determines the well-being and wealth of the family.
7. A girl with a bigger appetite often rebuked.
8. More often in the social imagery household chores are not even considered 'work' as one often comes across remarks such as, "my wife/mother does not work, she is a house wife".
9. A woman is not supposed to throw so many times the excess left over are consumed by them even if it is not required. Thus, the food consumed by them is not a balanced diet.
10. For example traditionally the juice of the sprout of a pine apple plant is prescribed for abortion. But, inadequate knowledge regarding the procedure and requisite quantity of intake had even led to death in rural areas (as narrated by an elderly Assamese woman).
11. Catfish.

12. When one interrogated her regarding other contraceptives, like condom, she told that she is not aware of it.
13. "Bodos are a race of the Mongolian people who are described to be inhabitants of a country north of the Himalayas and West of China. This land is known as *Bod*. The word *Bod* is supposed to mean a homeland" (Brahma, 2008).
14. Rabha is the name of an indigenous tribe in Assam. Besides Assam, their concentration is also found in the neighbouring states, like Meghalaya, West Bengal and in some parts of Bangladesh also. There are different clans within the Rabha tribe and they are: Rongdani, Maitori, Koch (or Pani Koch), Hana, Pati, Dahuri, Totla, Bitaliaetc. Rongdani, Maitori, Koch are the major clans maintaining their indigenous language and culture. The minor clans like Pati, Totla and Hana have lost own language. They have assimilated with the Axomiya to a great extent resulting in formation of a 'mixed dialect' within the Axomiya speech community (Basumatary, 2010).

REFERENCES

Basumatary, Phukan (2010). *The Rabha Tribe of North East India, Bengal and Bangladesh*. New Delhi: Mittal Publications.

Bora, Gayatri, Sharbani Barman and Jyotishmitha Barman (2015). "Maternal Anaemia: A prevailing burden in Assam, India", *Journal of Dental and Medical Science*, Vol. 14, Issue III, pp. 42-47.

Brahma, K. (2008). *Aspects of Social Customs of the Bodos*. Guwahati: Bina Library.

Das, D., J. Dhanoa and B. Cowan (1982). "Exclusive breast-feeding for six months: An attainable goal for poor communities". *Bulletin of the Nutrition Foundation of India* (India).

Dasgupta, M. (1987). "Selective discrimination against female children in rural Punjab", *Population and Development Review*, Vol. 9, pp. 35-60.

de Beauvoir, Simone (1949). *The Second Sex*, London: Vintage Books.

Dubey, Leela, (1997). *Women and Kinship: Comparative Perspectives on Gender in South and South East Asia*. United Nations University Press.

Dubey, Leela, (2001). *Anthropological Explorations in Gender: Intersecting Fields*, Sage Publications.

Government of Assam (GoA) (2014). *Assam Human Development Report 2014: Managing Diversities, Achieving Human Development*, Guwahati: Government of Assam.

International Institute for Population Sciences (IIPS) (1995). *National Family Health Survey*, India. 1992-93, IIPS: Bombay.

Nag, Moni (1994). "Beliefs and practices about food during pregnancy: Implications for maternal nutrition", *Economic and Political Weekly*, Vol. 29, No. 37.

Neogi, Suniti (2010). "Gender inequality, mother's health, and unequal distribution of food: Experience from CARE project in India", *Gender and Development*. Vol. 18, No. 3.

Registrar General of India (RGI) (1988). *Infant Mortality Differentials in India*, New Delhi.

Registrar General of India (RGI) (2011). *Maternal and Child Mortality & Total Fertility Rates*, New Delhi.

Saikia, J.P. and S. Prasad (2017). *Contemporary Indian Society*, Concept Publishing Company (P). Ltd., New Delhi.

Sen, Amartya (2003). "Development as capability expansion". In: Fukuda-Parr S., *et al.*, *Readings in Human Development: Concepts, Measures and Policies for a Development Paradigm*, New York: OUP.

Seshadhari, Subhadra (1994). "Assessment of Nutrition and Health Situations: A Household Level Perspective". In: Romy Barooah, Kathleen Cloud, *et al.*, *Capturing Complexity: An Interdisciplinary Look at Woman, Households and Development*, New Delhi: Sage Publications, pp. 231-48.

Sunny, Jose and K. Naveentham (2008). "A factsheet on women's malnutrition in India", *Economic and Political Weekly*.

Thapan, Meenkshi (1997). "Linkages between culture, education and women's health in urban slums", *Economic and Political Weekly*, Vol. 32, No. 43.

United Nations Development Programme (UNDP) (2011). *A Social Determinant Approach to Maternal Health: Roles for Development Actors*, Bureau for Development Policy.

World Bank (1996). *Improving Women's Health in Practise*, Washington: The World Bank.

13

A Sociological Understanding of Health-Seeking Behaviour of the Rural Women: A Study in Barsimaliya Village of Nalbari District of Assam

Purabi Bhagawati

Introduction

The term 'Health' has wide and narrow application, as it can be both positively and negatively used. Moreover, health is not just a feature of our daily life, it also appears frequently on the political landscape (Michael Bury, 2005). The political and economic, historical, socio-cultural, epidemiological state of a nation have played important role in terms of health scenario of a particular place. Thus, health scenario has been influenced by multiple other factors. However, health is also related to other complex ideas such as illness and diseases. There are various models that have been attached with the concept of health. The concept of medical model of health is one of them. Much of the focus of research and including sociological research is strongly influenced by the medical model of health. Of late the medical model of health basically means about the absence of diseases. In that context World Health Organisation has developed a holistic approach of health and it contradict the medical model of health's position to some extent. According to World Health Organisation, health is a state of complete physical, mental and social well-being and not merely the absence of disease or infirmity (www.who.int/about/overview/en), most medically related thought remains concerned with diseases and illness. The lay concept of health in modern societies would be strongly influenced by the modern times (Michael Bury, 2005). Herzlich has tried to provide a framework for understanding the links between way of life and the individual in lay concepts of health, subsequent work has explored their variation across different age and social groups (Herzlich, 1973: 22). Blaxter (1990) has provided important study on health and this study shows that health is not a single unitary concept, but one has a number of dimensions as applied to different areas of life and lifestyles (Blaxter, 2003, 2004). On the other hand, mental health is one of the important area of health. The one's behavioural aspect is the prime factor of mental health. Meanwhile social and epidemiological issues are also related with one's mental health. Hollingshed and Redlich (1958) attempted to show that mental disorder was not a random event, dependent solely on the individual's biological characteristics, but was patterned by social circumstances (including poverty) and social class. Thus, health can be seen as a comprehensive analysis of human life. Blaxter (2003, 2004) stated health as 'river stock' where psychological, physical or both dimensions of health has been drawn. In this chapter an attempt has been made to look the health seeking behaviour of socio-economically marginalised women who have been living in different geographical areas. Meanwhile, here it also tries to look how ecology and socialisation has made its impact on women's social production of diseases.

The popular mass has said that women enter the health care system by their reproductive organ. In the other words, for women, most of the time health care often focuses on reproductive health problems, where other health problems of women have been excluded. The U.S. Department of Health and Human Services at the National Conference on Women's Health in 1986 defined a woman's health issue as "any matter that affects the health of women exclusively, that predominately on women's health (at any age), or that affects women health differently from that of men". During the mid-nineteenth century women in USA irrespective of class, race and age have fought for better health care facility and that was the milestone of women health movement. This movement has brought significant change in terms of the conception of women health. Meanwhile after the movement the legislative authority in the USA has made noteworthy step by making hospitals emphasized research on women health related issues. Hence, health care was a major concern of second wave feminists in North America, Australia, New Zealand and Europe. But gradually the women's health movement has shifted to the Third World due to recession, structural adjustment policies and environmental deterioration. The Latin America particularly has very powerful and growing tradition of women health (L. Doyal, 1995). Thus, the women health movement has spread to different places and that is why, it is also influenced by the different cultures of different places. Kisekka (1992) and Tudiver (1986) stated that due to spread to the different countries, the practice of women health politics is also becoming increasingly international. The health movement was organised by women irrespective of her class position. But, it has been seen that the women belong to the poor economic background are more prone towards the ill health. Although over the period of time, women's life expectancy has increased in the developing countries also, but longer life does not mean healthy life all of the time. In India, according to the latest governmental statistical report, the life expectancy of both the man and woman are 64 and 67 years respectively. Jacobson (1992) and Smyke (1991) in their work stated that millions of women who belong to the poor economic background, in developing countries have been suffering from various chronic diseases, child birth related problem. Meanwhile the majority of such women have also been a victim of malnutrition, anaemic problem. Of late both the biological and social reasons are responsible for the poor health of women those who belong to lower socio-economic background in developing countries. As for instance, women are responsible for domestic tasks become more prone to be affected by the various water-borne diseases. Because domestic tasks are being considered only for women work. The World Health Organisation has pointed out at least 44 per cent of all women in Third World countries are anaemic compared with about 12 per cent in developed countries (WHO, 1992: 62). However, the political economy is also responsible for the poor health condition of women especially in Third World countries. The harsh decade of 1980 and the structural adjustment policies have also become conscientious for the poor health of women, specially in the Third World countries (Smyke, 1991; Vickers, 1991). Environmental degradation made many women's lives harder and millions are without access to clean water or sanitation (UNICEF, 1990). The environment has an important role as far as women's health is concerned. Because, it is the women who are relatively considered as close to the nature and majority of the domestic tasks also compel them to be closed with the nature. As for instance, the cleaning, washing, cooking are considered as women's work. However, women are central to maintain in health and well-being of their households through these kind of the activities. It is the women who have to take care each and every member of the family. Thus, in this way, somehow her health has been diminishing due to her own or the family's negligence. Hence, this picture is quite common in terms of poor socio-economic background women. Poverty has made the serious impact on both male and female health. But, it is the women who are severely being affected by the phenomenon of poverty. In this chapter an attempt has been made to study the health seeking behaviour of marginalised women. Here, the marginalised women mean those who are belonging to poor socio-economic condition, living geographically excluded and environmentally in the danger area.

Methodology

The data presented in this chapter were gathered during fieldwork conducted from January to May 2016 for a study on "Gendering Health: A study among the women in Nalbari District of Assam". The fieldwork has been done in three villages in the same district. Nalbari District is situated in between Kamrup and Barpeta District. For better administration, old Kamrup District has been divided into three Districts. Nalbari was declared a sub-division of undivided Kamrup District in 1967 (Census Report). According to 2011 Census, the total area of the district is 2,257 sq. km (Census, 2011). The total population of the district as per 2011 Census is 7,71,639; where 3,96,006 are male and rest 3,75,633 are women (*ibid*). The total Schedule Caste population is 60,216 where 29,562 is women (*ibid*). Again, according to 2011 Census the district has 23,364 ST population, and among them 11,672 is women. The studied village Barsimaliya is located under Barbhag Development Block. It is 18 km to the east of the headquarters of Nalbari District. From the local habitants, it has been known that once upon a time the area was covered with full big cotton *'simaliya'* trees. Therefore, the place is called barsimaliya, here *bar* means big and *simali* means cotton tree that provides shadow. The village is bounded by Bharamsing village in the east and the stream Baroliya in the west. Village Athghariya is situated in the north side of the village and Bharbhukiya is in the south side of the village. The majority of the population belong to Scheduled Caste. The main occupation of the village people is mainly fishing, cultivation. The economic condition of the inhabitants is poor. Meanwhile, the village is one of the severely flood affected villages in the District. Every year, flood has made huge damage in their life. Indeed, the village has been excluded from the mainstream area due to natural calamities. They have been struggling to survive with their limited resources and their economic insufficiency compel them not to care about their own health. In fact, the condition of women's health is more deteriorating. Thirty in-depth interview have been done to understand the health seeking behaviour of the people. The interview guide is used for in depth interview. Meanwhile, the male counterpart as for instance the head of the village, the village pharmacist also have been interviewed to know the health condition of their locality. All interviews were audio-recorded, transcribed, translated into English.

Theoretical Understanding on Women Health Seeking Behaviour

In this chapter an attempt has been made to see rural women's health seeking behaviour with the help of two theoretical perspectives. These are Pierre Bourdieu's concept of habitus and Symbolic Interaction Perspectives on Health. Habitus is a structured structure where one view and acts according to this. This structure is consisted of perceptions, dispositions and practices. However, it also generates and organises social practices and with the help of it, one could able to built the social world. An individual's early childhood socialisation has particularly strong effect in this regard because it provides the basis for apprehending and structuring all future experiences. As Bourdieu notes, the habitus is a system of durable dispositions that "tends to ensure its own constancy and defence against change through the selections it makes within new information by rejecting information capable of calling into question its accumulated information.... Through the systematic 'choices' it makes among the places, events and people that might be frequented, the habits tend to protect itself from crises and critical challenge by providing itself with a milieu to which it is as pre-adapted as possible, that is, a relatively constant universe of situations tending to reinforce its dispositions" (Bourdieu, 1980/1990: 60, 61). Habitus is the production of socialisation. The society reproduces its notions, norms, values from one generation to another and human beings as the agent of this socialisation have to internalise all of them. Meanwhile most of the cases the process of socialisation differs in terms of gender. That means the patriarchy mindset of society compels women to become subjugated in compare to her male counterpart. The socialist feminist tried to capture a holistic view on women's subordination and argued that both capitalism and patriarchy is the root cause of women's counterpart. In the early 1970s, Juliet Mitchell sketched a plausible two-system explanation of women's oppression. She suggested women's status and function are determined by their role in not only production, but, also reproduction, the socialization of children and sexuality. The roles are structured and restructured within the patriarchal and capitalist social world. Body and health is an important area, where the capitalist/market logic have vested interests. It reifies the patriarchal notions and construct the 'health market' accordingly.

Health Seeking Behaviour of Rural Women: An Analysis with the Habitus Concept of Bourdieu

Health seeking behaviour implies the action of an individual for getting cure of health related problems. It helps to understand the relationship between health care system and population. Health seeking behaviour in terms of illness behaviour refers one's wellness, recovery and rehabilitation with the help of patient's response towards their particular problem. Health seeking behaviour is an important dimension in terms of managing a health in a community. However, this aspect helps to understand the complex relationship of health, that is affected by other spheres of life as social, economic, political, environmental and technological dimensions. Hence, women's health seeking behaviour is different from the male health seeking behaviour and it also helps to understand the structure of society. As for instance, women's health seeking behaviour has been influenced by the patriarchal production of thought. According to Chatterjee (1988), there are four areas which determine women's access to and utilisation of health services. These are the need, permission, ability and availability. These factors produce the use of health services. The need implies at what point an ill woman seek to get better health care facility. Secondly, permission means the familial, communal and societal norms that dictate whether women can or cannot seek health services. Ability refers women's economic ability to access the affordable health care system. Last but not the least, availability of health services means whether women could able to access the existing health care system or not. In this study, it has been observed that the health condition of women is relatively poorer than her male counterpart. The socialisation process has played an important role in the studied village. The family and society give importance on women health at the time of reproduction. During the time of the interview, most of the respondent complained that their health-related issues are getting importance during the time of pregnancy. Thus, women's other health related issues are being neglected in a patriarch society. One of the women stated, *Frequently I fall in ill and I am getting used to it. During the time of illness, I have to engage myself in domestic task also. Because domestic task is considered as women's work only. I would not go to the hospital, unless and until severe illness will not occur.*[1] Naila Kabeer has defined the household as "the bundle of relationships in a society through which reproductive activities are organised" (Kabeer, 1991: 10). The term 'reproductive' includes not just biological, but also social reproduction—the maintenance of the well-being of those individuals located within the boundaries of the household (L. Doyal, 1995). Both in the rural and urban society much of the social production are performed by women and young girls. Food preparation, purchase and maintenance of household goods, laundry and care of clothing, socialisation of children, care and support of adults and maintenance and nurturing of kin and community ties are all part of social reproductive labour (*ibid*). In almost each and every case domestic tasks are considered as women's work. Meanwhile various feminist thinkers have articulated women's work with the help of role theory. Thus, women do not get time to take care of her own body, because most of the time she keeps herself busy in the domestic household work. It has been seen that majority of women neglect her own health and apparently there is also negligence from the family side also towards her health. As mentioned earlier the women are considered as the production of labour and this labour hardly get any care from the other member of the family. In the words of one of the respondents, *I try to reconcile myself with the diseases, I always try not to consult the physician.*[2] Women's economic dependence on her husband or other male members is one of the reasons for the negligence towards her own body. Most of the cases, women are not engaging in income generating activities and therefore, she has to depend on the other male members for the health expenditure as well. Although the public health care claims providing free of cost health care system, but in reality, it is not like that and day by day the out of pocket (OOP) expenditures related to health are raising. Another woman of the village stated:

> How can I consult my doctor without husband's permission. If, I am going to consult doctor, it needs money. But being the poor category, we have very limited amount of money and with that we have to manage the whole household expenditure including the husband's health cost also. The Doctor suggested him to take nutritious food including fruits. But, how can I manage all these foods? It has been very difficult for us to provide him all the foods that are suggested by the physician. Therefore, I avoid going to the government hospital, because once you go there, they will suggest a lot of medicines and have to buy them.[3]

The majority of the people in this village belong to the poor socio-economic background. Therefore, in most of the cases, they prefer to go for indigenous health practitioner or cheap medicines. In the words of one woman of the village stated:

> I had severe health related problem during the birth of first child. It was a premature baby and both the mother and child was in danger at the time of birth. At that time, hospital facility was not there as like today. I delivered the baby in the home itself and indigenous medicine was used for the treatment. Alas! I could not save my child

> life, the infant died on the third day of his birth. I still remember how the village people come forward and helped me. They used the different traditional model to heal me. As for instance, my body had been massaged with hot dust.[4] Another woman said, I believe both allopathic and indigenous medical practices. I use indigenous medicine to heal from the *'letha'*. Here *'letha'* means the diseases occur due to evil eyes of supernatural power on one's health, while in rest of the cases we use allopathic medicine.[5] Again another woman stated I use hermit's medicine when children fall ill. But in all the cases I don't use hermit's medicine. We believe in some supernatural power. We believe that when any *'batash'* touch to them, they immediately fall sick. The symptoms are fever, vomiting etc. The hermit provides *'tabij'* (it is a kind of ornament which is worn by an individual. Some kind of indigenous medicines have been used to make this instrument). We have beliet after using such *tabij*, one might be cured of the diseases.[6]

Thus, it has been seen that there are two reasons related to use of *bej's* medicine. Firstly, some of the people use it because they have belief on such medical practice. Secondly, there are other portion of women who use it because of the cheap rate. Because, the majority of women are not financially independent. However, it has been seen that people use the different medical systems in terms of thinking the nature of diseases. One of the respondents briefed, *I follow both Fakir and allopathic medicine. During the time of fever, I prefer to go to allopathic doctor and in terms of the body related pain, I go to the Fakir place.*[7] From the above discussion, it has been observed that early age socialisation and cultural notions of the particular place regarding the health have carried a significant impact on women's mind. The majority of the women reported that they have been taught in the early age of their life about do and don't do. During the interview, it has been noticed that the socialisation process teach women to behave in a subordinate way than her male counterpart. Thus, the structure of habitus has been developed. Bourdieu coined the concept of Habitus. Habitus is a part of the socialisation process where everything that we experience is understood and categorised according to what we have experienced in the past and events that we go through in childhood are particularly important in developing a 'matrix of perceptions' that inform how we come to view the world and more importantly how we react in different context (Jones, 1997; Swartz, 1997). Meanwhile socialisation has played an important role in terms of health behaviour also. Thus, women are one of the important agents of this socialisation. According to structuralism approach, the structure has very much effects of its agents. The agents behave according to the structure, although such notion of structuralism has been criticised by Giddens in his theory of structuration, where he mentioned about the duality of the structure. Meanwhile, as mentioned earlier the socialisation process compel women to behave in a subordinate way as compared to her male counterpart. Women's everyday health practices are the production of habitus. In Bourdieu's theory the field and habitus are working altogether. Because, the structure where habitus is working is called as a field. Fields are the contents of which the habitus operates. Swartz (2013) would refer to these as 'power areas', because for him, it is essential to understand the power relations within the fields. Similarly, in this study, the family and society are considered as the field. There are various power relations that have been seen within the family itself. The male folk are being considered as superior to his female counterpart. Such hierarchical nature of power also makes an impact on one's health behaviour. During the fieldwork, it has been noticed that majority of women try to reconcile with her ill health. In that concern, her economic dependence on her husband is one of the main reason of such health behaviour. The poverty has made a severe impact on one's health. But in that concern, it is the woman who is being severely affected. This study tends to look the health behaviour of rural women who belong to poor socio-economic background. These women are the worst survivor of the power structure and patriarchy domination. Due to economic dependence, they have been obeyed towards their husbands or other male members. Meanwhile the notions of patriarchy are quite strong in the village area. In studied village, the women never participate in marketing of agricultural items. It is considered that women have to stay inside the household and taking care of the family members. Thus, her idea of selfhood has been influenced by the notion of patriarchy.

Within the concept of selfhood, the concept of the body is quite relevant. The domination has made a severe impact on her body and mind. From the time of Plato's onwards various intellectual discussions have been developed around the body. Plato illustrated between body and the soul (Alexander Howson, 2005). Turner stated that human body has been implicitly conceptualised in sociology as a relatively stable organic entity onto which social categories are imposed and has not been explicitly incorporated into sociological theory (Turner, 1984). However, Frank has affirmed that in the last quarter of the twentieth century the body has acquired greater significance within Sociology (Frank, 1990). Now, the question comes, what is the body? Thinkers like Bury (1995) defined through a Cartesian standpoint and asserts that body could be known and understand through rational inquiry (*ibid.*). Howson and Inglis (2001) identify three moves of the particular importance of the body in sociology. The concept of body is related to one's own identity. Meanwhile socialisation process plays an important role in the development of body and identity concept. To understand the body, identity and self-one could not undermine the social understanding or socialisation process of an individual. To adapt to the situation of society one has to internalise some basic features of that society. As for instance, an ill person has to adopt certain behaviour, that is adaptable by society. Charmaz (1991) and Radley (1991) stated that sometimes circumstances compel the ill person to ignore their ill health. Meanwhile sometimes situations demand to give more importance on other matter rather give concern on illness. But after long years of ignoring, minimizing, struggling against and reconciling themselves to illness, they adopt a sense of wholeness, a unity of body and self in the face of loss (Kathy Charma, 1995). From the field, we have seen that many women neglect their ill health and they try to reconcile themselves to illness. Most of the women reported that their poor economic condition does not permit them to consult a doctor. Meanwhile, a kind of acceptance towards illness has been seen in their nature. This study tends to look the health through a gendered lens. One of the respondents stated:

> "I don't have any care towards my health. From the morning to evening I have been busy with the domestic

> task. Therefore, I don't get much time to take care of my health. I generally visit the PHC when the illness become severe, otherwise, I won't go. A huge expenditure is related in terms of treatment. Because, the government health care facility is no longer a free of cost business".[8] Similarly another woman stated, "I generally don't care about my health. With the ill health, I have done all kinds of household related activities. Sometimes, I am working as daily wage labour. I have been suffering infection on my leg. The infection was started from the working in the agriculture field. One day while I was working in the field, a bamboo stick hurt on my leg and gradually the injured place tend to swell. Some liquid kind of material came out from the injured place. Agriculture is the main way of livelihood. So, I have to go to the agriculture field with this injury also."[9]

Thus, in most of the cases, situations compel women to neglect her own health. In those cases, her embodied notion of socialisation helps to act like that. Embodiment behaviour has been shaped by the structure and through an agency that behaviour or nature could be reflected (Park, 2005). Sociologists have used Foucault's embodiment of agency through the concept of power and knowledge. The body follows social practices, norms that have been produced under the influence of a discourse (Foucault, 1972). Thus, many thinkers tried to relate the concept of the body with the embodiment. An embodiment is a physical and mental existence. With the help of this, people could relate themselves with other people of the world. Embodiment is a lived matter of gender (Hughes and Witz, 1997). Embodiment represents the everyday experience of human being. As, per women health study, is concerned the study of the embodiment is important. Meanwhile the embodiment is shaped by the day-to-day practices, values and social construction. We can articulate our embodied experience through language, emotions, memory and speech. Embodiment is "an existential condition in which the body is the subjective source or inter-subjective the ground of experience" (Csordas, 1990a: 143). Henrietta Moore has pointed out that embodiment is the essence of identity (Moore, 1994a: 31). Human embodiment has also relation with the expression of inner feelings, selfhood and identity and all of these are interconnected. An attempt has been made to study women's everyday experience of her health through the phenomenological theoretical paradigm. Edmund Husserl is commonly considered the founder of phenomenology. Husserl used the term lifeworld to refer to the world of existing assumptions and people are experienced and made meaningful in consciousness (Wager, 1973:63). Husserl tries to explain how our consciousness is directing our thought. Following Husserl, Alfred Schutz emphasised that humans do not experience the world as an 'objective reality', in fact human's ideas are always being influenced by the socialisation process, norms, values. Therefore in the present study, an attempt has been made to see how women's socialisation process do have an impact on her health-seeking behaviour. Meanwhile to know women's perception of her body, this theoretical understanding has been selected. It has been seen in both the village that the majority of woman have admitted that they have been socialised in such a way which makes them behave in a particular way. One of the women stated,

> "From my childhood, my mother used to tell me to take food in the last, especially after consumption of male members. I have been following this even after my marriage also. Thus when any good food comes to our house I prefer to give the major portion of it to my husband and sons."[10]

In the patriarchal set up, women have very limited right over her body also. Her body become the commodity of the male. She is often considered as the tool of reproductive activities. Specially socio-economically marginalised women's right to health is more often violated. During the fieldwork in both the village, irrespective of caste, religion most of the women do not have right over her own body. A woman stated:

> "I don't have any right over my body; I can't say no to my husband in terms of physical relationship".[11] In similar tone another woman stated "I never enjoy any rights over my own body. Every time husband will become more important. He even forces me to establish the physical relationship with him. Moreover, all the household

> decisions are made by him. In a nutshell, he is the dominant member of the family."[12]

Women's Accessibility Towards Public Health Care System and Doctor-Patients Relationship

Health Behaviour is also influenced by the degree of access to effective services. Because with the improvement of effective health services, the superstitions, various stigmas become diminishing over the period of time. That also helps to change the health culture of a society. The biomedical model of health has been considered as the most scientific and dominant health practices and gradually it becomes the normative model of health practices. In this study an attempt has been made to see whether women could able to access better health facilities or not. Could she able to go to the PHC without depending on her husband. Thus through this the power dynamics in the household has been examined. One of the woman stated, *"every time during my illness time I have to take permission from my husband whether go to the hospital or not"*. In the studied village a strong patriarchy system has been seen by the inhabitants. As mentioned earlier the majority of the inhabitants are belong to Scheduled Caste and fishing is their prime livelihood. But the interesting fact that coming during the fieldwork is that the women are not allowed in terms of selling the fish in the market. They are simply being excluded from the marketing activities. Similarly, the majority of women reported about their economic dependence on the husbands and sons. The primary health centre is situated quite far from this village. Again there are no transportation facilities to go to the PHC. Therefore, the whole village depend on a village pharmacist. Labhita Das (35 years old) briefed about her experiences:

> "Except the pregnancy-related cases, I generally avoid going to the doctor. Actually, the Primary Health Centre is situated quite far from our place. For us, it is very difficult to get both the medicines and doctors. Therefore, for us Md. Samcher Ali is just like a doctor. He did service in the medical department under the government of Assam. So, he has knowledge about the health related issues. Every evening he usually visits this place with a medicine bag.

> He is the only hope for us during the time of illness. He provides treatment for almost each and every health issues except the pregnancy. Before consulting the district doctors, most of the villagers take the suggestion from him. He is just mentoring us".[13]

In the village, it has been observed that people generally follow allopathic medical systems. Although there are different kinds of indigenous medical practices but the majority of women have trust in this model of medical practice. However, this medical system is the default and most prestigious form of women health care. The question is how this hegemony came about? According to Italian social theorist Antonio Gramci (1970), Hegemony is domination that is achieved through consent rather than by force. In allopathic medical systems physicians have rarely forced women to accept them as their primary medical practitioners. Thus, it became the default medical system. Being an inhabitant of the remote village they have another option of healing method, which is coming under the indigenous medical practice.

The health seeking behaviour of women is also determined by the doctor-patients relationship. Such relationship is the determining factor in terms of women going to the hospitals or not. Because during the fieldwork, it has been noticed that majority of women do not want to visit the government hospital because of the rude behaviour of doctors and other para-medical staffs. Forty years old Parbatee Das of this village stated:

> "So far I have not satisfied with the behaviour of doctors in our Primary Health Centre. Doctors give importance to the people who could be able to express their health problem lucidly. We are illiterate people and we even don't know how to speak. I have the experience of being neglected by the doctors."

Therefore, most of the time these women decide to use medicine from the village pharmacist, rather going to the Primary Health Centres. Thus, the behaviour of doctors and other paramedical staffs are also playing the significant role in terms of women's health seeking behaviour.

Concluding Remarks

Health is one of the essentials of life without which nothing can be achieved. WHO views health as an absence of disease, injury or distress. Meanwhile, most of the studies have focused on lay person's concept of health. Such concept is very important to understand on one's everyday health behaviour. Many individuals consider health to be a state of functional fitness and apply this definition to everyday lives (M. Thamilarasan, 2016). Good health is a prerequisite for adequate functioning of any society. A sound health can help to produce better quality of work. DuBuos (1981) explained health can be defined as the ability to function. In a family, a woman's health is important for functioning the family. Woman's fitness is required for the family because she has to take care each and every member of the family. There are various social, political, cultural and religious issues that determine woman's health. In this study with the help of empirical analysis, it has been seen that culture has played an important role in terms of women's health. The village's cultural construction of health has made significant impact on women's health seeking behaviour. Meanwhile, along with culture the socialisation process also works to make the health seeking behaviour. Since from the childhood every woman has to internalise a strong patriarchy notions through socialisation, which also shapes their health seeking behaviour. Through this study, it has come out that majority of women choose indigenous health practices, because of its cheapness. Again, women's reproductive health is getting more importance both from the state and family, after the period of pregnancy, her health is being neglected. This negligence is also playing an important role in terms of their health seeking behaviour. Apart culture and socialisation the other factors, i.e., the interaction between doctor and patients also become important to shape a health seeking behaviour of women in a society. Most of the women do not want to visit the primary health centre due to the negligence of doctors and other para-medical staffs. Thus, there are various factors, viz. cultural, socialisation, structural that have been continuously determining the women's health seeking behaviour. Moreover, her understanding of health and body is also help in terms of seeking the health care behaviour.

NOTES

1. An in depth Interview with one 17 years woman from Barximaliya Village during the fieldwork of February 2016.
2. Thirty one years old woman's narratives about her health during the fieldwork at Barximaliya in February 2016.
3. Thirty five years old age woman of Barximaliya village narrated her experiences during the time of fieldwork in May 2016.
4. Forty years old woman of Barximaliya village narrated about her experiences with health during the time of fieldwork in February, 2016.
5. Twenty seven years old woman narrated her health problem during the fieldwork at Barximaliya village in February 2016.
6. Twenty nine years old woman of Barximaliya village narrated about her experiences related with her health during the fieldwork in May 2016.
7. Twenty five years old woman from Barximaliya Village of the district narrated her views on health during the fieldwork in May 2016.
8. Nineteen years old woman of Barximaliya expressed her understanding regarding health during the fieldwork in January 2016.
9. Forty years old woman of Barximaliya Village narrated her understanding regarding health during the fieldwork in January 2016.
10. Thirty five years old woman of Barximaliya stated her views during the time of fieldwork in January 2016.
11. Twenty two years old woman from Barximaliya expressed her view during the fieldwork in January 2016.
12. Thirty years old woman of Barximaliya village narrated her experiences regarding health during the field visit in January 2016.
13. Labhita Das 35 years old women narrated her story.

BIBLIOGRAPHY

Ahmed, Yasmeen (1995). "Environment degradation and natural diseases: Who are the worst victims?" In: Shamim, Ishart and Salahuddin, Khaleda (eds.), *Towards Beijing and Beyond: Women Shaming Policies in Areas of Concern*, Dhaka: Centre for Women and Children Studies.

Akram, M. (2014). *Sociology of Health,* New Delhi: Rawat Publication.

Beaglehole, R. *et al.* (1993). *Basic Epidemiology*. Geneva: World Health Organisation.

Blaxter, M. (1990). *Health and Lifestyle,* London: Routledge.

Blaxter, M. (2003). "Biology, social class and inequalities in health: their synthesis in 'health capital'", In: S.J. Williams, L. Birke and G.A.

Bendelow (eds.), *Debating Biology: Sociological Reflections on Health, Medicine and Society,* London: Routledge, pp. 69-83.

Blaxter, M. (2004). *Health,* Cambridge: Polity Press.

Burke, Peter J. (1980). "The self: Measurement implications from a symbolic interactionist perspective." *Social Psychology Quarterly,* 43:18-29.

Bury, Michael (2005). *Health and Illness,* Cambridge: Polity Press.

Census Report (2011). India: 15th August, 2014., www.censusindia.com.

Chatterjee, Meera (1988). *Implementing Health Policy,* New Delhi: Manohar Publication.

Cregan, Kate (2006). *The Sociology of Body,* London: Sage Publications.

Csordas, T.J. (1990). "Embodiment as a paradigm for anthropology", *Ethos,* 18: 5-47.

Doyal, Lesley (1995). *What Makes Women Sick: Gender and the Political Economy of Health,* London: Macmillan Press.

Fentherstone, Mike *et al.,* (1991). *The Body: Social Process & Cultural Theory,* Sage Publications.

Foucault, Michel (1975). *The Birth of the Clinic: An Archaeology of Medical Perception.* Tr. A.M. Sheridan Smith. New York: Random House.

Grosz, Elizabeth (1994). *Volatile Bodies,* Australia: Indiana University Press.

Haider, Raana (1995). *A Perspective in Development: Gender Focus,* Dhaka: VPL.

Herzlich, C. (1973). *Health and Illness: A Psychological Analysis,* London: Academic Press.

Hewitt, M. (1983). *Biopolitics and Social Policy: Foucault's Account of Welfare.*

Hollingshead, A.B. and Redlich, F.C. (1958). *Social Class and Mental Illness,* New York: Wiley.

Howson, A. and Inglis, D. (2001). "The body in sociology: Tensions inside and outside sociological thought", *The Sociological Review,* 49(3): 297-317.

Howson, Alexander (2005). *Emboding Gender,* London: Sage Publications.

Hughes, A. and Witz, A. (1997). "Feminism and the matter of bodies: from de Beauvoir", Butler, *Body and Society,* 3(1): 47–60.

Inglis, D. (2000). *A Sociological History of Excretory Experience: Defecatory Manners and Toiletry Techniques.* Lampeter: The Edwin Mellen Press.

Irshad, Ashequa (2002). "Women & environmental degradation", *Social Science Review,* Vol. 19, No. 2, pp. 211-218.

Jacobson, J. (1991). "Women's reproductive health: The silent emergency", *Worldwatch Paper 102,* Washington DC: Worldwatch Institute.

Jahan, Momtaz (2008). "The impact of environmental degradation on women in Bangladesh: An Overview", *Asian Affairs* 30.2.

Kabeer, N. (1991). *Gender, Production and Wellbeing: rethinking the household economy* Discussion Paper 288, Brighton: Institute of Development Studies, University of Sussex.

Kisekka, M. (1992). "Women's organised health struggle: the challenge to women's association", In: M. Kisekka (ed.), *Women's Health Issues in Nigeria*, Zaria, Nigeria: Tamaza Publishing Co.

Last, J.M. (1995). *A Dictionary of Epidemiology.* 3rd edition, Oxford: Oxford University Press.

Moore, H. (1994). *A Passion for Difference.* Cambridge: Polity Press.

Shilling, Chris (2003). *The Body & Social Theory,* London: Sage Publications.

Smyke, P. (1991). *Women and Health,* London: Zed Press.

Sujata, V. (2014). *Sociology of Health and Medicine: New Perspectives,* New Delhi: Oxford University Press.

Thamilarasan, M. (2016). *Medical Sociology,* New Delhi: Rawat Publication.

Tudiver, S. (1986). "The strength of links: international women's health networks in the eighties", In: K. McDonnell (ed.). *Adverse Effects: Women and the Pharmaceutical Industry,* Penang, Malaysia: International Organisation of Consumer Unions.

Turner, Bryan S. (1984). *The Body and Society,* New York: Sage Publications.

UNICEF (1990). *The State of the World Children, 1989,* Oxford: Oxford University Press.

Vickers, J. (1991). *Women and the World Economic Crisis,* London: Zed Books.

World Health Organisation (1992). *Women's Health: Across Age and Frontier,* Geneva: WHO.

World Health Organisation, 12 September, 2016, www.who.in

14

Women and Health: A Study of Women Labourers in a Tea Estate of Assam

Upasana Borthakur

Introduction

Health is a state of complete physical, mental and social well-being and not merely the absence of disease or infirmity. Women's health involves their emotional, social and physical well-being and is determined by the social, political and economic context of their lives. However, health and well-being exclude the majority of women. A major barrier for women to the achievement of the highest attainable standard of health is inequality, both between men and women and among women in different geographical regions, social classes and ethnic groups. Women have different and unequal access to and use of basic health resources for the prevention and treatment of childhood diseases, malnutrition, anaemia, diarrhoeal diseases, communicable diseases, malaria and other tropical diseases and tuberculosis, among others. Women also have different and unequal opportunities for the protection, promotion and maintenance of their health. The prevalence of poverty and economic dependence among women, their experience of violence, negative attitudes of men towards women and girls, racial and other forms of discrimination and indecisiveness etc. are social realities which have an adverse impact on their health. Lack of food and inequitable distribution of food among girls and women in the household, inadequate access to safe water, sanitation facilities and fuel supplies, particularly in rural and poor urban areas, and deficient housing conditions, all overburdened women and their families and have a negative effect on their health.

Health is an important factor that contributes to human well-being and economic growth. Currently, women in India are confronted with a multitude of health problems which ultimately affect the aggregate economy's output. Gender is one of the many social determinants of health which include social, economic, and political factors that play a major role in the health outcomes of women in India. Therefore, the high level of gender inequality in India bears negative impact on the health of women. The role that gender plays in health care access can be determined by examining resource allocation within the household and public sphere. The low status of and subsequent discrimination against women in India can be attributed to many cultural norms. Societal forces of patriarchy, hierarchy and multigenerational families contribute to Indian gender roles. Thus, women in India face unique gender discrimination. Gender inequalities, in turn are directly related to poor health outcomes for women. Differential access to healthcare occurs because women typically are entitled to a lower share of household resources and thus utilize healthcare resources to a lesser degree than men. Women are negatively affected by the geographic bias within implementation of the current healthcare system in India. A disparity in access to maternal care between rural and urban population is one of the ramifications of a highly concentrated urban medical system. The National Heath Policy (2002) envisaged the revival of the primary health system by providing some essential drugs under Central Government funding through the decentralized health care system. In 2005 India enacted the National Rural Health Mission. Some of its primary goals were to reduce infant mortality and also the maternal mortality ratio. Additionally, the NRHM aimed to create universal access to public health services and also balance the gender ratio. But despite all these efforts by the Governmental and Non-Governmental Organizations, women in India, especially those in rural and urban poor areas, illiterate, and women from the marginalized sections of society are prone to more ill health and unaware of the modern medical system. The scribe in this chapter makes an attempt to analyse the health condition of women workers in tea plantations of Assam. For this purpose, the researcher selected one tea estate in Dibrugarh district and through simple random sampling interviewed 122 women workers to get an account of their health awareness and health status. The empirical investigation was carried out during November and December 2016.

The tea industry is an export oriented, labour intensive agro-based industry which occupies an important role in the economy of Assam. This industry is the gift of the colonial administration, which paved the way for the early start of tea plantation in Assam. Most of the workers in the tea industry are tribals from east, south-east and central India—Mundas, Oraons, Gonds, Santhals, Kols etc. brought in by the British over the last two centuries. Known as '*adivasis*' their population is estimated to be around 50 lakh. These '*adivasis*' are the most marginalized communities in Assam today. More interestingly about half of the workforce comprises women, whose nimble fingers are considered better at plucking tea leaves. According to Rasaily (2014), employment of women in plantations historically was sought by the planters in order to "contain the male labour force" and to "ensure a steady reproduction of cheap labour" as recruitment costs were expensive. As Engels (1993) notes the strategy of setting up of 'family units' of single men and women; conducting 'depot marriages' were some of the coercive measures for recruiting men and women that enabled the production and reproduction of labour in the plantations. Thus, one of the important features of tea industry in India is the proportionately higher levels of female employment in cultivation and production. In the early period, the recruited labourers were given inhuman treatment. The tea planters exploited the labourers in many ways. The condition of the workers has remained almost the same for years, since the British brought the ancestors here to work in the plantations. The labourers suffer from illiteracy, poverty, poor health and even lack of awareness of most of the things in life. The prevalence of vector borne diseases soon after monsoon, for instance is a yearly affair. Tuberculosis, gastrointestinal diseases, diarrhoea are common and despite the management's welfare activities, the well demarcated labour colonies breed diseases because of lack of hygiene, water stagnation, poor drainage and overflowing sewers. The women workers in the tea plantations are the worst affected. Maternal mortality is the highest among the garden workers. Besides, they suffer from anaemia, high blood pressure, under-nourishment etc.

Review of Literature

There is quite an extensive literature on the health condition of the tea industry labourers. However, not many studies are available on the health condition of the women workers engaged in tea industry workers in Assam. Here, the researcher has tried to review the limited literature available on the health conditions of the industry labourers. Intensive study was done by Medhi (2006) on health problems and nutritional status of tea garden population of Assam. The study highlighted high incidence of under-nutrition and prevalence of infectious diseases among the tea garden population. Poor socio-economic condition and unhygienic living conditions make the tea garden population vulnerable to various communicable diseases and malnutrition. The study highlighted prevalence of under-nutrition among children, thinness among adults, worm infection, skin infection, tuberculosis, back pain and micronutrient deficiency, disorders like anaemia among the tea garden labourers. Hazarika (2006) highlighted the prevalence of hypertension among tea garden workers, which is emerging as a major health problem in India. Consumption of alcohol, intake of extra salt in food and beverages, and habit of taking tobacco were found to be potential risk factors for hypertension. Mahanta (2006) highlighted the high rate of consumption of alcohol by the tea industry workers, who had no formal education or were school drop-outs and whose parents were illiterate. Bhowmik (2002) examined the condition of the tea plantation industry in terms of its productivity and labour standards. He also examined the implementation of the Plantation Labour Act (PLA), 1951 towards the welfare of tea workers. It emphasized that the workers are in many ways marginalized. They are paid very low wages and have to work in poor conditions. The tea growing areas in India were covered with thick, unhealthy forest where diseases like malaria and black fever were rampant in the early period of tea plantation. The study highlighted that the Plantation Labour Act was not properly implemented in Assam as the housing facilities; especially sanitation facilities are not adequate to meet the needs of the labourers. Bhadra (1997) has observed that the tribal workers of tea plantation still practice traditional health culture. He also observed that in those plantations where medical facilities are better and easily accessible, there is a keen inclination among the workers towards modern medical facilities. Biswas (2002) revealed that there is high degree of under-nutrition among tea workers of Assam where females were the worst sufferers. Moreover, these hard working labour forces with chronic energy deficiency may result in huge loss in work capacity. Dutta (2001) conducted a study regarding "Morbidity and Curative Measures among the Tea Labourers". She stated that 30 different diseases from which the tea labourers suffered like influenza, dysentery, gastroenteritis etc. are reported to occur in a relatively higher frequency during monsoon. The frequent diseases among children include diarrhoea, cough and cold, flu, ringworm, skin diseases and malnutrition etc. Nutritional deficiency seems to be an important cause for most of the infant deaths. Likewise anaemia is more frequent among women. Tuberculosis is also another frequent disease among the women. Kar (1990) has discussed health and sanitation among the tea labourers in Assam. He noted the causes and treatment of diseases. He found that the workers live in an unhygienic condition. Poor sanitation, inadequate and impure drinking water supply, inadequate and unhealthy housing etc. are the normal living conditions of the workers which have been the main causes of diseases suffered by the tea labourers in Assam. Women workers in the tea plantations of Assam grapple with critical health issues. According to health survey of Assam, the upper regions of the state that comprise Golaghat, Dibrugarh, Jorhat, Sivasagar and Tinsukia which are the major tea growing areas recorded very high maternal mortality rate. Child marriage, less span of time between the next child, inexistent maternal healthcare, lack of positive diet charts are some of the crucial reasons suffixing the demonic MMR and IMR. According to UNICEF, consumption of tobacco based substance and alcohol is higher among tea garden workers. Thus anaemia, hypertension, substandard food habits are some of the critical health issues faced by the women labourers. Almost 87-90 per cent of women workers are anaemic which are caused by nutritional deficiency or low iron storage resulting from a previous pregnancy and heavy menstrual blood loss. Child marriage, elopement is very common among tea garden workers and remains a challenge despite interventions by Adolescents Girls' Club, Mothers' Club etc. Lack of awareness is also one of the reasons why teenagers elope, often resulting in early pregnancy and desertion of the young girl. Alcoholism, mostly among men, is yet again a major problem, resulting in an economic drain, poor health and even domestic violence.

From the above review of literature, it is quite evident that the health conditions of the women workers in the tea plantations is not good. The present study was conducted in a tea estate to get a more scientific account of the health conditions of the women workers in the tea plantations. The selection of the sample garden has been done through multistage sampling technique. First one district, namely Dibrugarh is selected purposively as more than 30 per cent of the tea plantations in Assam is located in Dibrugarh district. Then Modarkhat Tea Estate of the Lahoal division is also selected purposively. After the selection of the garden, the targeted respondents of the garden are selected through simple random sampling. There are a total of 5 labour lines in the Modarkhat Tea Estate. They are Ek number Pakka line, Do number Pakka line, Kenduguri line, Mura line and Godabahar line. Through simple random sampling, the researcher entered every third household in each labour line and interviewed the women of the household. In this way the total respondents came to around 122 which cover around 10 per cent of the population. Besides personal interviews, focus group discussions and observation were other sources of data collection.

Profile of the Sample Tea Garden

Modarkhat Tea Estate is located in Dibrugarh District in Upper Assam. It is 22 km away from Dibrugarh town. The tea estate covers an area of 194.22 hectares. The tea estate was established in 1913 by Late Nandeshwar Chakravarty, a native of Assam. Modarkhat Tea Estate belongs to M/s. Modarkhat Tea Co. (P) Ltd. Its head office is situated in Dibrugarh. The plantation is located in the plains with the settlement of labourers, staff quarters, administrative office, factory, educational institution, hospital, canteen etc. A large number of labourers are employed in the tea estate as tea pluckers and manual workers. Besides permanent workers a large number of casual workers are also employed in the peak season. The total number of permanent workers in the tea estate is 491 including both male and female and the casual workers employed in the peak season are 652.

Healthcare Services Available in Modarkhat Tea Estate

According to Plantation Labour Act, 1951, every tea garden should have medical services and educational facilities. In Modarkhat Tea Estate there is one garden hospital which was established in 1946. The labourers working in the plantation attend the hospital for necessary medical services. There are two wards, one for the male and the other for the female patients. There are 13 beds for the inpatients. With regard to the composition of the staff, during the present investigation, there was one visiting doctor, two nurses, one pharmacist, one health assistant and four health attendants. It is learnt that because of lack of proper infrastructural facilities and absence of resident doctor in the tea estate, all the major cases including delivery cases are referred to the nearest Lahoal Block Hospital or Assam Medical College Hospital, Dibrugarh. There is also 'Ashakarmi' workers in the tea estate who are a part of the NRHM Scheme to take care of the pregnant and new born babies. They organise immunization camps every month for the new born babies of the tea estate workers. Besides these, every month health camps are organised in the tea estate by the Oil India Limited and the workers come to the camps for free check-up and medicines.

Social Background of the Women Workers

Age Structure

Women from different age groups were interviewed. Out of the 122 women interviewed, 25 per cent of the women belonged to 25-29 age group and 2 per cent of women belonged to 60-64 age group. Table shows the percentage distribution of women in different age groups.

As regards the marital status of the respondents it was found that out of 122 respondents, majority of the women were married, only 12 were widowed and one was unmarried. Again nearly 80 per cent of the women interviewed live in nuclear families.

Table 14.1: Age structure of the women respondents of Modarkhat Tea Estate

	Numbers	*Percentage*
20–24	19	15.57
25–29	31	25.40
30–34	16	13.11
35–39	14	11.47
40–44	13	10.65
45–49	15	12.29
50–54	7	5.73
55–59	5	4.09
60–64	2	1.63

Source: Field Study.

Caste, Religion and Other Beliefs

The tea industry labourers are the migrated section of the society but have settled permanently in Assam and play an important role in the demography of Assam. They belong to different ethnic groups, tribes which include Mura, Tanti, Gond, Kharia, Karmarkar, Barhai, Guala, Pattar, Kurmi, Bhumij. In this tea estate around 25 per cent of the respondents belonged to Mura tribe, followed by Karmarkar and *Kharia* tribes. Almost all the women workers under investigation are Hindus and only 11 per cent of the workers were Christians. Sadri is the mother tongue of the women respondents. The management has build a big temple in the garden premises where different *pujas* like *Durga Puja, Kali Puja, Lakshmi Puja, Rash Puja, Annapurna Puja* are sponsored by the management for the labour class. Besides these *Tusu Puja, Gram Puja, Karam Puja* etc. are celebrated by the labourers themselves in the labour lines. There is also a church for the Christians in the garden premises, where the Christian workers celebrate Christmas, Good Friday and do Sunday Mass.

Education

Education is the decisive factor of socio-economic and cultural advancement of a community. Higher percentage of literacy reflects the socio-economic background of a community. But the standard of education of labourers of tea plantation is very poor. The socio-economic condition is one of the factors that are responsible for the low level of literacy of the labourers. Lack of education adversely affects the health awareness and health seeking behaviour, contributing to higher incidence of diseases. Various researches have shown a positive relationship between health and education. However, according to Plantation Labour Act, 1951, every tea garden should have one primary school in the garden premises, but most of the tea garden workers are illiterate especially the women workers. Now-a-days, few workers have become conscious regarding their children's education and have started sending their children to school. There is one primary school in the garden premises established in 1946 and there are three teachers. However, most of the women workers, that the researcher interviewed, were illiterate. The women workers have different reasons for their illiteracy. Most of the workers mentioned that their parents were indifferent towards their daughters' education. In the tea garden community as both the parents are working, so, the responsibility of looking after younger siblings rests on the hands of daughters, which ultimately forces them to discontinue education. This is the case even today, but now-a-days, the mothers are becoming conscious of their daughters' education. In the following table 14.2 the educational background of the respondents is given below:

Table 14.2: Educational background of the respondents

Education	*Numbers*	*Percentage*
Illiterate	107	87
Able to read and write	7	5.73
L.P.	1	0.81
M.E.	2	1.63
High School	3	2.45
12th Pass	2	1.63

Source: Field Study.

Economic Status

There is a general impression among the people that the tea industry workers are very poor and illiterate. The tea workers are manual workers engaged in the tea industry as permanent and casual workers. Some families have two or more permanent workers in the garden and thus their total income is higher than the others. On the other hand, in some families, there are only casual workers whose economic status is very poor. The economic status of plantation workers of Modarkhat Tea Estate is not so high. The workers are paid wages on daily basis at the rate of Rs. 126 fortnightly. Besides, the permanent workers get some fringe benefits like ration at subsidized rates, firewood, medical facilities and free housing. Therefore, the monthly income or the daily wages including other fringe benefits is the primary source of income of the plantation workers. The workers consider this income as low as their entire earnings is spend on maintaining household expenditure and fulfilling other necessities of life. In this tea estate only 2 per cent of the husbands of the respondents worked outside the plantation to make an additional income to their household. The rest both husband and wife are working in the tea estate as permanent and casual workers.

Living Standard of the Women Tea Garden Workers

The standard of health and well-being varies very much with the environment and living conditions of the population. It has been observed by social scientists that there is a close relationship between health problems and socio-economic and environmental conditions of the people. An attempt has been made by the researcher to evaluate the relationship between socio-economic environment of the tea garden labourers and the health conditions of the women workers.

Housing Condition

Housing condition plays an integral part in the maintenance of human health. Section 16 of the Assam Plantation Labour Rules, 1956 along with the Plantation Labour Act, 1951, amended by Act No. 58 of 1981, prescribes the provisions for housing facilities in the garden (Kaniampady, 2003). The permanent workers of the Modarkhat Tea Estate are provided with housing facilities by the management under the provision of the PLA in the adjoining areas. The casual workers live with their families in the houses built by them. Different types of houses were observed in different residential clusters in the field during the time of investigation. Most of the houses provided by the garden authority are *pukka* houses, having brick wall, corrugated iron sheet roof and unpaved floor. There are only two rooms with a kitchen and a verandah. But the houses are in dilapidated condition with broken windows and doors. Lime washing, painting and varnishing are not done in the houses. The provision of ventilation in the houses cannot be considered as sufficient because the rooms, even during the day time remain dark and the floor damp. Also there is no electricity in the labour lines barring a few exceptions. During the rainy season, at times through the rotten roof, water enters within the house. The labourers also extend the quarters by using bamboo to cope with increased size of the family without any prior approval of the management. Some labourers also live in mud houses with corrugated Iron sheet-roof. Thus, it is observed that the housing condition is relatively unhygienic. Apart from this, the drainage system of the houses under investigation seems to be very poor. Besides cowshed and pig-shed are generally built attached to the dwelling houses. Although very few labourers own cows, pigs, goats, hens, but the manner in which they are kept seem to have an adverse impact on their health. Thus, the labourers live in unhygienic and inadequate conditions.

Sanitation

Hygiene and sanitation are very important for a person to remain healthy. Lack of hygiene and sanitation facilities leads to various communicable diseases. Therefore, proper toilet and bathroom facilities are absolutely essential for a healthy society. The garden authority of the Modarkhat Tea Estate provides *pakka* latrine to each household. But there are no proper bathroom facilities for the labourers. Generally, the workers cover their tubewell areas and use it as the bathroom as the women cannot bath in the open. So, the women take their bath in the early morning or in the evening after coming from work in the dark. Thus, it becomes very unhygienic and inconvenience for women workers because of lack of bathroom facilities.

Drinking Water

Water plays a direct as well as indirect role in the transmission of micro-organisms or parasites which cause illnesses. Almost all diseases are linked to unsafe water and lack of adequate sanitation measures. Drinking water is one of the several routes for transmission of diseases like diarrhoea, cholera etc. The present study found that 100 per cent of the workers of the tea estate use water from tube-wells for drinking purposes. The tube-wells are provided by the garden authority in the labour lines, one for every four families, and from these tube-wells the labourers collect water for various purposes. It was also found that few labour families have their own tube-wells and use its water for drinking purposes. The labourers are prone to various waterborne diseases as they do not purify the water before drinking. In reality because of their low level of education and health consciousness, they are not aware of the fact that unsafe drinking water transmits various communicable diseases and therefore, it should be purified before drinking.

Food Habits

Human body requires a balanced diet to remain healthy. Food stuff contains substances known as nutrients that perform various functions in the body. These include proteins, fats, carbohydrates, vitamins and mineral salts. According to Kaniampady (2003), proteins, fats and carbohydrates are also sometimes called "proximate principles". Human beings require a sufficient amount of proximate principles, vitamins and minerals to enable them to live and thrive. A well balanced diet should contain all these factors in correct proportion and in adequate amount. However, dietary habits of different people have been determined mainly by the income of the people of different populations. During the present investigation it was found that the main diet of the labourers consists of rice, wheat (*atta*), vegetables and black tea with salt. Sometimes *dal* is also added to their food but not always. Meat, fish and eggs are taken occasionally during the payment period or when they have money in hand. So, meat is rarely purchased from the market by the people. The adults, irrespective of sex, working in the tea garden take principal meals twice a day: one meal before going to their duty and the other after returning from their duty. Black tea with salt is also taken with two principal meals. Similarly, the labourers are provided with black tea with salt by the management during their working hours. They consume large amount of salt which causes disorders like hypertension. Moreover, milk and milk products and fruits are almost missing in the diet of all age groups. This leads to deficiency of several nutrients such as calcium, iron, protein, vitamins, fats etc. in them. Thus, in the present study it was found that in all the labour families under investigation there is a huge deficiency of calorie, carbohydrates and protein in their diet. Therefore, the labourers suffer from nutritional deficiency.

Almost all the labourers have the habit of consuming alcohol or *'haria'* which has detrimental effects on the lives of the workers. Drinking is an accepted way of life among the tribals. They drink *'haria'*, which is an alcoholic drink locally brewed in their houses. In this regard Roy (1975) observes that undistilled rice or millet beer usually has a high nutritive value and half a litre of rice beer supplies 5 to 10 per cent of daily requirements of calories, proteins, iron, calcium and vitamin. Yet continuous excess intake of *'haria'* and other alcoholic drinks can lead one to alcoholism. As a matter of fact, alcoholism is by and large considered a disease. Very often it affects the proper functioning of the brain. It is a depressant drug and slows down the activities of the brain. Alcoholism may lead to considerable absenteeism from work, poor productivity, family break down, and neglect of care of children etc. During the present investigation it has been observed that the labourers, irrespective of their sex, by and large are in the habit of taking alcoholic drinks, especially the locally fermented *'haria'*, more or less regularly. Some of them get so much addicted to it that they spend a major part of their earnings, very often at the cost of their basic needs, on *'haria'*. This not only affects their basic economic condition and health, but also the peace and tranquillity of the family. It often leads to quarrels between husband and wife leading to domestic violence. Drinking of alcohol is very common among the women interviewed and nearly 20 per cent of the women workers are in the habit of drinking alcohol and they themselves prepare it in their houses.

Like alcohol, taking tobacco is also a common habit of the tea industry labourers, which has adverse effect on their body. A large population of the studied population (90%) takes tobacco and only 10 per cent of sampled labourers do not take it. Tobacco is very harmful for our health and is called the silent killer. A high rate of alcohol and tobacco consumption is found among the respondents of the tea garden. A considerable amount of income is spent on the consumption of alcohol and tobacco by the labourers of Modarkhat Tea Estate. Further, betel nut is another favourite among the labourers and almost all the labourers have the habit of taking it. It is seen that the women workers carry a small bag, containing betel nut, pan, and tobacco, and consume it at any time.

Health Condition of the Women Labourers

The women workers of the tea plantation often remain busy with their work in the tea beds for a larger part of the year. The working hours of the women workers are from morning 8 to 4 in the evening. They have to wake up early in the morning, do all household chores and prepare food and pack their lunches and then go to work. After the whole day's work in heavy sunlight and sometimes even rain, when they return to their homes, they have to prepare for dinner and look after their children. On the whole, the women workers, by and large, do not get time for recreation and relaxation. This continuous excessive strain, coupled with an imbalance and under nutritious food habit has contributed towards the frequent incidence of a number of diseases among the women. Most of the women workers have been found to suffer from diseases like backache, chest pain, knee pain, high blood pressure, cough and cold etc. Interestingly, most of the women have taken these ailments as part and parcel of their working life, and as such they generally do not go for any kind of treatment for the same. One of the problems that the researcher faced is that the women workers are themselves not aware of their health problems. When the researcher talked with the general nurse of the garden hospital then it was known that most of the women workers of the tea estate are anaemic. Besides anaemia, other health diseases of women workers are high blood pressure and some cases of tuberculosis. In the present investigation it was found that 90 per cent of the women workers are sufferers of anaemia. The main reason of anaemia is lack of proper nutritious food and also lack of proper care taken after childbirth. In this study, as many as 40 per cent of the women were found sufferers of high blood pressure. The hospital nurse reported 5 cases of tuberculosis. The excessive salt intake leads to high blood pressure and lack of proper hygiene and sanitation leads to tuberculosis. During the present investigation it has been observed that the people by and large do not provide any special nutrient food to pregnant women, neither during pregnancy nor after childbirth. With regard to the child birth, it may relatively be noted here that the people, by and large, have been found to prefer delivery at home. During the present investigation the researcher found that the women in the higher age group had home based deliveries with the assistance of midwives. But the women in the younger age group are having deliveries in hospitals. Another finding of this study is that right from conception till child birth and immunizations of children the NRHM Ashakarmi workers are engaged with the women workers. Now-a-days, the NRHM has send directions to the garden authorities to make a Mothers' Club consisting of women members of the tea garden community. In Modarkhat Tea Estate also a Mothers' Club is formed consisting of 12 members, but, it is not effectively working for the women workers.

Conclusion

From the above discussions it is quite evident that there is a close connection between socio-economic conditions and ill-health among the plantation labourers, especially women workers. Nature of work, living conditions and type of food intake are clear manifestations of the morbidity patterns and mortality data of the plantation labour. Nutrition, health and hygiene are synonymous to each other, but without good nutrition and proper hygiene, health cannot be at its best. Besides education and economic condition also has an important bearing on the health of women. Wherever people are educated, their health consciousness also increases. But, in Modarkhat Tea Estate 87 per cent of the women workers under investigation were illiterate. And the main income of the plantation workers in Modarkhat Tea Estate is only from the plantation and only few are engaged in subsidiary income. So with this meagre income it becomes difficult for them to make both ends meet leave alone for taking care of themselves or buy nutritious food items. Fruits, milk, meat and other protein rich food rarely find a place in the diet of women workers. So, most of the women workers are undernourished and their children malnourished. Most of the women are also anaemic as they lack iron rich food and are not taken care during prenatal and postnatal period. Housing and sanitation facilities are also not adequate in Modarkhat Tea Estate. There is no electricity in the labour lines. Besides, there is no proper drainage system and during rainy season the entrances of the houses become slippery causing inconvenience. Bathroom is completely absent in the labour quarters which is substituted by make shift bathroom near the tube-wells. This causes inconvenience to women workers and it is also not hygienic.

The health facilities available in Modarkhat Tea Estate are also not adequate. The infrastructure of the garden hospital should be improved and be fully equipped with all the modern technologies of healthcare. One thing that should be immediately taken care of is the appointment of a permanent resident doctor which was absent at the time of present investigation. The general nurse whom the researcher interviewed told that even simple delivery cases are not done in the garden hospital due to the absence of resident doctor. The Mothers' Club formed by NRHM should be more active and should organise awareness camps in the labour lines. The more active women workers should take initiative and spread the information regarding health, hygiene, maternal health care and ill effects of alcohol and tobacco. Thus, it has been observed in the present investigation that women's health is affected not just by their biology, but also by their social conditions, such as poverty, illiteracy, family responsibilities, ignorance about health awareness, addiction to alcohol and tobacco, unhygienic living conditions, absence of proper sanitation etc. The tea plantation women workers are thus most marginalized section of the society. Moreover, they have been enjoying low status in the patriarchal plantation society.

REFERENCES

Bhadra, R.K. (1997). *Social Dimensions of Health of Tea Plantation Workers in India,* Dibrugarh: N.L. Publishers.

Bhowmik, S.K. (2002). "Productivity and labour standard in tea plantation sector in India", In: A. Sivananthiram and C.S. Venkata Ratnam (eds.) *Role of Social Dialogue,* ILO.

Biswas (2002). "Study on nutritional status of tea garden workers of Assam with special emphasis on body mass index and central obesity", *Journal of Human Ecology,* 13: 299-302.

Borgohain, Parijat (2013). "Occupational health hazards of tea garden workers of Hajua and Marangi tea estates of Assam, India", *The Clarion,* Vol. 2, No. 1.

Deb Nath, R. (2002). *Social and Cultural Life of Labourers in Dewan Tea Garden,* Unpublished M.Phil. Dissertation, Assam University, Silchar.

Dutta, B.M. (2001). "Morbidity and curative measures among the tea labourers: A case study in Upper Assam", *Bulletin*, Department of Anthropology, Dibrugarh University, No. 29, pp. 77-98.

Engels, D. (1993). "The myth of the family unit: Adivasi women in coal mines and tea plantations in early twentieth century Bengal", In: Peter Robb, *Dalit Movements and the Meaning of Labour in India*, Delhi: Oxford University Press.

Hazarika, N.C. (2006). *Hypertension and its Risk Factors in Tea Garden Workers of Assam*, Regional Medical Research Centre, North Eastern Region, ICMR, Dibrugarh, Assam.

Kaniampady, E. (2003). *Status of Working Women in Tea Plantations: A Case Study*, New Delhi: Akanksha Publishing House.

Kar, R.K. (1990). "Health and sanitation versus culture: An appraisal of tea labour in Assam", In: B. Chowdhuri (ed.), *Cultural and Environmental Dimensions on Health*, New Delhi: Inter-India Publications.

Mahanta (2006). *Tobacco and Alcohol Use among the Youth of the Agricultural Tea Industry in Assam*, Regional Medical Research Centre, North Eastern Region, ICMR, Dibrugarh, Assam.

Medhi, G.K. (2006). *Study of Health Problems and Nutritional Status of Tea Population of Assam*, Regional Medical Research Centre, North Eastern Region, ICMR, Dibrugarh, Assam.

National Health Mission, Ministry of Health and Family Welfare, Government of India, http://nrhm.gov.in/

National Health Policy (2002). (India), http://mohfw.nic.in/

Rasaily, Rinju (2014). *Women's Labour in the Tea Sector: Changing Trajectories and Emerging Challenges*, National Research Programme on Plantation Development (NRPPD).

Sahoo, D., K. Konwar and B.K. Sahoo, (2010). "Health condition and health awareness among the tea garden labourers: A case study of a tea garden in Tinsukia District of Assam", *The IUP Journal of Agricultural Economics*, Vol. 7, No. 4.

Timung, J. and Juliana Sarmah (2013). "Nutrition, health and hygienic practice of women tea plantation workers of Assam", *Asian Journal of Home Science*, Vol. 8, No. 2.

Index